THE
BUREAUCRATIC
EXPERIENCE

THE BUREAUCRATIC EXPERIENCE

Third Edition

Ralph P. Hummel

University of Oklahoma

St. Martin's Press
New York

Cover design: Douglas Thompson
Cover photograph: Joel Gordon

Acknowledgments

Figure 1.1, "Gross City Product (Lagged 1 Year) Vs. Number of AFDC Recipients in New York," Office of State Comptroller, Office of the Special Deputy Comptroller for the City of New York, "Trends in Public Assistance Caseload and Expenditures in New York City with Comparisons to Selected Counties in New York State," Report No. 36-85, November 27, 1984, submitted to the Financial Control Board of the City of New York.

"Morale of Justices in New York is Low," Copyright © 1976 by the New York Times Company. Reprinted by permission.

"Klassen Told by a Senator that Mail Service is a Joke," Copyright © 1973 by the New York Times Company. Reprinted by permission.

Stress Diagram, Michael Diamond, "Bureaucracy as Externalized Self-System: A View from the Psychological Interior," *Administration and Society*. Vol. 16, No. 2, August, 1984. Copyright © 1984. Reprinted by permission of Sage Publications, Inc.

"Haigledygook and Secretaryspeak," Copyright 1981 Time Inc. All rights reserved. Reprinted by permission from TIME.

David Stockman quote, Copyright © 1985 by the New York Times Company. Reprinted by permission.

In Memory
of
Pat Boughton

This edition of *The Bureaucratic Experience* contains original
essays by:

Michael Harmon
Jay White
Michael Diamond
Sandra Fish
Conrad Rutkowski

Preface

Everyone has trouble with bureaucracy. Citizens and politicians have trouble controlling the runaway bureaucratic machine. Managers have trouble managing it. Employees dislike working in it. Clients can't get the goods from it. Teachers have trouble getting an overall grip on it. Students are mystified by the complexity of it.

It would be useful to all of us—citizens, clients, politicians, administrators, functionaries, teachers, and students—to have a clear framework for organizing our thinking about bureaucracy and our dealings with it. The framework should be one that can be easily kept in our heads. It should not be esoteric, it cannot be Pollyannaish. It should not be complex but essential. It should encompass the nature of bureaucracy, and it should have clear practical applications.

The framework proposed is this:

First, bureaucracy—whether public or private—is an entirely new way of organizing social life. It succeeds society, just as society has succeeded community.

Second, bureaucracy, a world into which we are recruited, differs from society, the world into which we are born, in five ways: (1) socially, (2) culturally, (3) psychologically, (4) linguistically, and (5) power-politically. Bureaucracy is a new society and a new culture. Bureaucracy's functionaries represent a new personality type and speak a new language and new thoughts. Bureaucracy is a new way of exercising power, defying politics.

Third, bureaucracy, because it differs from society in these five ways, poses special difficulties for people depending on where they stand. Grouped according to the type of problem they face, these people are: (1) the citizen as taxpayer, voter, and nominal boss over bureaucracy, (2) the politician as immediate but still nominal boss, (3) the manager as the wielder of bureaucratic power, (4) the employee as the tool of bureaucratic power, and (5) the client as recipient of bureaucracy's goods and victim of bureaucracy's power. Individuals in each of these groups must make different adaptations to bureaucracy if they are to succeed in dealing with it or working in it.

The assumption of the book is this: We will be better able to live and work *with, in,* or *against* bureaucracy IF we (1) view it as an entirely new world, (2) become aware of the practical impact of its differences from the world with which we are familiar, and (3) understand how that impact will vary for each of us depending on the form of our involvement with bureaucratic life.

For a book that originated as a lone protest against life in modern organizations, one intended to do no more than lay bare the underlying realities producing the agonies of the bureaucratic age, the first edition of *The Bureaucratic Experience* received an overwhelming response from readers. This response made me realize that I was not alone, that many practitioners and scholars out in the world were working, thinking, and writing along similar lines.

The result was twofold. First, the second edition contained not only the reworked core chapters of the first edition, which expressed the development of my own thoughts, but also the work of a number of writers pursuing the critical study of bureaucracy and modernity from similar points of view. These writers have since established their own well-known works on specific subjects and themes. Second, the knowledge that many of us shared not only the same impressions of life in the bureaucratic age but the same methodology for exposing its roots brought a number of us together into a network of mutually supportive researchers, which continues as the Institute for Applied Phenomenology. In the second edition of *The Bureaucratic Experience*, a number of phenomenologists addressed the problems of modern bureaucracy together for the first time. This did not exclude the findings and approaches of behavioral scientists, and, along with a psychoanalyst, several of them joined us in this work.

The third edition expresses a deepening concern for how readers can be enabled to set aside obstacles and defenses against benefitting from a critical analysis of bureaucracy that often challenges what they have had to become—as bureaucrats or as clients. The "What People Can Do" sections at the end of chapters 1–5, written by Michael Harmon, Jay White, Michael Diamond, Sandra Fish, and Conrad Rutkowski, aim at showing ways of dealing with insights that may seem painful and unacceptable but that are necessary because they allow us to confront, and perhaps overcome, what appears irresistible and inevitable in the bureaucratic experience.

Perhaps as a reflection on our times, the greatest debt in the making of this book is owed to anonymous men and women in greater and lesser bureaucracies across the United States. Not even all the institutions could be listed here.

Over the course of the three editions, I owe debts for intellectual and physical survival to: Howell Baum, Peter Berger, Renee Berger, Morton Berkowitz, Paul Bernstein, Bayard Catron, Raymond Cox, Fred Dallmayr, Robert Denhardt, Stephen Dracopolous, John Everett, Michael Diamond, Glenn Cowley, John Forester, Sandra Fish, Frank Fischer, Claudette Ford, James Glass, Michael Halperin, Charles Hayes, Hans Held, Marc Holzer, Patricia Ingraham, Robert Isaak, Hwa Yol Jung, Jong S. Jun, Louis Koenig, Douglas LaBier, Charles Levine, Donna Lavins, Bert Lummus, Tommie Sue Montgomery, Dail Neugarten, the late Max Mark, Bruce Marquand, Edward Mazze, Roger Mazze, Brinton Milward, Kirsten Moy, Carl Nelson, H. Mark Roelofs, David Rosenbloom, Barry Rossinoff, Conrad Rutkowski, David Schuman, Howard Schwartz, Jay Jayfritz, Eli Silverman, the late Kalman Silvert, Michael P. Smith, Patricia Snow, Kathryn Speicher, Harry Steinberg, Clarence Stone, Peter Vaill, Richard VrMeer, Dwight Waldo, Stephen Wasby, Michael Weber, and Jay White.

Ralph P. Hummel
Spruce Head Island,
Maine
1986

Contents

THE
BUREAUCRATIC
EXPERIENCE

Introduction: Understanding Bureaucracy

This book is a practical guide to bureaucracy. It is practical because a group of twenty-five student interns in the New York City Urban Corps challenged an academician to be practical.

THE CHALLENGE

The challenge came in the form of an invitation. Would I, asked a voice at the other end of the telephone, come down to New York's City Hall and tell interns about to enter the city bureaucracy what to expect? No matter how down-to-earth an academician is in the classroom, there is only one reaction to such a request: stark, naked panic. After years of work in generalizations and abstractions, I was asked to give practical advice *that would be tested*. Not only was my own reputation at stake with the interns, who would soon enough encounter the realities of bureaucracy, but the interns themselves would be tested by seasoned bureaucrats.

The credibility of the academic world and its relevance to society had been very much on my mind. I had just become director of a small consulting firm on urban educational and administrative problems. Half the reason for the existence of that firm was my own experience that academicians had created around themselves their own little world of unreality. The other half was the remnant of an earlier faith that academicians still *did* have something to tell practitioners. Here was my first personal test.

What was bureaucracy all about? What could an individual expect the first day he or she walked into an office? What *should* he or she expect in order to survive?

What could I tell newcomers about modern bureaucracy?

THE KEY

Half a century ago, sociologist Max Weber recoiled from the bureaucratic future in horror. Like George Orwell and Aldous Huxley he saw a strange

1

new world in which not the brave but the dehumanized would survive. What if we started taking seriously Weber's classic characterization of bureaucracy and his condemnation of its inmates? After all, he did foresee a future populated by nonentities—"Specialists without spirit, sensualists without heart; this nullity imagines that it has attained a level of civilization never before achieved."[1]

Planted like time bombs through his famous essay on bureaucracy, temporarily defused by the neutral language of his "constructive" insights, lay the fragments of Weber's vision of a terrifying reality.

Bureaucracy* gives birth to a new species of inhuman beings. People's social relations are being converted into control relations.[2] Their norms and beliefs concerning human ends are torn from them and replaced with skills affirming the ascendancy of technical means, whether of administration or production.[3] Psychologically, the new personality type is that of the rationalistic expert, incapable of emotion and devoid of will.[4] Language, once the means of bringing people into communication, becomes the secretive tool of one-way commands.[5] Politics, especially democratic politics, fades away as the method of publicly determining society-wide goals based on human needs; it is replaced by administration.[6]

Daily experience with bureaucracy showed this picture matched reality. The time had come, I decided, to set off the time bombs. And—as bureaucrats themselves reacted to the resulting explosions[7]—it has become increasingly necessary to show what goes into the building of bureaucracy as the bomb that threatens humanity.

Newcomers deserve to be told they are not facing minor adjustments when they enter or deal with bureaucracy but a challenge to alter all their orientations and behaviors. Old-timers in bureaucracy deserve to be told what lurks behind the pressures that threaten to turn them not only into one of the most severely criticized category of jobholders anywhere in the world[8] but into the most suspect of human beings.[9]

A president may say this of bureaucrats:

You may have been told that government workers are clockwatchers; you will soon find that the vast majority of them are dedicated not to their pay checks but to the job to be done. You may have heard that government positions involve nothing but plodding routine tasks; you will see some of the most exciting, interesting work in the world being done here. You may have read that public servants are unimaginative, security-seeking, uncreative, skilled only at the techniques of empire building; you will quickly discover that we have far more than our share of lively minds, endowed with vigor and courage.[10]

But bureaucrats themselves find it useful to draw radical distinctions

*With Max Weber, I here use the term "bureaucracy" as a shorthand for all modern organization, public or private, including business and industrial corporations as well as public service agencies organized according to the rationalized principles of modernity.

between what it takes to survive in bureaucracy and what it takes to live social life on the outside.[11] Especially those who survive and are successful know that:

1. Life in bureaucracy is radically different from life in society.
2. Unique pressures—social, cultural, psychological, linguistic, and political—shape the bureaucrat's life and determine what he or she will become.

One way of achieving an overview of the distinctions is to visualize them in terms of misunderstandings and understandings of bureaucracy:

Misunderstandings	*Understandings*
Socially—	
Bureaucrats deal with people.	Bureaucrats deal with cases.
Culturally—	
Bureaucrats care about the same things we do: justice, freedom, violence, oppression, illness, death, victory, defeat, love, hate, salvation, and damnation.	Bureaucrats aim at control and efficiency.
Psychologically—	
Bureaucrats are people like us.	Bureaucrats are a new personality type, headless and soulless.*
Linguistically/Cognitively	
Communication with bureaucrats is possible: we all speak the same language, we think the same way.	Bureaucrats shape and inform rather than communicate; they are trained to think the way computers think.
Politically—	
Bureaucracies are service institutions accountable to society and ruled by politics and government.	Bureaucracies are control institutions increasingly ruling society, politics, and government.

The issue is not whether there are among bureaucrats those who are dedicated to getting the job done, those who do exciting and interesting work, and those of lively mind and hearts endowed with vigor and courage. Such dedication, excitement, and interest, such hearts and minds do exist. The question is whether they exist because of or despite bureaucracy. If bureaucracy enables, what are the kind of social life, the

---

*The terms "headless" and "soulless" here evoked strong protests from some employees of modern organizations. It may be worthwhile to point out that these terms reflect a tendency that bureaucratic life forces on bureaucrats, rather than the actual characteristics of specific individuals.

kind of values, the kind of psyche, the kind of speaking and thinking, the kind of politics that are enabled? And what qualities of human life are disabled or destroyed? No one denies the monumental accomplishments of modern civilization, with bureaucracy—public and private—at its spearhead. But the question human beings will inevitably ask is: Who or what is being speared?

Newcomers or outsiders, in order to deal with bureaucracy, need to understand just how the bureaucratic experience differs from ordinary social life. If bureaucrats are to understand just what sacrifices this most powerful of human organizations requires of them as human beings, they themselves need to learn just what it is that bureaucratic structures around them require of them.

In sum, the bureaucratic experience that awaits us differs from the social experience behind us in five ways: socially, culturally, psychologically, linguistically/cognitively, and politically. Each of these five differences deserves exploration in depth. The rest of this introduction provides a survey; it is based on the lecture I delivered to those twenty-five interns. Chapters 1 through 5 provide the details.

BUREAUCRACY AS A STRANGE NEW WORLD

Anyone who has set out from familiar daily life to tangle with bureaucracy knows that bureaucracy and society are worlds apart. The distance can seem as far as that from the earth to the moon. It is not impossible to get there and back, but surviving the journey requires learning not only a new set of behaviors but a new mode of life. We must be attuned to both the home world and the new world.

The Bureaucratic Experience

People have difficulties with bureaucracy. This is true for the administrator who suddenly finds himself or herself in charge of and held responsible for an instrument of purported power and control that eternally squirms and wriggles to escape the grasp. It is true for newly hired workers in a bureaucracy who have to learn a new set of behaviors, norms, and speech patterns to get along and keep their jobs. And it is true for the outsider who wants to do business with a bureaucracy—get a tax refund, register a birth or death, secure a passport, license an enterprise, obtain police protection, or enter a child in school. Quite similar problems exist for the manager trying to control a corporation's sales force; the employee learning to talk, act, and think the way employees typically talk, act, and think at IBM, GM, or ITT; and the customer attempting to get Macy's credit department to correct a mistake the computer made.

If we have experienced bureaucracy in any of these roles, and none of us can long avoid such contact, we have to admit to ourselves that we have great difficulty with bureaucracy—attuning to it, communicating our needs to it, and obtaining satisfactions from it. No matter how astute we are, these difficulties exist, and we may feel that if only we could explain the reasons for such tensions we might be able to do better for ourselves in future contacts.

BUREAUCRATIC SOCIETY

The fundamental reasons for our difficulties were spelled out by Max Weber in warnings to which we seem not to have paid much attention. Perhaps to do so would result in too painful a recognition of the vastness of the chasm between social life and bureaucratic existence. Bureaucracy in its modern form, Weber concluded, constitutes the creation of a new world of human interaction. A transformation of normal human life began specifically with the development of modern organization.

In this new world of organized human interaction, it is entirely possible that a baby entrusted to welfare agencies may die of neglect even though in the words of a welfare administrator "everyone concerned did his or her job conscientiously."[12]

In normal human life, Weber points out, people relate to one another through the meaning each attaches to his or her actions—a meaning to which the other responds.[13] Responsibility means acting in keeping with mutually defined meanings. The bureaucrat, on the other hand, is restricted to those actions permitted by the job rules and program requirements. These are defined systemically and from the top down. As a welfare administrator said in the case of the baby cited above—an eight-month-old who died weighing only seven (7) pounds: "There was never a complaint filed with the state's Central Registry charging neglect or abuse."[14]

In the organized system, the bureaucrat is not officially allowed to tune in to the subjective meanings and needs that a client may be trying to convey. The bureaucrat must tune in only to those meanings and needs that have official standing. The result: it is possible for a baby to die even though advocates for the homeless may charge that the baby "spent repeated nights without shelter sleeping on the floor" of a welfare office and that "he was constantly seen dying by Human Resource Administration workers, but none intervened to protect him."[15]

When social interaction becomes organized, those actions become rational that are logically in line with the goals of the organization. This is what Weber meant when he said, "Bureaucracy is *the* means of transforming social action into rationally organized action."[16] Personal responsibility becomes systemic accountability. The system may have faults, but this does not mean we can assign blame to persons operating the system according to rules defined by those faults.

Thus the press may roast the Pentagon bureaucracy for being unable to find an officer who would shoulder responsibility for a crash that, in 1985, killed 248 soldiers aboard a chartered plane at Gander, Newfoundland, but such criticism is simply inappropriate.[17] Accountability, like the military's transport system as a whole, is systemic: the system might be maldesigned but, at best, the dutiful officer is accountable to that system and not responsible to outsiders with their separate social values.

That generals act like bureaucrats rather than warriors may be frustrating, but it is surprising only to the uninitiated.

In the case of the dying baby, the government charged with his care could honestly report that while the system had weaknesses—which could be corrected after the fact by introducing nurses and physicians to welfare offices—all the system's workers did their jobs properly.[18]

The goals of the bureaucratic social system may in themselves be human or humane. It is just that other human and humane goals not encompassed in the system's objectives cannot be considered by those functionaries who carry out its objectives—at least not in their official capacity. Such goals or needs stand logically outside the goals and needs of the bureaucratic system. They are, in the system's terms, "illogical" and therefore "irrational." It is one of the great ironies of bureaucratic interference in social life that those most in need of whatever help bureaucracy might be able to offer also feel least effective in dealing with it. A study for the U.S. Congress showed that only 46 percent of people with an income below $5,000 felt themselves to be highly effective when dealing with bureaucracy; the figure was 69 percent for those with an income over $15,000.[19]

Great care must therefore be taken, it would seem, in the design of the objects of bureaucratic systems so as to give a chance to human interaction at the functionary/client level. But this may not be enough. Bureaucracy's need for control may impose a form of social interaction incompatible with situations in which people need to care for each other. It may be true, as defenders of public bureaucracy have argued, that "Governments gets the messy jobs, and government agencies have many goals imposed on them,"[20] goals that private bureaucracy—business—can't handle. But the problem may be that *any* type of organization that insists on rationally organizing social interaction may be systemically unfit to take *care* of goals and policies that require caring human interaction.

In summary, bureaucracy changes the way human beings relate to one another as social beings:

1. Bureaucracy replaces ordinary *social interaction*, in which individuals act by mutually orienting themselves to each other, by *rationally organized action*, in which individuals orient themselves to goals and meanings defined from the top down.

2. Bureaucracy replaces mutually defined *meaning* of social action by orientation toward systems *functions*.

The extent to which the bureaucratic world is not the normal human world can also be understood psychologically. Weber himself pointed out that bureaucratization favors the development of "the [new] personality type of the professional expert."[21] Because Weber did not develop this theme further in psychological terms, we may have missed that he was speaking about the creation of a new, truncated type of human being.

THE BUREAUCRATIC PERSONALITY

Clients find bureaucrats cold and impersonal. But clients have an escape. They can sacrifice what bureaucracy has to offer. They can cut down on dealing with bureaucratic personalities. Most clients, except the most dependent, can turn to other aspects of life—like economic enterprise, social life, and politics. Their own personality is shaped by other than bureaucratic demands.

Bureaucrats are not so lucky. Their job contract with bureaucracy soon becomes a psychological contract. This they cannot escape. Pulled on a daily basis between the human demands of social life and the organizational demands of work life, they live in the tension between two personalities. One is integrated and in charge of itself. The other is fragmented by division of labor and hierarchy and under the control of others. (See Chapter 3.)

Two forces originating in organizations' structure shape the bureaucratic personality. First, there is always someone else who is in charge of what you do (hierarchy): deciding whether what you do is socially right or wrong. Hierarchy relieves you of personal conscience and guilt. In psychological terms, hierarchy acts as the individual's superego. Second, what you do is predefined by job description, rules, and the division of labor. This relieves you of having to decide for yourself what work activity is most appropriate for the task at hand. In psychological terms, job definition replaces ego function, the function of mastering the world out of one's own sense of what works.[22]

Individuals respond quite differently to modern organization's demand that, when push comes to shove, members must check their conscience and sense of mastery at the plant gate or office door. One consultant reports this response from bureaucrats to whom the institution's demand for ego and superego control was pointed out[23]:

Now, clearly, they would make this argument: Yeah, there are those people who work there whose ego may be questioned in terms of the fact that they are conformist or that they are terribly compliant civil servants, and therefore will do whatever their superiors tell them to do.

But this total collapse in front of bureaucracy's demands is not the experience of most:

Their experience was more often that political appointees in leadership positions, for example, would make things difficult for them, but that they could make things difficult for those political appointees, given their position in bureaucracy over time and the history they have in their organization, and so forth. So in that sense what they were describing was this tension: given the constraints how can they maintain ego integrity or self integrity?

Psychologically, then, the bureaucrat lives a daily life suspended in the tension between organization structure and self. Psychology itself, however, cannot tell us anything about the ultimate degree to which bureaucracy is the enemy of self. Human beings, it could be argued, have always had to adapt themselves to their environment. Yet, in the bureaucratic environment, which human beings themselves constructed, they may have overemphasized essentials of human nature that so finally challenge other essentials as to nearly destroy human nature. There is something fundamentally wrong with bureaucracy and not with the individual bureaucrat. The individual always retains his or her human potential. This becomes apparent only when the psycho-logic of bureaucracy is pushed to its logical conclusions. The result becomes clear in two ways: when bureaucracy pushes a human being to the ultimate extreme by "terminating" him or her, and when bureaucracy's basic values themselves are changed as has happened in recent attempts to humanize bureaucracy.

Douglas LaBier, a Washington psychoanalyst dealing with government employees, describes the pain of a perfectly well-adapted federal bureaucrat when the environment became less bureaucratic:

A federal bureaucrat went along for years perfectly happy in his role of giving pain to other bureaucrats on behalf of his boss. This individual's sado-masochistic personality fitted his official role of "hatchet man." The hatchet man's boss upheld a strictly top-down chain of command by a reign of terror. Finally the boss was replaced by a new boss who believed in letting employees help in deciding policy as part of a participative management style.

No longer afforded a legitimate channel for expression the hatchet man's previously "well adjusted pathology" now "erupted as the work environment changed to become healthier."

The hatchet man now began to actively interfere in the work of the division, badmouthing people behind their backs, sabotaging projects that were being worked on, trying to disrupt communications by impeding the flow of memos, and the like. Finally, in pain, he went to see the psychoanalyst, who asked not the usual questions about childhood, but: "Has anything changed in your work lately?[24]

The symptoms and the pathology are specific to the hatchet man and his situation, but the pain is universal. An entire new movement of psychoanalytically oriented organization analysis beginning in the 1970s has found that bureaucracy produces pain. (See Chapter 3.) The efforts of psychoanalysts focusing on work is to alleviate such pain. But there is something that psychoanalysts are specifically prevented from doing by their own competence in dealing with the psyche. This is to undertake the social and cultural analysis that shows *why* bureaucracy is an ultimate challenge to all human beings.

The origin of emotional tension at work, of pain, of an ultimate challenge to the humanity of people lies in the structure of modern organizations itself. It is not to be sought in the individual weaknesses of inmates. This becomes most clear when the bureaucracy "terminates" a bureaucrat. A former contract administrator for a private bureaucracy— the office of mining company[25]:

I didn't really mind getting fired. The company had been in trouble for a long time. What I did mind was passing my boss every day in the hallway and his being unable to look me in the eye, say hello, much less smile. I still had two weeks to go before I'd actually have to leave. He'd see me coming down the hall and he'd turn away.

How did that feel?

Why, it makes you feel like you're nobody—a *nonentity*!

The challenge of bureaucracy to all humankind is not essentially a psychological one. Bureaucracy is not satisfied with disordering the psyche by breaking away large chunks of it and reordering the psyche by distributing it over in organizational structures. Bureaucracy also challenges an individual's entire being. The Greeks had a word for it: being = *ontos*. The fundamental challenge of bureaucracy is not merely a psychological one, it is an ontological challenge. The individual submits to it in agreeing to the initial work contract. Once major functions of the self are placed outside the self—conscience in hierarchy and mastery in job definition—the individual has surrendered his or her being to the organization. This also explains how the organization retains its hold over the individual. An individual trained in letting the organization make decisions of conscience and mastery for her or him over many years loses the ability to refer to her or his own standards for what is right or wrong and whether work is done well. Without the functions originally surrendered to the organization and now lodged there, she or he is—nobody. Not accidentally do we speak of "incorporation." The driving force for all social relations, political power, and administrative control in bureaucracy therefore is the experience of a nameless fear that without one's job one will cease to exist. The driving force of bureaucracy, its hold over humankind, is existential anxiety.[26]

In summary, bureaucracy radically alters the psyche of human beings:

1. Bureaucracy replaces autonomous *personality* with organizational *identity*.
2. Bureaucracy takes the functions of *conscience* (superego) and *mastery* (ego) out of the individual's psyche and distributes them across organizational structures: *hierarchy* and the *division of labor*.
3. Bureaucracy, in creating *dependency* of the individual self on structures of the organization (in effect, mingling self and organization), controls its functionaries by manipulating the *existential anxiety* over loss of being that a separation from the job threatens.

BUREAUCRATIC CULTURE: PARADOX OF NEEDS

Modern organization was designed to take care of human needs; yet everywhere in modern organization human needs lie in chains. This paradox of bureaucracy is already evident in the new type of action and the new type of personality required. Each person involved with bureaucracy—administrator, employee, client—experiences this paradox in his or her own way. Each stands in a different location in relation to the bureaucracy and therefore has his or her own perspective.[27]

The daughter of an eighty-five-year-old woman admitted to a Bakersfield, California, hospital with a heart attack is told three weeks later that her mother is being moved to a nursing home:[28]

I said what she needs is acute-level care and they said, Well, they can give her the same care over there. And I said, Well, I *know* they can't because they're not equipped for that, you know. So—uh—she said, I'm sorry—this is one of the sisters at the hospital. She said, we're losing money on her and Medicare won't allow her to be here any longer. So, she said, she has got to go. [Two days after the phone call, the woman was moved out.] . . . And they strapped her down, and put her in the ambulance, and took her over to the convalescent hospital. Well, I stayed with her all day, and I came home about 9/9:30 that night, and in three hours they called me and said she was dead.

A hospital spokesman, denying that the woman was moved for economic rather than medical reasons:

We have the responsibility, too, to remind the physician of his responsibility to let the patient and the patient's family know where they stand in terms of the benefits of an insurance plan, or Medicare plan, versus the economic resources that have been expended toward the patient's care.

The physician who approved the woman's discharge:

Question: Was that based on medical reasons or what you call pressure from the hospital to get her out of here?
Physician: I think I can honestly say I just felt pressure to release her. I'll never be coerced into doing something like that again.

The case, an entirely predictable result if we understand the bureaucratization of human needs, is not unique. These instances are the result of a government-mandated program in which physicians are asked to place patients in standard categories—diagnostic-related groups or DRGs—for which typical length of stay in hospital has been established. If length of stay exceeds the norm, the hospital is no longer reimbursed by Medicare.

The origins of the cultural paradox lie in this: The client approaches the bureaucracy with a full set of human needs. These are interrelated. But a policy or program is designed to satisfy only one or a few of them. More important, there is the essential difference of how needs are defined by a living human being and an organization, constructed by humans but not human itself.

You and I as human beings define our needs according to *projects*— something we as yet hope to accomplish in our lives. Literally: project = a plan that throws us ahead of ourselves on behalf of ourselves. We are not what we have just finished being yesterday but what we intend to be tomorrow and are becoming today. In short: life goes on. (Or, it will, if bureaucracy lets us.)

In contrast, bureaucracy defines needs not by projects for the future but by standards of policies and programs defined in the past. The legislation, the policies, and the programs that bureaucracy administers set standards of yesterday for what it takes for a human being to become a "case" today—to be served or controlled. The evidence for becoming a case, including assessment of need, is determined by rational, scientific, and legal standards; these look to the past: to what already is. The artificial construct that is the organization cannot encompass the ongoing fullness of human life, which looks not only backward, but lives ongoingly in the present, and looks in anticipation toward the future. This is so simply because organization is not life. Bureaucracy in its administrative function must, to follow the policy standards that authorize it to act, look at human needs not as if they were part of an ongoing *project* of a living subject but as if they were *finished characteristics* of a dead object.

This backward-looking orientation of bureaucracy is often obscured by the actual experience of bureaucrats. In actually applying the standards of the past—for example, those of the lawbooks or of the precinct captain's orders of the day—the cop on the beat must hurl himself or herself into the future and its not-yet-defined possibilities. In short, the officer must make contact with reality. That reality creates itself ongoingly before the officer; to survive on the job he or she must deal with it. The cultural tension within which the bureaucrat lives is defined by being torn between past enactments of a *model* of reality and present encounters with reality itself. No work at all can be done if the bureaucrat clings strictly to the enacted model of reality without hurling himself or herself into reality itself. Yet in even touching what is real—the objects and people in front of us, with whom we must deal—we desert the previously enacted model of that reality. That is why it is in the interest of managers and administrators—the police captain, for example—to have their subordinates do *nothing* rather than be accused of corrupting the pure model of mandated actions and values that is inevitably tainted by contact with reality.

Thus the City of New York saw to it that all work of two "supercops" was halted when they succeeded in stopping the heroin flow in one precinct by permitting heroin to be available for their informers; the story is told in *The Supercops*. All work of bureaucrats is measured by past standards, not by current exigencies that rise out of reality. Examples abound; they may not be as extreme as the above, but their very subtlety testifies to their omnipresence.

All too often, studies have found that confidence and potential efficacy is reduced as future opportunities are increasingly defined by standards determined by the past. In the case of those who have allowed themselves to be defined as "the poor," the experience of the past—"the culture of poverty"—closes in on them.[29]

But the middle class does not escape unscathed. It cannot fail to strike an ironic eye that the often praised ability of the middle class to adapt to and even manipulate bureaucratic rules may merely subject members voluntarily to the past orientation of the bureaucratic environment, whereas their lower-class fellow citizens are forced into it.[30]

A past orientation, in fact, also characterizes top-level bureaucrats. When Robert S. McNamara, and his generation of computer geniuses, took over the Department of Defense in 1961, they also assumed that the defense needs of the nation could be satisfied by designing programs that would efficiently adhere to previously established and well-defined, measurable goals. Following the advice of economists[31] instead of soldiers, McNamara then went ahead to conduct a war by past standards and by the numbers—the Vietnam War. He lost it to those who treated war not as a means to achieve past ends but as a way of shaping a future whose exact character could not be known.

The Bureaucratic War

Since Max Weber, we have recognized two cultures at war with each other in modern civilization. One still clings to what we hold worthwhile in ordinary social life. The other, rising culture defines what the bureaucratized believe worthwhile in the all-encompassing world of modern organizations.

The traditional values of human life, as the contemporary philosopher and sociologist Jürgen Habermas has said, focus on "justice and freedom, violence and oppression, happiness and gratification, poverty, illness and death, . . . victory and defeat, love and hate, salvation and damnation.[32] They are ultimate values: they define what Life is all about.

In contrast Weber summarized the norms of bureaucratic life as "precision . . . stability . . . stringency of discipline . . . reliability . . . calculability of results . . . formal rationality . . . formalistic impersonality . . . formal equality of treatment."[33] These are instrumental values: they promise to serve as instruments by which human beings can achieve some ultimate values. By design bureaucrats are intended to be instruments. They are expected to fulfill their tasks without anger or predisposition.[34] Or as Weber says elsewhere:

Sine ira ac studio, without hatred or passion, and hence without affection or enthusiasm. The dominant norms are concepts of straightforward duty without regard to personal considerations. Everyone is subject to formal equality of treatment; that is, everyone in the same empirical situation. This is the spirit in which the ideal official conducts his office.[35]

But from the beginning there is this question: Can neutral—in a specific sense: heartless—administration take care of basic human needs that are never experienced in a neutral way? It is not with formal rationality or even with the demand for formal equality of treatment that I, as the average client, approach bureaucracy. I want *my* needs taken care of, ill-defined and even contradictory as they are. I experience myself in my own unique way, through my own personality, with my own unique set of problems. I do not easily present myself as a "case" to the bureaucrat, to be processed following universal rules. The quality of my life, my problems, my needs do not lend themselves easily to definition, measurement, and decision.

In contrast the bureaucrat's experience of me is quite different. Viewing the world through a perspective shaped by bureaucratic values, the bureaucrat sees me not as a distinct individual with qualitatively unique problems and needs but as number 98 of a class of cases whose claim to service or control can be logically determined and quantitatively measured.

To the registrar of births and the county clerk, the addition of a new family member is just "another birth," the addition of a simple mark in a book of accounts. To me the birth of my daughter is an event full of affection, enthusiasm, anxiety, joy, emotion, passion, and import. She is *my* daughter. She has my eyes. My feelings about her, awakened by her from within me, make me laugh and cry. She is my future, my burden, my redemption—the transcending testimony of enduring love, my wife's and mine.

To the Social Security official, a man's death is just another form filled out; to his wife it is the death of her beloved or hated husband and all he meant and all the things they ever did together and were to each other.

To the welfare case worker, you and I are "cases" or we are not "cases." If we are not "cases," the "case worker" is not allowed, on eventual pain of losing his or her job, to recognize us or our troubles.

Even if we are cases, our troubles are troubles only if they fall within the bureaucracy's predefined cases of trouble. Bureaucracy encases us. We obtain its services or we are subjected to its controls if we fit its framework. To the extent that none of us ever fits perfectly into frames preconstructed to us by the reason of others, we can say, with the wrongly accused: We wuz framed! Originally designed as the tool of humankind, bureaucracy has turned humankind into a tool for its own ends.

Two basic critiques have been launched against bureaucracy as the result of the observed culture conflict:

1. We *value* life differently from bureaucracy.
2. We *know* life differently from bureaucracy.

The first is a simple cultural critique. Its tradition goes from Max Weber to Jürgen Habermas. Cultural critique juxtaposes patterns of values. It simply points out that bureaucracy finds different things worthwhile than do the rest of us who are outside it. These values—such as efficiency—were at one time considered tools for achieving human ends. Today, critics not only question whether a modern organization's internal values are compatible with human beings' values but point to instances in which bureaucratic values have distorted human values. For example, the closest the Pentagon has come to satisfying the human longing for peace has been to offer something sold as the bureaucratic equivalent: "permanent prehostility." This literally means always being ready for war, which is not everyone's idea of peace.

The second critique is more basic. If human beings outside bureaucracy *know* life in ways radically different from the way bureaucrats can know life, then the adequacy of all modern civilization for knowing what human life is can be put into question. For bureaucracy is the vanguard of modern civilization; it is *the* modernizer wherever it goes because it hones modern ways of valuing and knowing to a sharp cutting edge. Critics such as Edmund Husserl and Martin Heidegger point out that ways of knowing define reality.[36] If we accept modernity's method of knowledge—knowing the world by reference to laws of nature and human nature outside of ourselves[37]—we can no longer legitimately know those experiences of what it means to live life and be human that stand apart from such laws. On the practical level this means that I, as a client, am permitted to know myself only in bureaucratic terms. If I cannot accept the bureaucratic way of knowing me—taking cognizance of me—then I will simply not receive its goods. Or, in the extreme, if I don't know enough to get out of bureaucracy's way, it will simply steamroller over me. This critique is the more basic one because it puts once again in the forefront of our thinking the question: *How* do we know *what* we are as human beings? The suggestion is that modern knowing leaves us largely unknown to ourselves. Bureaucracy stands in the way of knowing our humanity.

BUREAUCRATIC LANGUAGE AND THOUGHT

Bureaucracy's values and bureaucrats' way of knowing cut straight to the heart of how we speak and think in the modern world. As outsiders, as clients, we hear ourselves addressed from the top down in language that rings strange in our ears. Our very way of thinking about ourselves is questioned by the way we are challenged to think if we want to make contact with a corporation or government agency. The ordinary human being recoils from that encounter with bureaucratic language and thought in essentially the same way as this man trying to track down his delayed Social Security checks in Washington, D. C.:

Well, I'll tell you something about this town. They got a secret language here. You know that? Bureaucratese. Same thing we used to call doubletalk. These government people, they don't hear you. They don't listen. You start to say something and they shut you out mentally, figuring they know right away what you're going to say before you say it. . . .*

Here a client puts his finger on central experiences of all those dealing with bureaucratic language:

1. That bureaucratic language is *different* from ordinary language. It is, in fact, encoded in terms all its own. To the outsider these are secret terms, the language is a *secret language*.
2. That bureaucratic language is a *power language*. Bureaucrats address clients as if they had the right not to listen to them, assuming, rather, that clients must listen to them. This implies the presumption of power, that the bureaucrat has the means to enforce a speech situation in which he or she speaks (predefines) and others listen (are predefined).

Later we discover that the secret of bureaucratic language lies *behind* its technical terms, its jargon, and its affinity for acronyms in the way bureaucrats are taught to *think*. Reasoning deductively from general rules and by analogy from previously established case norms, bureaucrats speak a language that differs from ordinary speech exactly because it is created on a knowledge base that is top down and prior to experience: derived from the universal laws and rules that constitute modern knowledge of reality.[38] We will conclude that:

1. In bureaucracy a new form of speech arises that is top-down instead of reciprocal in defining reality; *information* replaces *communication*.
2. In bureaucracy a new form of thinking comes to predominate: *analogous thinking* in which bureaucrats are trained to recognize reality only to the extent that aspects of it match a previously conceived model of reality; *analogous*

*For the full text of these observations, see the report of Pasquale Plescia in Chapter 4.

thinking replaces *thinking* with its original commitment to the exploration and discovery of new realities and possibilities.

In a new classic example of dependence both on top-down speech as definition of reality and on analogous thinking, employees of an airline simply denied as unreal the repeated reports by two passengers of a crashed plane that they had seen two fellow passengers fall out of the broken fuselage into Boston Harbor. A computer printout had not contained the names of the extra passengers. If they were not on the printout, they were not real.

As long as people trust that kind of knowledge and distrust their own experience that things in reality work quite differently from the way the rules say they should, bureaucracy retains the power to define reality through top-down speech. However, as we enter postmodernity, we find problems in industrial production and the provision of human services that cannot be defined top-down.[39] Then new forms of speech, new ways of speaking to each other, new words arise from the bottom up and do battle with top-down words and thoughts that seem increasingly detached from reality. This also calls for a new focus on politics.

Politics: The Revolt Against Control

Politics is the enemy of administration. This is why wherever possible, bureaucracy attempts to transform politics into administration. As early as 1917, Max Weber asked questions such as these about the fate of politics:

Given the basic fact of the irresistible advance of bureaucratization, the question about the future forms of political organization can only be asked in the following way:

1. How can one possibly save *any remnants* of "individualist" freedom in any sense?. . .
2. How will democracy even in this limited sense [of a check and control on bureaucracy] be *at all possible*?
3. A third question, and the most important of all, is raised by a consideration of what bureaucracy as such *cannot* achieve. [How are politics and political leadership still possible in the sense of] battle for personal power and what follows from that power: personal *responsibility for his own cause* [which] is the lifeblood of the politician as well as of the entrepreneur [?].[40]

By the end of our century, the replacement of politics by administration and the resulting loss of political vision has become epidemic. While political theorist Sheldon Wolin could write of the nineteenth-century, "At bottom the century desperately longed to transcend the political,"[41] twentieth-century organization theorists and political scientists could report solid and growing fulfillment of that longing. Wherever organization became dominant, democracy had to be, as Weber anticipated, redefined. While Wolin points to Lenin's redefinition of democracy as "'bureaucratic' in the sense that the Party is built from the top downwards,"[42] we can point to the rationalist redefinition of democracy by American political scientist Robert Dahl and others who empirically observed that democracy actually works as rule by shifting minorities—later called the plurality of elites.[43] Politicians, political scientists, and other students of modern organization today observe not only the bureaucratization of democracy but of citizens, of politics through campaign management and technology, of interest groups, of courts, of Congress and other legislatures, even of the president.[44] The same president who praised bureaucrats also complained of the bureaucratization of everything that came before him:

Sooner or later it seems that every problem mankind is faced with gets dumped into the lap of the president right here in the center of it all. But by the time it reaches here, the problem has been dissected, sanitized, and cast into a series of options—almost as though they were engraved in stone. What is missing is the heart behind them, what they mean in human terms.[45]

In fact a number of presidents have limited their political potential by checking off alternatives presented on "option papers." This is a bureaucratic approach to politics that assumes that choices are already present in the environment when, in reality, not even problems emerge fully shaped from the environment.

As a leading consultant and scholar on bureaucracy has noted, "Underlying every public debate and every formal conflict over policy there is a barely visible process through which issues come to the awareness and ideas about them become powerful."[46] Political scientists have only of late issued warnings about keeping this process alive. Examining the increased use of staff by members of Congress, Michael Malbin warned that members of Congress were increasingly denying themselves the opportunity to get a sense for what was going on in other people's districts by personal contact with other members of Congress.

A representative system would require elected members from one district with one set of needs and interests, to talk to members from districts with different needs and interests, if the members hoped to achieve anything. Indirect communication, such as we see today, was not what was envisioned: direct communication among elected members was considered essential to informed deliberation.[47]

Similarly, political scientist Raymond Cox, a longtime staffer in the Massachusetts legislature, cautioned against applying bureaucratic standards to legislative performance: "A legislature may be entirely functional without being either efficient or productive.[48]

Ironically, it has been in business that a politics of focusing on how problems are shaping up received its most potent recognition in recent years. After decades of making policy from alternatives presented them by middle managers, engineers, and executive staff, the American automotive industry suddenly was confronted in the 1970s with the fact that its huge bureaucratic machinery had lost touch with reality. American car buyers were turning to Japanese products that actually functioned as cars. That is, Japanese cars had the ability to get you from one place to another with greater reliability than American cars. After defending itself like any bureaucracy against any input from reality that would endanger internal values, the industry finally turned to a single outside consultant—James Harbour, who had been beating on its doors for years—to hear what made Japan so much better. Within a few years, much of the American auto industry had begun to balance a system of top-down policymaking based on quantity with a bottom-up system of "political" consultation with workers who could tell management *what* was actually going on in the production line. By 1982, 41 percent of all American companies having more than five hundred employees reported they had worker-management participation programs. In these the goals of management could be brought in touch with knowledge of reality that only hands-on workers could have. Similar revolts against bureaucratized politics can be observed in the public sector.[49]

The problem with the bureaucratization of politics is simply this: bureaucracy, both private and public, is infested with the modern bias toward believing that what is real is measurable. As early as the turn of the century, the philosopher Edmund Husserl, himself a mathematician, predicted that an increasingly mathematized civilization would eventually lose touch with the physical things it was measuring. The civilization had come to believe that all human activities could be predesigned according to universal laws. The model was physics. But an increase in mathematical knowledge *about* physics ultimately led to a neglect of the knowledge *of* the physical that comes to the worker when he or she lays hands on a wheel and an axle and tries to fit the two together.[50] Similarly, in official politics and public service, faith grew in policy clearly predefined and programs with measurable performance standards. These would produce intended results all by themselves. This faith now is challenged by the bureaucratic experience of those who actually lay their hand on things or on clients.

The collision between bureaucracy and politics can be summarized in terms of two opposing tendencies observable in modern civilization today:

1. There is a tendency to "rationalize" politics, to conduct it as if it were a rational process of making decisions among clear choices already formed in people's minds. This leads to the evaluation of politics and politicians according to bureaucratic standards. The central standard is measurability.
2. There is a countertendency to "derationalize" politics: to give renewed care to

those processes by which human beings define who they are, what their problems might be, and what possibilities arise out of conflict between what is already here and what is still possible. This leads to a conduct of politics according to a concern for how problems are framed *before* decisions are made about alternatives. The mode is one of discovery. New possibilities are evoked; the body politic is convoked. The central standard in politics as much as in economics, private production, or public service is quality: from *qua* = *what* things are.

Five Foundations of Conflict

Bureaucracy continues its victory march around the globe. It changes human life socially, culturally, psychologically, linguistically/cognitively, and politically. It takes human needs and promises to erect a huge storehouse of goods and services that satisfies these needs. Only the most advanced modernized countries, and others modernizing but with a strong culture of their own, begin to suspect the cost: that, in order to satisfy human needs, bureaucracy must change them. The mentality is best expressed in the words of an American commander in Vietnam:

> We had to destroy the town in order to save it.

Bureaucracy, as one psychoanalytic organization theorist has pointed out, is an externalized self system that promises to construct an outer world of total security for a species of beings whose psyche is destined to struggle between both love and war. In its most grandiose worldwide structure—the nuclear balance of terror supported by computerized armies and armies of computers, the ultimate bureaucracies—bureaucracy has produced permanent worldwide readiness for war as its answer to human longing for peace. Even at this early a stage of examining the bureaucratic experience, we can see that both its solutions to human problems and its methods are shot through with paradoxes like this.

Socially, bureaucracy brings people physically closer to each other than ever, by making them more interdependent; yet it does this by pushing them farther apart through replacing *mutually oriented social action* by *rationally organized action.* Strangers fill positions next to each other without ever looking at each other, each looking upward and outward for hierarchy or the system to tell him or her what to do. Ironically, this system of getting work done is the most powerful yet devised in human history—for that kind of work that can be conceived of and organized from the top down. Only the extent of informal organizations and actual work behavior that falls outside of the formal structure indicates just how much this top-down social structuring of work relies for its success on the voluntary associations of its workers as social beings and on the bottom-up knowledge of reality that only hands-on workers can have.

Psychologically, bureaucracy rips control over conscience and mastery out of the psyche of the individual bureaucrat and deposits these functions in organizational structures: hierarchy and division of labor. What sense of self is left to the individual comes in terms of organizational *identity*—what the organization says he or she is—not *personality*—who a person becomes when left to grow and utilize all of individual psychic potential. In the absence of the inner strength of knowing who we are that comes from an autonomous personality, we suffer recurrent attacks of existential anxiety whenever separation from the bureaucratic home is threatened. This anxiety also explains why we stay with bureaucracy even when it destroys us, and it is the basis for managers' manipulation of employees.

Culturally, bureaucracy replaces ordinary human cultural values with values of its own: values compatible with the inner needs of the bureaucratic machine. Permanent prehostility as a quantitatively measurable but qualitatively inadequate substitute for peace is only the most blatant and globe-spanning example. Ultimately, bureaucracy, like modern science and technology, places a faith in *quantitative* measurement as a standard for what is real where there used to be a faith of human beings in the inner *qualitative* experience of human life. However, this triumph of quantity is today being challenged, beginning with the decline in quality when control over quantitative aspects of time and space is exaggerated beyond human tolerances and below the utility of products in the mass production of goods.

Linguistically/cognitively, bureaucracy commands through the top-down definition of reality: defining what things are. By instilling the practice of analogous thinking, bureaucrats are trained to act only when they recognize aspects of *reality* matching predefined *models* for action. Top-down speech and analogous thinking, however, preclude the discovery of new problems and the shaping of solutions continuously adapted to a changing reality.

Power-politically, bureaucracy reaches its peak. Max Weber called it *a control instrument* without compare. Created as the tool and servant of politics, bureaucracy today redefines politics by imposing on it bureaucratic standards. But especially in its encounter with politics, bureaucracy's limits become intolerably obvious. The more bureaucracy relies on the rationalization of everything—which ultimately means placing its faith in the most rational of all mental constructs: the world of numbers—the more it becomes detached from physical, social, and psychological reality. Politics, itself seduced into the process of rationalization and bureaucratization, shows its potential for being the single most important human tool for getting in touch with new realities exactly when rationalization and bureaucracy achieve their triumph. There is potential for both release and tragedy here. If humankind has to learn the lesson of reason's detachment from reality in an event as global as the current international security structure—for example, in a massive failure of a proposed Strategic Defense Initiative (Star Wars) system—it will be too late to celebrate a politics that focuses not on end-states but on human possibilities.

The personal and professional lessons that might be drawn from the analysis of bureaucracy as a separate culture with its own norms, behaviors, psychology, language, and political structure cannot even be outlined in an introductory essay such as this. In general, however, each of the persons most concerned with tackling the problems bureaucracy presents—manager, functionary, and client—might begin to recognize that the challenge is not one of making minor adjustments, such as "humanizing" management, "psyching out" the job in order to keep it, or "getting access" to get the goods.

Managers who "humanize" or "personalize" some of their relationships with their hierarchy (they obviously cannot personalize *all* relationships given the size of most bureaucracies) are not simply stepping on the toes of some people who will be jealous of such relationships from which they are excluded. They are, in fact, subverting the basic structure of modern organization: they are opening up to question the taken-for-granted value system that provides most functionaries with guidelines for success, attacking the identity of functionaries as organizationally defined and thus frightening the excluded to their very core, and factually and legally engaging in "corruption" in the true sense of the word by propagating emotional relationships that threaten death to rationalistically legitimated ones.

For functionaries the problem is not merely one of making a minimal adaptation to the bureaucracy. In most cases they must allow themselves to be brainwashed into new norms, change their personality structure from self-orientation to dependency, make bureaucratic language and thought their own, submit and uphold the hierarchic power structure, and cut themselves off from personal empathy and relationships with clients. To the extent they do not, the probability of official failure rises.

Clients are in the most difficult position. Without the institutional support given to recruits into bureaucracy, clients must learn a new language, think alien thoughts, tune in to new norms, bow properly to immense institutional power, understand and flatter the bureaucratic personality, and try to become a "case." Paradoxically, especially in social policy bureaucracies, only to the extent that clients surrender their humanity are they given the bare promise of material support by which to uphold that humanity.

Each of these problem areas deserves separate investigation.

NOTES

1. Max Weber, *The Protestant Ethic and the Spirit of Capitalism*, trans. Talcott Parsons (New York: Scribner's, 1958), p. 182.

2. Max Weber, *Economy and Society: An Outline of Interpretive Sociology*, 3 vols. Guenther Roth and Claus Wittich, eds. Ephraim Fischoff trans. New York: Bedminister Press, 1968). All of the points made here are in the essay entitled "Bureaucracy," pp. 956–1005. On the transformation of social relations, Weber writes, p. 987: "Bureaucracy is *the* way of translating social action into rationally organized action."

3. Ibid., p. 975: "Bureaucracy develops the more perfectly, the more it is 'dehumanized,' the more completely it succeeds in eliminating from official business love, hatred, and all personal, irrational, and emotional elements which escape calculation."

4. Ibid., p. 998: Bureaucratization favors development of "the [new] personality type of the professional expert." P. 968: Bureaucracy develops "the official's readiness to subordinate himself to his superior without any will of his own."

5. Ibid., p. 992. This is my expansion on Weber's comment regarding bureaucracy's interest in secrecy, extending even to the use of a "secret script." See Chapter 4.

6. Ibid., pp. 987 and 991. See also p. 1403.

7. The book has now been used by all strata of civil servants at the federal, state, and local levels, in quasi-independent agencies, and in the private bureaucracy of corporations. This third edition if fundamentally a response to their input.

8. For example, a congressional survey showed that 65 percent of the public and 57 percent of elected officials agreed with the statement, "The trouble with government is that elected officials have lost control over the bureaucrats, who really run the country." Source: U.S. Congress, Committee on Government Operations, Subcommittee on Intergovernmental Relations, *Confidence and Concern: Citizens View American Government* (Washington, D.C.: U.S. Government Printing Office, 1973), part 2, p. 115, and part 3, p. 61. Similarly 73 percent of citizens and 80 percent of elected officials agreed that the federal government had become too bureaucratic. Ibid., part 2, p. 114, and part 3, p. 60.

9. Here bureaucrats are caught in a classic bureaucratic paradox: they may do their work well and yet the work itself may be criticized. A study that reports that 69 percent of a bureaucratic office's clients were "satisfied with the way the office handled your problem" says nothing about whether the clients wanted to be handled at all or whether the bureaucracy created the problem. Perhaps the office was the Internal Revenue Service, the local police station, or the county jail. See Charles T. Goodsell, *The Case for Bureaucracy—A Public Adminstration Polemic*, 2nd ed. (Chatham, N.J.: Chatham House, 1985), p. 23, reporting analysts' explanations for lower satisfaction in generalized attitudes toward bureaucracy in contrast to higher specific satisfactions. (Study cited: Daniel Katz, Barbara A. Gutek, Robert L. Kahn, and Eugenia Barton, *Bureaucratic Encounters* [Ann Arbor: Institute for Social Research, University of Michigan, 1975.]) Questions about human satisfaction with bureaucracy cannot be asked from within the bureaucratic framework, when what is suspect is the framework itself.

10. President John F. Kennedy quoted in Bernard Rosen, "Who Needs Bureaucrats?—In the National Interest," *The Bureaucrat—The Journal for Public Managers*, vol. 12, no. 1 (Spring 1983), pp. 41–43; citation from pp. 41–42.

11. Every civil servant I have ever taught has acknowledged the problem of attuning oneself to the realities inside the organization as distinguished from and often opposed to the realities outside the organization. People, situations, and things to be trusted are simply different in modern organizations than they are in ordinary social life. In fact, the issue of trust looms ever large for inmates of bureaucracies. For example, the 1979–80 Federal Employees Attitudes Survey asked bureaucrats to respond to the statement, "Employees here feel you can't trust this organization." Out of a survey of 13,799 bureaucrats, a total of 42.4 percent agreed, 16.2 percent were undecided, and 41.4 percent disagreed. Source: U.S. Office of Personnel Management, 1979–80 Federal Employees Attitudes Survey, "Measures of Trust, Efficacy, Participation, Authority and Communication and Their Distribution" reported in David Nachmias, "Determinants of Trust Within the Federal Bureaucracy," in

David Nachmias, ed., *Public Personnel Policy: The Politics of Civil Service* (Port Washington, N.Y.: Associated Faculty Press, 1985), pp. 133–43; citation from p. 139.

12. Barbara Basler, "A Blind and Deaf Infant's Short Life on the Rolls of New York's Homeless," *New York Times*, Dec. 20, 1985, pp. B1 and B5; citation from p. B1.

13. Weber, *Economy and Society*, p. 4.

14. Basler, p. B5.

15. Ibid., p. B1.

16. Weber, *Economy and Society*, p. 987.

17. "The Broken Chain of Command," editorial, *New York Times*, Dec. 21, 1985, p. 26.

18. Basler, p. B5.

19. U.S. Congress, Committee on Government Operations, Subcommittee on Intergovernmental Relations, *Confidence and Concern: Citizens View American Government* (Washington, D.C., U.S. Government Printing Office, 1973), part 2, pp. 275–76.

20. H. Brinton Milward, and Hal G. Rainey, "Don't Blame the Bureaucracy!" *Journal of Public Policy*, vol. 3, Pt. 2 (May 1983), pp. 149–168; citation from pp. 154–55.

21. Weber, *Economy and Society*, p. 998.

22. The technical terms "superego" and "ego" used here are Sigmund Freud's. But any modern psychology focuses on the conscience and mastery functions.

23. Personal communication with Prof. Michael A. Diamond of the University of Missouri, who has served as consultant for federal and state governments.

24. Case paraphrased from personal communication with Douglas LaBier, Jan. 2, 1986. The case is discussed in Douglas LaBier, *Modern Madness: The Emotional Fallout of Success* (Reading, Mass.: Addison-Wesley, 1986).

25. Personal communication with Cynthia Confer, Jan. 13, 1986.

26. The differentiation here between a psychological concept of anxiety and an ontological one is derived from a comparison of Sigmund Freud and Martin Heidegger on anxiety in R. P. Hummel, "Anxiety in Organizations: Heidegger and Freud," paper delivered at the annual scientific meeting of the International Society for Political Psychology, June 1983, Toronto, Canada.

27. The theory of how social place affects what we get to see of reality belongs to the sociology of knowledge. See especially Karl Mannheim, *Ideology and Utopia*, various editions, and Peter Berger and Thomas Luckmann, *The Social Construction of Reality* (Garden City, N.Y.: Doubleday, 1967).

28. This case is reported from a transcription of an ABC "Nightline" television broadcast, Feb. 4, 1986.

29. See Frank Riessman, Jerome Cohen, and Arthur Pearl, eds., *Mental Health of the Poor* (New York: Free Press, 1964).

30. As against the "culture of poverty" argument, it might be argued that some of the poor, because they tend to personalize human relations while middle-class people are better able to relate to one another impersonally, may actually escape bureaucratization. For the personal/impersonal difference between lower class and middle class, see Herbert Gans, *The Urban Villagers* (New York: Free Press, 1965).

31. McNamara was reported to have been strongly influenced by the work of economists Charles J. Hitch and Roland N. McKean, *The Economics of Defense in the Nuclear Age* (Cambridge, Mass.: Harvard University Press, 1960). My thanks to Gideon Sjoberg for pointing this out.

32. Jürgen Habermas, *Toward a Rational Society* (Boston: Beacon Press, 1971), p. 96.

33. Weber, *Economy and Society*, pp. 956–958; cf, pp. 224–225. Similar norms hold for bureaucracy in private enterprise. See ibid., "The Conditions of Maximum Formal Rationality of Capital Accounting," pp. 161–64.

34. Max Weber, *Staatssoziologie—Soziologie der rationalen Staatsanstalt und der modernen politischen Parteien und Parlamente*, 2nd ed., ed. Johannes Winckelmann (Berlin: Duncker & Humblot, 1966), p. 45.

35. Max Weber, *Economy and Society*, p. 225. Here *sine ira ac studio* is rendered differently. The German terms Weber used in the Staatssoziologie compilation are *ohne Zorn und Eingenommenheit*.

36. For example, Edmund Husserl, *The Crisis of European Sciences and Transcendental Phenomenology*, tr. David Carr (Evanston, Ill.: Northwestern University Press, 1970), p. 32,

and Martin Heidegger, *What Is a Thing?*, Trs. W. B. Barton, Jr., and Vera Deutsch (South Bend, Ind.: Regnery/Gateway, 1967).

37. This refers to Husserl and Heidegger's point that with the advent of modern physics what constitutes knowledge for the entire civilization is not based on qualities *inside* of things, as ancient Greek physics (valid up to Galileo) used to assume. Instead, knowledge is based on *external laws*, which measure quantities of things and their relations. Scientific knowledge of this sort denies the validity of the inner experience of life.

38. See Husserl and Heidegger, above, footnote 37, as well as the discussions of culture and cognition in chapters 2 and 4 based on Heidegger.

39. This theme is further developed in R. P. Hummel, "The Two Traditions of Knowledge: Quality Management and the Crisis of Quantity," in Don Calista, ed., *Bureaucratic and Governmental Reform*, vol. 9 of *Public Policy Studies Series: A Multivolume Treatise* (New York: JAI Press, 1986).

40. From Max Weber's essay "Parliament and Government in a Reconstructed Germany," Appendix II of *Economy and Society*, pp. 1381–1469; citation from pp. 1403 and 1404. The last paragraph has been retranslated by the present author from the German "Parlament und Regierung im Neugeordneten Deutschland: Zur politischen Kritik des Beamtentums und Parteiwesens," in Max Weber, *Gesammelte Politische Schriften*, 2nd ed., ed. Johannes Winckelmann (Tübingen [West Germany]: J.C.B. Mohr (Paul Siebeck), 1958), pp. 294–431, from pp. 322–23, because of omissions in the original translation. The material in brackets represents a synthesis of Weber's third point, which he himself neglected to put in question form.

41. Sheldon Wolin, *Politics and Vision: Continuity and Innovation in Western Political Thought* (Boston: Little, Brown, 1960), p. 416.

42. Wolin, op. cit., p. 425, citing Lenin, *Selected Works*, Vol. II, pp. 447–48, 456 (Footnote 1).

43. Ralph P. Hummel and Robert A. Isaak, *The Real American Politics* (Englewood Cliffs, N.J.: Prentice-Hall, 1986), pp. 88–89, 104–105, and 109.

44. For a thorough survey, see David Nachmias and David H. Rosenbloom, *Bureaucratic Government U.S.A.* (New York: St. Martin's Press, 1980).

45. John F. Kennedy, quoted by Lou Harris in *The Anguish of Change* (New York: Norton, 1973), p. 15.

46. Donald Schön, *Beyond the Stable State* (New York: Norton, 1971), p. 123.

47. Michael Malbin, *Unelected Representatives: Congressional Staff and the Future of Representative Government* (New York: Basic Books, 1980), p. 247.

48. Personal communication with Prof. Raymond Cox of Northern Arizona State University. See also Raymond Cox and Michael R. King, "American State Legislatures: Models of Organization and Reform," paper presented at the annual meeting of the Midwest Political Science Association, Chicago, April 17–20, 1985.

49. See Hummel, "The Two Traditions of Knowledge," cited in footnote 39.

50. See Ralph P. Hummel, "Bottom-Up Knowledge in Organizations," paper delivered at the Conference on Critical Perspectives in Organization Theory, Sept. 5–7, 1985, Baruch College, City University of New York.

1

Bureaucracy as the New Society

Bureaucracy is the means of transforming social action into rationally organized action.

—Max Weber[1]

What does it mean in a practical sense when we warn a newcomer to bureaucracy in Max Weber's words that "bureaucracy is *the* means of transforming social action into rationally organized action"? In juxtaposing social action and rationally organized action, it is clear that Weber is warning us about a *difference* between society and bureaucracy.*

HOW PEOPLE ACT

The Citizen versus Bureaucracy

The man in the street experiences that difference every day. It has to do with the coldness and impersonality with which he is typically treated by the street-level functionaries of a bureaucracy. Before he walked into the doors of, say, the New York Motor Vehicles Department, our man in the street was a proud car owner, a man of substance because he could own a car, a man with some degree of self-esteem because he just steered that car through difficult traffic—in other words, a human being with class, status, and unique personality. Once inside the door, he is told to stand in line, fill out forms just so, accept the rejection of the way he filled out

---

*As throughout the book, each difference between society and bureaucracy is here first treated experientially. Analysis of the difference in social relations begins in the second section of the chapter.

25

his forms, told to stand in the same line again to wait another hour or so, required to answer the questions of the man or woman behind the desk, directed to another line, and so on.

They made me feel like a kid, like I didn't have a brain in my head. The whole thing didn't make sense. First one line, then another. Then they sent me back to my insurance agent for my F-1 form I didn't know I was supposed to have. I told them I just took off the day to get my license plates and couldn't take off another. Couldn't they just give me my plates and I would mail in my form? No! The rules say . . . blah, blah . . . another day shot.

—Man interviewed outside a Motor Vehicles Department office[2]

"They made me feel like a kid. . . ." The client here commits his first and almost universal error in misunderstanding bureaucracy. Actually, he is turned into less than a child in the eyes of the bureaucrat. He is turned into a "case." The bureaucrat has no time and no permission to become involved in the personal problems of clients. From the bureaucrats' point of view, the more they can depersonalize the client into a thing devoid of unique features the more easily and smoothly they will be able to handle cases before them.

Here is where the client commits a second mistake of misunderstanding. In the world from which the client has just come, the world outside the bureaucracy's door, there are many areas of life in which it is absolutely necessary to take into account the unique personality of the person with whom you are dealing. Friendship and salesmanship are two of these areas. When you go to a friend for help, he or she helps you in a personal and intimate way precisely because you are unique—because you are you, a friend. If you are trying to sell door-to-door, whether it is cosmetics or life insurance, you had better take into account the unique state of mind of the individual you are selling to. It may make a difference to know that a housewife's husband has just put her on a strict budget or that the person you are trying to sell life insurance to has just that day lost a relative.

Yet when the Avon representative and the sales people from Prudential walk into the Motor Vehicles Department, they see themselves treated in exactly the opposite way from how they would treat their clients, their customers. The normal assumption, the second misunderstanding engaged in, runs along the following lines:

Those goddamn bureaucrats behind the counter got it soft. They got Civil Service, can't get fired. I knock myself out with every customer; they can just kiss me off. They should have my job for a while, they'd try harder.

—The same man interviewed outside the Motor Vehicles Department[3]

The misunderstanding is typical. What the client here fails to understand is that the pressures on the bureaucrat behind the counter are such that the very same behaviors that a client finds objectionable guarantee the bureaucrat "success" within the rules of his or her bureaucracy—not just this bureaucracy, an organization running on the modern bureaucratic model. In Weber's words, "Bureaucracy develops the more perfectly, the more it is 'dehumanized'."[4]

This kind of statement seems to fly in the face of all common sense. Is not a public service bureaucracy, especially, set up to provide public service? The answer has to be yes. By definition it is set up to provide service. But it is also set up to be a bureaucracy!

The Bureaucrat and the Client

There are many ways of giving public service. The Salvation Army gives public service. Parishioners in your local church collect money to give to the poor at Christmas. Society women hold a charity ball. You give to a poorly dressed man holding out his hand on a street corner. Whether any of these ways of giving are bureaucratic remains to be examined. The last two examples are likely to be unbureaucratic.

SERVICE WITHOUT A SMILE

Bureaucracy is a particular strategy, chosen from among others, through which public service can be given. Weber indicated the chief characteristic of bureaucracy as a specific organizational strategy for giving service: it is characterized by "rationally organized action" not by "social action." In fact, it transforms social action into rationally organized action.

In brief, the way bureaucrats relate to clients is analagous to the way people in one country relate to people from an entirely different country. Bureaucrats can't help the way they act—if they want to remain employed members of bureaucracy. There is something innate in bureaucracy that turns bureaucrats into people who provide service coldly, impersonally, without a frown or a smile.

The newcomer to a bureaucracy, intending to keep the job, and the client approaching a bureaucracy, wanting to get service and still remain sane, had better understand the difference in the codes of behavior built into society and bureaucracy; that is, the conflict of "social action" versus "rationally organized action."

The alternative, even for the experienced bureaucrat, can be eternal puzzlement. A social worker for Catholic Charities talks about her attempts to get humane, personal attention for her clients from welfare case workers:

In dealing with clients we would eventually have to take certain clients down to welfare, Social Security, the board of education and they would see a caseworker.

Still, no one is interested in what your problem is. The caseworker screens you like you have applied for a Banker's Trust loan.

Eventually you get pretty tired of all the bullshit questions and ask, Are you so inhuman that you can't deal with the client as a person? Then, being the dedicated caseworkers that they are, they'll give you some crap about the manual not allowing for that.

If you still continue along this line of questioning the caseworker—or, as they call it, harassment of the caseworker—they will read you the rules and regulations of the welfare department.

All of this keeps you in line and keeps them uninvolved. . . .

Bureaucracy, as you say, is *the* means of transforming social action into rationally organized action. Which is what any well-organized agency will do, in that they cut through the bull and get to *their* main objectives, not *yours*.[5]

Ultimately, functionaries who cannot accept the restrictions of bureaucratic service leave, or are forced to leave, the bureaucracy. A former social worker tells of the frustrations that led to her being fired:

For two and a half years, I was a social worker for a private child caring agency which cared for dependent and neglected children. Since these children were all from New York City, our agency was funded by the City of New York and thus we were bound by the rules of the Bureau of Child Welfare of the city's Social Service Department.

My job was to provide casework services to the children and their families. The goal was to come up with some long-range plans for the child—hopefully to reunite him with his family or to place him in a long-range foster home. I had a regular caseload and visited the families every two weeks.

I had a difficult time adjusting to some of the rules set up by both New York City and the agency that employed me. We always had to become somewhat detached from our clients. It was not my job to get involved in determining how much welfare money my clients received. Almost all of them were receiving public assistance and it was easy to see that it wasn't enough.

I recall using my own money to buy Christmas gifts so that the parents would give them to the children when they spent the holidays with them. I occasionally brought food with me to my clients because it was easy to see that their public assistance allotment wasn't enough.

I never told this to my employer.

Our agency had a rule that the parents could come and visit the children every other Sunday. I remember feeling frustrated over this, as I felt that it was hardly enough contact. I remember asking how this decision was arrived at and being told by my supervisor that he didn't know: it had always been that way.

I always felt that the bureaucratic process placed a great gap between the social worker and the client. This created much frustration because I guess I felt some human feelings toward these people and couldn't give them what I wanted to. There were too many regulations and forms that got in the way of what I considered to be a good relationship based on needs and feelings.

Thus, I didn't last long.

—*Elaine G., currently personnel director*
for a detention shelter for juveniles[6]

Despite puzzlement, resentment, and an overpowering sense of frustration, both the Catholic Charities social worker and the child care agency social worker put their finger on essential characteristics of bureaucracy. Their only problem is that they perceive these essentials as pathology.* In their own words, these essentials are:

1. Bureaucracies "get to *their* main objectives, not *yours.*"
2. "Regulations and forms" get in the way of "a good [social] relationship based on needs and feelings."

Why is this so? Why should this be so?

WHAT PRICE EFFICIENCY?

Bureaucracy is an efficient means for handling large numbers of people—"efficient" in its own terms. It would be impossible to handle large numbers of people in their full depth and complexity. Bureaucracy is a tool for ferreting out what is relevant to the task for which the bureaucracy was established. As a result, only those facts in the complex lives of individuals that are relevant to that task need be communicated between the individual and the bureaucracy.

To achieve this simplification, the modern bureaucrat has invented the "case." At the intake level, individual personalities are converted into cases. Only if a person can qualify as a case is he or she allowed treatment. More accurately, a bureaucracy is never set up to treat or deal with persons: it "processes" only "cases."

Once this is understood, the uncanny fact is explained that within a bureaucracy you will never find clients in the form of human beings. They can have existence for the bureaucracy only as truncated paper ghosts of their former selves—as cases.

This simple fact of bureaucratic life is seldom communicated to prospective clients in any explanatory way. Clients continue to assume they are addressing the bureaucracy for help as they define it in all their complex individuality. The intake section of a bureaucracy usually resembles a theater of war. In fact it *is* a theater of war. The war is one between two cultures. It is conducted by two totally different personality types, according to two totally different rules of war. The opposing armies cannot even shout threats or imprecations at one another very well; their languages are too different.

---

*The citizen of the social world typically has this difficulty of being unable to believe that the dehumanizing characteristics of bureaucracy are the result of design rather than the result of a systems breakdown. This is exactly equivalent to the story of an old Italian immigrant to the United States who remembers: "When I first came to New York, off the boat, I thought the people were crazy. They couldn't even speak Italian." This observation neglected the fact that Americans were all crazy the same way: they all spoke English.

The Client as "Case" and the Policymaker

What is a case? A case is never a real person. A case is a series of characteristics abstracted from persons; it is a model of those characteristics that a potential client must display in order to qualify for the attention of a bureaucracy, whether for service or control. Definitions of what constitutes a case have far-flung impact not only directly on clients—who are accepted or rejected by comparison to these definitions—but on policy formation.

For example, case definition was crucial when one of the watchdog organizations appointed to keep an eye on New York City's finances noted a strange phenomenon in 1984: the City's public assistance "caseload" was continuing to rise at a time of high economic growth at both the national and local level.[7] In its attempts to explain such public assistance growth and to forecast future trends, the state's Office of the Special Deputy Comptroller for the City of New York needed to do two things: define what constituted "public assistance" and define under what conditions people could be expected to become "cases" that would add to the city's financial burden: that is, its caseload.

The Deputy Comptroller's Office defined public assistance as including benefits to indigent people under two major programs: Aid to Families with Dependent Children (AFDC) and Home Relief (HR).

AFDC was defined as providing "assistance to families with dependent children that are deprived of support due to the death, prolonged absence, incapacity or unemployment of a parent."

HR was defined as providing "financial assistance to indigent persons who do not meet Federal eligibility requirements for the AFDC program, including persons with substantial physical or mental impairments, unemployed young adults with limited training or work experience, and families with very low incomes." It also was defined as providing "temporary assistance to persons who are awaiting eligibility determination for the Supplemental Security Income (SSI) program, a Federally administered program which provides assistance to certain aged, blind or disabled individuals." These, of course, are summary definitions based on operational case definitions authorized for case "intake."

USING THE CASE IN POLICY ANALYSIS

Without definitions of who is likely to come onto the city's "case rolls," it would be impossible to explain or predict the financial load on the city's coffers. Using such definitions, the Deputy Comptroller's Office was able to construct an econometric model to explain the relationship between

Figure 1.1: Gross City Product (Lagged 1 Year) vs. Number of AFDC Recipients in New York City

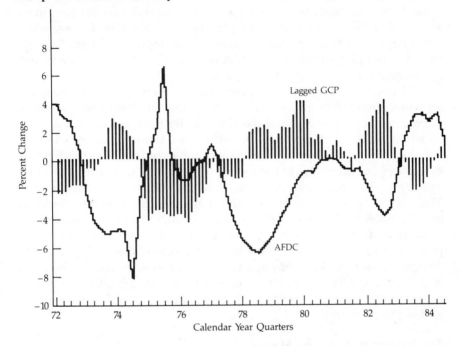

caseload and fluctuations in the city's economy as measured by Gross City Product, an indicator of the city's economic strength.*

By lagging Gross City Product one year behind the number of cases of AFDC, technical staff concluded that any trickledown effect of prosperity on the poor was delayed. Based on the past pattern of such delay, staff was able to predict that the growth in the city's AFDC caseload would level off or possibly decline over the near term, a trend already evident in a recipient decline of ten thousand between May and October of 1984—a drop of about 1 percent.

Even for those less than interested in whether the City of New York can survive carrying its public assistance caseload there is a lesson here. The "case" is not only the basic definition of whether a person in need officially can come to exist to the eyes and ears of bureaucracy; it is also the basis for all calculation of future needs of a bureaucracy and of the entire political system as it engages in providing government services and controls. By the time a human being is allowed to enter a bureaucracy as a case, that human being already no longer exists as a human being. That

*Gross City Product is defined as the total output of city goods and services adjusted for inflation. It is analogous to Gross National Product.

human being becomes a list of specific characteristics that the bureaucracy has been authorized by law to recognize as a case. Given our bias today toward measurement and numbers, such characteristics are believed to be more real if they can be defined in terms of calculations. For example, imposing an age range on who is meant by unemployed "young" adults makes it possible for all future calculations of an agency's needs and operations to be based on the *same* unit of calculation.

Herein lies not only a fundamental difference between people's self-perception when they stand in society and the client's official status as perceived by bureaucrats as the clients enter bureaucracy. In ordinary social life, each of us considers ourself to be a unique human being. In bureaucratic life, each of us is examined not according to our individual differences but according to a standard of sameness: Does each one of us measure up to those universally *same* characteristics that constitute a case? This trust in being able to create units of analysis based on sameness out of a population defining itself in terms of differences has, of course, fundamental and ultimate impact on this ultimate policy question: Can a policy and an administrative system based on calculations of *sameness* be designed to satisfy the needs of a population defining itself on the basis of *differentness*? To the extent that this is not possible, the calculations may be exact and even aesthetically pleasing, but they will have little or nothing to do with reality.

The Functionary and the Manager

The dehumanization of the functionary-client relationship is hard to understand, especially in public service agencies. After all, such agencies were set up to serve clients, or so clients keep saying. The classic remonstrance from a client with taxpayer consciousness is and always has been: "You're *my* employee. My taxes pay your salary. Now let's get some service around here!"

Bureaucracy as Organization

Yet this attitude ignores the nature of bureaucracy. After all, why do we have bureaucracy? If we stop thinking of it for a moment in its negative, dehumanizing role and compare bureaucracy to previous forms of organizing administration, we are left with one answer only. Bureaucracy, as a form of organization, is the most powerful instrument yet developed for getting people to work together on monumentally large common tasks. Modern bureaucracy harnesses more power than any, and possibly all, of the great projects of antiquity. As a form of organization, it makes possible the control of literally millions of people. And all these millions can be directed to one big project—bigger than building the pyramids, larger than the Roman Empire.

We live, as Weber pointed out, in an age of "universal bureaucratization."[8] "In a modern state," he wrote, essaying the impact of World War I on the process of bureaucratization, "the actual ruler is necessarily and unavoidably the bureaucracy. . . . "[9] Similarly, in a more recent work, Henry Jacoby explores, as the book's title indicates, "the bureaucratization of the world."[10]

What underlies this triumph of bureaucracy is its ability to amass and direct power. It does so better than any competing organization. And it does so whether in the private sector, as in the organization of modern business and industry, or in the public or political sectors, as in public service or the management of campaigns. The world over, those countries that have resisted "modernization"—that is, the introduction of bureaucratic organization and its norms—have been pushed aside and into the backwaters of history by modern, bureaucratized countries. In this sense the organization of China's Communist party is as much a triumph of bureaucracy as *the* form of modern organization as was the conquest of countries and continents by Western European nations in the nineteenth century.[11] Similarly, the state apparatus of one of the world's largest political organizations, the Soviet Union, has become one of the most successful control mechanisms in the world for exactly the reason that Weber predicted when socialism was first introduced in Russia: "Increasing 'socialization' today unavoidably means increasing bureaucratization."[12]

BUREAUCRACY AS CONTROL

What does the victory of bureaucracy as a control instrument of unparalleled power mean to people in everyday life? Listen to the complaint of a functionary in the personnel department of the Cleveland, Ohio, Board of Education.

For a long time, I felt my role within the bureaucracy was to deal with human needs. In recent years, accountability has become so important, however, that I now must spend more and more time completing forms and compiling records. In many instances this work is duplicated by others and there is less time devoted to rendering service.

My program director is caught up in this control situation and is constantly seeking new control methods and reactivating dormant rules. We had the sign-in and the sign-out procedure, the daily log, weekly, bi-weekly, monthly and yearly reports; now, we have a management information retrieval system.

When similar information about all workers in the program is placed in the system, management can then analyze this data and attempt to control the daily work schedule and work distribution. Before all this paperwork there was more productivity. It seems that accountability and productivity are not compatible.

—*Richard W., curriculum specialist*[13]

Here a functionary has put his finger on two countervailing pressures of bureaucracy that express themselves in the meaning of "rationally organized action."

VISIBLE VERSUS INVISIBLE ACTION

In bureaucracy, action is rational on two grounds: first, if an action is a *logical* means to a clearly defined end; second, if and only if action is performed in such a manner that its means-ends logic is *visible*. Action within bureaucracy must not only be action; it must also be subject to control. If it is not subject to control, it is not action. Or, rather, it may be action, but bureaucracy itself cannot take official notice of it.

This double aspect of action as defined in the modern era stems from our concept of science and pervades all the kinds of technology that institutionalize action. Science recommends this definition; technology, including modern bureaucracy as the technology of management, enforces it.

A social scientist, like sociologist Talcott Parsons, will include the double demand for both logic and visibility in a definition:

Action is rational in so far as it pursues ends possible within the conditions of the situation, and by the means which, among those available to the actor, are intrinsically best adapted to the end *for reasons understandable and verifiable by positive empirical science.*[14]

And a bureaucracy will enforce the double aspect by insisting both that work be done in a manner suitable to an overall purpose and that it be done in a visible manner so it can be checked and controlled from above.

Functionaries have a hard time accepting the double aspect. "Why," they typically ask, "do I have to spend hours filling out reports when anybody can see that I've got my work done." The demand for visibility is especially irritating to civil service personnel whose work is already highly visible to them. A battalion chief in the New York City Fire Department complains:

When the fire's out, the fire's out. Anybody can see that. We've done our job. There's a lot of satisfaction in that.

I don't even mind going over what happened at a big fire with the captains involved. I think it's necessary to debrief. You learn from that. Other people can see things that happened that you missed.

But then there are the reports. And the second guessing from upstairs. And the insisting on regs [regulations]: does your watch guy have his shirt buttoned, are shoes shined, are buttons on?

If I've got a good team that turns out a topnotch performance at a fire, I'm going to hassle them about a missing button?[15]

Yet bureaucracy is a control instrument and a control instrument without compare. Control is the source of power for this type of organization, and it is natural that those charged with control will emphasize the visible portions of what their subordinates do. As a result, instituting standard operating procedures and basing assessment of performance on observed compliance with these is a natural and normal solution to the problem of control experienced by an organization that grows larger and larger.

The results of such emphasis on the visible are also inevitable. Eventually control comes to mean largely checking that procedures are followed—instead of looking at impact.[16] In other words, for the sake of visible procedures that can be easily supervised by control personnel (management), the first condition of modern rational action—that action be logically connected to some end or purpose—is finally abandoned. Formality conquers substance.

The Organization and Citizens

A classic example of the loss of substance is the way teachers are forced to organize their teaching in most public schools. In an essay on alienation and bureaucracy, Michael P. Smith puts his finger on exactly that point at which the demand for controllable, visible work, with no other reason for being than its visibility, actually destroys work that is purposeful:

In many urban school systems excessive bureaucratization also has resulted in the routinization of teaching practices, which, in turn, has added to the deindividualization of the learning process. Even those teachers and principals who are person-oriented rather than task-oriented can be constrained by the weight of procedural strictures and paper work emanating from the central headquarters staff. In the St. Louis public school system, for example, teachers at the elementary level are required to organize their entire work week according to a printed form. Such behavior leaves little room for spontaneity or that leap of imagination we call creativity.[17]

The bias in favor of the visible, which can be recorded on paper and preferably in numbers, inevitably leads to results contrary to human intentions simply because less visible and qualitative aspects of human relations are left out of account. The following summary of a qualitative study of four high schools in the San Francisco Bay area is not atypical:

We have inadvertently designed a system in which being good at what you do as a teacher is not formally rewarded, while being poor at what you do is seldom corrected or penalized.[18]

"Every 50 minutes," the principal investigator said, "1,500 people play musical chairs. Like clockwork, people are moving from one place to another and, in the course of four to five minutes, must switch from thinking about the industrial revolution to the solution of a quadratic equation."[19]

How does this feel from a student's perspective? A star pupil, Charlotte Krepismann:

What it all comes down to is that the average student is remarkably unquestioning, accepting as normal that one moves from little box to little box [sometimes with the teacher in mid-sentence].[20]

This early training for service in bureaucracy—by inculcating an acceptance of hierarchy and division of labor—does ultimately have its comeuppance in adult reality. But by then the victim is safely removed from the school, and the school can continue to pride itself in its internal fragmentation not only of social relationships but of the meaning of the entire formal school experience. Political scientist and educational administration specialist David Schuman reports, for example, that his own in-depth study of college graduates showed these adults most critical of one thing: the fragmenting experience of their college life, disabling them from making coherent sense of real life, which after all is experienced in its totality.[21]

These examples contain two truths about the nature of bureaucratic action:

1. In bureaucracy, action can be recognized and rewarded even though it has become totally detached from people, as in the contrast between person-oriented and task-oriented school personnel.
2. In bureaucracy, action can be recognized and required even though it has become totally detached from an object—the teaching process from what is being learned, for example.

BUREAUCRATIC ACTION

What is bureaucratic action? Social action is normally initiated by a human being who has certain intentions or purposes. The action is intended to convey such goals or purposes and is addressed to a social partner whose understanding of the action is a key part of the purpose. Social action, then, consists of a human initiator with intentions, the action itself, and a human co-actor with understanding.

For most functionaries, bureaucratic action is reduced to the action itself. They are asked to leave their intentions out of it, and the people whose intentions are contained in the action are several rungs up the hierarchy, far removed from the functionary. The intentions, origins, causes of action are a mystery to the functionary. Action passes through him or her like water through a sieve—except that the functionary's job description is a sieve designed not to interfere with the flow and to channel it to a predetermined place. What that place is, who the victim or beneficiary of a policy is, or who becomes a "case" for a program—such issues, like the issue of whether the end of the action will or will not be

appreciated by the recipient—are not the official concern of the functionary.

In fact, action for the functionary ceases to be action. Instead, action
becomes functions, or operations, within a system. Bureaucratic behavior
is not primarily related to the logical point or purpose of the original
program or policy. What makes the functionary's action an operation or
function is determined by whether or not what he or she does meets the
rules and standards of the next higher job description that encapsules the
functionary in the division of labor. The functionary's actions are as
distant from the ultimate outcome as from the·original intent. It is not
social action at all, for it is separated from the bureaucratic actor's own
intentions and cares nothing for the understanding of the recipient client.
If social action is what you do *with* people, bureaucratic behavior is what
you do *to* things.

Bureaucratic action, therefore, is motion amputated from origin and
purpose. It is, however, never uncontrolled motion. I first understood
this difference between action and motion when a disgruntled client told
me about a bureaucracy with which he was having difficulty, "They went
through a lot of motions, but I didn't get any action."

The novice bureaucrat especially must keep this difference between
social action and bureaucratic action in mind if he or she is not to be
eternally puzzled by a fundamental absurdity of bureaucracy: if there is
ever a conflict between actually rendering a service to clients and thereby
endangering internal control within the organization, control must be
first. That is the bureaucratic imperative for self-preservation.* The
alternative is that the bureaucracy dies, as nearly happened to New York
State's Urban Development Corporation, which the former governor said
was intended to render service even at the risk of bankruptcy.†

CONTROL RELATIONSHIPS

All of the often-complained-about structural characteristics of bureaucracy—like the division of labor, which gives no single functionary enough
power to do anything alone but allows him or her to specialize, or the
requirement that the functionary treat clients not personally but as
cases—are derived from the imperative of control.

The division of labor, for example, has two purposes. On the one
hand, it makes a functionary capable of developing highly specialized

---

*For a detailed discussion of control as the bureaucratic imperative in public service, see
Chapter 2. But it should be obvious even at this point that, without its much vaunted claim
to be the most powerful instrument of control in the history of the world, bureaucratic
organization loses its raison d'être.
†The rise and fall of this almost unique bureaucracy, which abdicated the prime imperative
for maintaining control as the means for self-preservation, is traced in Chapter 2.

skills. The advantage of this may be that the bureaucracy can bring to bear on a specific problem an individual who has the ideal capabilities to resolve that problem. It makes possible the development of the expert. On the other hand, because of specialization, it is often impossible for one expert to solve an overall problem without the cooperation of other experts. And to mobilize this cooperation we need the manager.

We now have arrived at a most important insight into the whys and wherefores of the structural arrangements of bureaucracy. People's work is divided not only to make them expert and more efficient but also to make them dependent on managerial control.

If you want to survive as a bureaucrat, you will never forget that the prime relationship you engage in is that between you and your manager, not that between you and your client. And that functionary-manager relationship is a control relationship. The successful manager never forgets this.

In many public service bureaucracies the choice between service and control is being made every day. A police officer on the beat may truly want to render a service to a citizen.[22] In fact, contrary to popular misconception, the kinds of behavior of which police are most proud and which they recall with great self-respect are instances of personal service they have rendered to citizens. An anonymous patrolman in a Midwestern city provides an example:

The things you really do for people, you never get credit for.
I remember picking up this kid out of the gutter three times. High on dope. The fourth time, I start taking him in. His mother comes running up to me and says the kid is going into the army in a couple of days. The medical corps. He'll straighten out. He'll never be on the stuff again. I'm supposed to give him another chance. Three times before!
I must've been out of my skull. I let the kid go. Kid goes in the medical corps, gets his training. Now he's in medical school, becoming a doctor. Once in a while he still keeps writing me letters saying how I saved his life.
Imagine me putting that into my day report![23]

Here is a clear-cut case of an officer of a public service institution rendering an individual citizen a human service. No matter how laudable the patrolman's humanity might be, however, his act also represents a clearcut breakdown of bureaucratic control. It is a threat against the very existence of the police department as a modern organization that is at least potentially under the control of legitimate political authority.[24]

Against this deterioration of control, managers who intend to keep their jobs as sergeant, lieutenant, or captain of police will defend themselves by such techniques as introducing the use of "shoo-flies" (internal police spies), tightening up on the number of times a patrol officer has to report in by radio, and demanding more written reports on how and on what time was spent. All these assertions of control, of course, take time away from service. But it is a choice a manager cannot help but make.

WHAT THE EXPERTS SAY

What people experience, experts should explain. In the preceding, we have seen that social relations—how humans encounter humans—differ radically between bureaucracy and society. How has this difference been explained by the experts?

Max Weber

The classic, and still leading, expert on bureaucracy is Max Weber, who also gives us a definition of social action outside bureaucracy that underlies much of current sociology.

SOCIAL ACTION

In *Economy and Society*, the theoretical groundwork for his sociology, Weber offers this definition of action and social action:

We shall speak of "action" insofar as the acting individual attaches a subjective meaning to his behavior—be it overt or covert, omission or acquiescence. Action is "social" insofar as its subjective meaning takes account of the behavior of others and is thereby oriented in its course[25]

What does he mean, and how is what he means relevant for any attempt to distinguish between social action in bureaucracy and in society?

If we take Weber personally, his meaning becomes clear: I am engaged in action when I do something and attach some sort of meaning to what I do. For example, I may be swinging an ax and hacking away at a piece of wood. This behavior, in itself just a physical exercise, becomes action when I attach to my swinging and hacking the intention of ending up with some kindling for the fire.

So far Weber's point about action is merely definitional. He is simply saying to us: this is how I shall define "action" in a purely arbitrary way. But, of course, he has a hidden purpose, and this becomes apparent when we look at the definition of *social* action.

Social action is action not simply of the sort to which I, as the actor, attach my personal meaning. It is action in which I take into account the meaning that *others* may attach to it.

For example, if I am in the woods by myself and want some kindling, I may swing and hack at anything that comes along. If Joe is with me, however, I do not want him to misunderstand my wild swinging and hacking as an attack on him. I therefore chop in a very organized way at one piece of wood at a time, hoping Joe will recognize in my care and

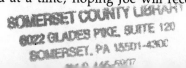

direction the meaning I attach to my action: "Hey, Joe, I'm chopping at this piece of wood, you see? Not at you!" When I so design my actions that I take into account how others might react, I have begun to transform action, with its purely personal meaning, into social action, which is intended to have meaning for myself and at least one other person.

From this, Weber progresses to the form "social relationship." "The term 'social relationship' will be used to denote the behavior of a plurality of actors insofar as, in its meaningful content, the action of each takes account of that of others and is oriented in these terms."[26] Now we have at least two actors, you and I, for example; and each of us acts in such a way that the other can understand the meaning of the action. I, for example, am now writing these words with the intention of having you understand them. And, you, to the degree that you want to engage in a reader-author (social) relationship with me, read with the intention of understanding me. To the extent that we each direct our actions toward the other, we are engaged in a social relationship.

Now let us ask ourselves to what extent bureaucrats are allowed to engage in either social action or social relationships with their clients. To answer the question, we can simply ask ourselves:

1. To what extent do bureaucrats intend to have their actions understood by clients?
2. To what extent do bureaucrats intend to engage in relationships with clients in which all action rests on mutual understanding?

In our ordinary human life, we treat people as people. We try to understand them and give them a chance to understand us. But what of the bureaucrats' position? Do they wait—*can* they wait—until they are engaged in a relationship of mutual understanding with their clients? The fact is that the machinery of bureaucracy must grind on long before that. What Weber meant to tell all of us working in and living with bureaucracy is that the pressures we feel from being unable to deal with clients as human beings are not occasional. They are not symptomatic of something gone wrong in bureaucracy. They are built into bureaucracy. They are essential to bureaucracy if the great claims of modern organization to greater efficiency and their ability to manipulate large masses of people are to be achieved. Bureaucracy *is* the rational organization of action.

That leaves us with one more of Weber's terms to understand. What is rationally organized action?

Rationally Organized Action

Weber clarifies the character of rationally organized action in another essay, "Some Categories of a Sociology of Understanding," in which he distinguishes between social action, defined as "action based on mutual understanding," and "institutionally commanded action."[27] The first type of action is most developed in that sociohistoric stage of development traditionally called "community." It is also called "communal action" (*Gemeinschaftshandeln*). "We shall speak of communal action," writes Weber, "wherever human action is related in terms of its subjective meaning to the behavior of other human beings."[28]

"Institutionally commanded action" (*Anstaltshandeln*)[29] gradually replaces communal action as community becomes "society"—that is, as human relationships become "socialized." In this new form the actions human beings engage in are designed by others. Individuals are expected to obey society's rules even if they did not have a chance to contribute to their design. In a final stage there is the probability that they can expect to be *forced* to obey.

In the first kind of action, two individuals are considered to be of the same mind, sharing an understanding of each other, because they have contributed to that understanding. In the second type of action, two individuals are of the same mind because they are *forced* into it.[30] This is the kind of action already prefigured in society. Society imposes general rules for proper social behavior, but personal discretion is allowed, providing plenty of room for actions based on mutual understanding. As society becomes more bureaucratic, however, rationally organized action finally collapses that room: in its never-ending search for control over its functionaries, bureaucracy must destroy discretion.

Rationally organized action thus dominates the step that follows community and society in the history of human existence. These stages and their dominant types of action can be portrayed as follows:

community = communal action based on mutual understanding.
society = social action: general rules mixed with discretion for exercise of understanding within the rules.
bureaucracy= rationally organized action: design of all action from above; shrinkage of discretion.

The insight that bureaucracy is a new type of social relationship, first outlined by Weber, is subsequently developed in three directions. Talcott Parsons and the functionalists accept rationally organized action as a necessary condition of the large-scale organizations into which human beings have fitted themselves for survival in the twentieth century.[31] Jürgen Habermas, a successor of both Weber and Karl Marx, criticizes the decline of true social relationships of a personal kind and penetrates the farthest of any academician into the consequences of the new form of human relationships in spheres such as education, technology, and politics.[32] But the third direction in which Weber's insight is developed contributes most intimately to the understanding of our personal experience with bureaucracy. This direction is pursued in the phenomenological sociology of Alfred Schutz.

Alfred Schutz

Phenomenology in this context refers to nothing more than a technique for reducing our experience of life in bureaucracy to its basics. Phenomenology begins with ordinary everyday experience, brackets out the accidental and unessential, and ends up by exposing the fundamentals of any experience.

Where Weber distinguished between social action as constituting ordinary social life and rationally organized action as constituting bureaucratic life, Alfred Schutz asks how such differences are experienced by ordinary human beings. He observed that such ordinary experience divides relationships I have with you into two types: in one I perceive you and myself as part of the same group, as part of a "we"; in the other I perceive you as alien to me, as part of a "they." Phenomenology thus points to two essential and different types of human relationships: the "pure we-relationship" and the "they-relationship."

WE-RELATIONSHIPS

In the pure we-relationship I create my social life with others who have intentions similar to mine. In the they-relationship the social world has been preconstructed for me and my contemporaries, and the problem becomes to get to know them in terms of the significance and role already assigned them by the system. It is easy to see that the we-relationship describes the situation between close friends, whereas the they-relationship describes that between bureaucrat and client, with the bureaucrat being forced to think of the client in terms predefined by the bureaucracy.

The same distinction can be observed between creative or revolutionary political action and institutionalized political action.[33] In creative politics at least two individuals must go through the effort of determining what each of them wants or intends. If their goals or intentions are similar, they then can work out a shared social act that will bring them together, laboring toward those goals. Once this act has worked for them in achieving their shared goals, they may want to repeat it under the assumption: we have done it once, we can do it again. But at that point, institutionalization of politics begins. The second time around, the problem of achieving a want or intention does not have to be apprehended anew. All the participants have to do is identify the want or intention. If it fits into the category of a want or intention previously accomplished by a political action, all they need to say is: "It fits under Political Routine No. 1001B; let's do Political Routine No. 1001B." Typical routines of action replace original and creative action. Bureaucracies and specifically their organizational structures are such routines frozen into permanently repeated patterns; that is, they are institutions. What makes social life appear human is a kind of intimacy I gain from interacting in depth with my consociates—the members of the little world whose center I am and which I enlarge by including you in the we-relationship. In fact, the more I make an effort to understand you in your complexity and the closer to you I feel, the more meaningful and satisfying life in the social world appears to me.

THEY-RELATIONSHIPS

They-relationships tend toward just the opposite pole. Routines, stereo-typing, recipes for action coded in work rules—and the evenhanded application of these to *all* comers—dominate they-relationships. The relationship between bureaucrat and client is easily recognized as the extreme example. Not that human relationships of a personal sort are never used, but they represent a deviation. The bureaucrat who becomes deeply involved in the life of a client is regarded as either undependable or corrupt.

When we think of bureaucracy in the value-free sense, neither condemning nor approbating, we think of the organization of human labor into methodically applying overall institutional goals and functions. The essential characteristics of such a human apparatus can be defined in terms of the inner logic it must come to possess if it is to carry out its predetermined purposes. These terms will be spelled out in the next section, but it already is evident that bureaucracy is the ideal type of the Schutzian they-relationships of the world of contemporaries, located at the polar opposite end from the we-relationships of consociates. In the world of contemporaries, Schutz writes, "we never encounter real living people at all."[34] It is not the face-to-face we-relationship in which "the partners look into each other and are mutually sensitive to each other's response."[35]

Schutz's concept of the they-relationship corresponds to Weber's concept of action that is not social. If we recall the example of the clerk in the license plate office, pressed by office rules and the number of clients, Schutz's concept helps us understand more closely the situation the clerk is in:

I cannot assume, for instance, that my partner in a They-relationship will necessarily grasp the particular significance I am attaching to my words, or the broader context of what I am saying, unless I explicitly clue him in.[36]

For me, as a hard-pressed clerk, there just isn't enough time to penetrate through the cloak of anonymity that having to treat people as cases has thrown over them. "As a result, I do not know, during the process of choosing my words, whether I am being understood or not. . . . "[37]

Few bureaucracies have standards for the functionary's behavior that test the client's understanding of what the functionary has done or said. Schutz points out, "In indirect social experience there is only one way to 'question a partner as to what he means,' and that is to use a dictionary. . . . "[38] This again argues the one-directionality of communication in a bureaucracy. Functionaries are allowed to uttter any statement they like from within a repertory assigned them by the organization. They need not see to it that this organizationally approved statement is understood. On the other hand, clients have to bend over backwards to learn the bureaucratic language.

TWO SEPARATE WORLDS

According to Schutz, the worlds of we-relations and they-relations remain distinct. As a client dealing with a bureaucrat, our ideal type of they-relationship, I am not allowed to know him intimately "unless, of course, I decide to go to see him or to call him up; but in this case I have left the They-relationship behind and have initiated a face-to-face situation."[39] As Schutz indicates, travel between the two worlds involves a special effort on the part of the client to gain personal access to the functionary. Of course, an infinite number of devices—ranging from failure to hand out a telephone number to claims of bureaucratic secrecy, purportedly intended to protect the client's anonymity—protect the bureaucracy and its functionaries from becoming accessible to what Weber called social action and Schutz calls the we-relationship:

In the We-relationship I assume that your environment is identical with my own in all its variations. If I have any doubt about it, I can check on my assumption simply by pointing and asking you if that is what you mean. Such an identification is out of the question in the They-relationship.[40]

Ultimately in the world of contemporaries (here used to include the world of bureaucracy), "we never encounter real living people at all. In that world, whether we are participants or observers, we are only dealing with ideal types. Our whole experience is in the mode of 'They.' "[41] In other words, we are dealing only with cases. But cases are artificial constructs that bureaucracy requires real people to become before they can be considered for service. The motorist must have an insurance form, a driver's license, and an application form, and must be free of driving tickets before qualifying for a license plate; that is, before flesh-and-blood uniqueness can become a generalized case that the bureaucracy is predesigned to handle. In Schutz's words:

Observation of the social behavior of another involves the very real danger that the observer will naively substitute his own ideal types [case characteristics] for those in the mind of his subject. The danger becomes acute when the observer, instead of being directly attentive to the person observed, thinks of the latter as a "case history" of such and such an abstractly defined type of conduct. Here not only may the observer be using the wrong ideal type to understand his subject's behavior, but he may never discover his error because he never confronts his subject as a real person.[42]

The results of the functionary-client relationship can be disastrous. A mother and her children applying for welfare may even suffer and die because the mother is one child short of becoming a "case." A patient is denied treatment at a hospital, not on medical grounds, but on grounds of being an insurance card short of qualifying financially for admission.

But these are extreme cases. More widespread, and affecting us all, is the ever-present pressure of a multitude of bureaucracies demanding that we think and act at all times like cases.

In conclusion, Schutz can show us, through his exposition of they-relationships, that in bureaucracy social life has ended. And he shows us the reasons why. If we first define what social life consists of— what Weber called social action and Schutz the we-relationship—then it becomes possible to measure the distance away from these standards of social life that human beings are forced to go.

Michael M. Harmon

DECISION-RULES AND KNOWLEDGE

The distance between extreme they-relationships and we-relationships can be portrayed on a spectrum suggested by the work on decision-rules of public administration theorist Michael M. Harmon. Five kinds of rules, Harmon says, are or can be employed in making and legitimating decisions in public organizations: hierarchy (unilateral decision), bargaining or market rules, voting, contract, and consensus.[43] There is one major benefit in thinking of how different decision-rules work in organizations: it becomes obvious that we get different kinds of knowledge depending on which decision-rule we use.[44] Consider the decision-rules distributed over a spectrum, as in Figure 1.2.

The kind of knowledge mobilized by the hierarchical setup permits only the knowledge of the superior, not the subordinate, to become the official basis for action.

As we move to contracting, each contracting partner has an autonomous power base and is respected for what he or she says on the grounds of that base. An exchange of knowledge is possible, though only on the basis of an assumed zero-sum game rule: what you win, I lose. Knowledge tends to be highly controlled still: I only let you know what I believe to be in my interest to let you know. Over this relationship, to keep individuals from killing each other, looms in the contractual system an umpire with enough power, as Thomas Hobbes said, to keep them all in awe. Hierarchy is still there, but knowledge arises from the contracting partners, not from the top down.

In bargaining, we move a step further from situations of domination and distrust. It is conceivable to think of two natives of different countries meeting on a desert island and bargaining food for services, or the like, without necessarily having a third party watch over them to threaten death and destruction if a bargain is not kept. Perhaps rational perception of one's own self-interest can function as a disinterested third party, if neither bargaining partner considers it in his or her interest to break off bargaining altogether. Very likely, however, bargaining also holds a hidden hierarchical agenda: each partner is likely to want to get the better of a bargain, thereby raising him- or herself to a superior position relative to the other (represented by the dotted circle in Figure 1.2).

Voting also mobilizes knowledge and, especially, judgments of bottom-line individuals; however, the separation of voters from one another prevents, at least during the act of voting itself, any communication about the definition of problems or solutions. As public administration specialist Frederick Thayer points out, democracy is a hierarchical system. Quite clearly he is right: the division of labor in the act of voting separates people from one another and representative government itself constructs a hierarchy at each election. While knowledge may flow upward in elections (that is, in *political* action), official *governmental* action is shaped by knowledge that flows downward from those authorized to aggregate it and use it.

CONSENSUS AS TRUE WE-RELATIONSHIPS

Only consensus operates on the possibility that a true we-relation is possible; that is, on the assumption that knowledge can be shared among

Figure 1.2: Decision-Rules

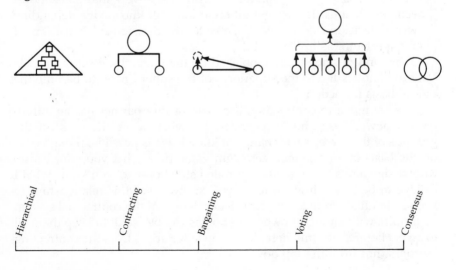

participants in a situation and that this knowledge is not simply additive (you tell me what you know, I'll tell what I know) but synthetic. Many heads in a consensual relationship are better than one, not simply because there are more sources of knowledge but because qualitatively superior problem definition can arise from such relationships.

Ultimately, Harmon argues, all parties gain from relationships in which assessment of a situation and the process of working out solutions are shared by all. "Even managers may get a surprise: they may actually gain power to solve problems by slackening the reins of topdown control over employees," Harmon says.[45] Much of organization development and of Japanese management rests on consensual decision rules. In fact, "decisions" as such tend to be avoided and become unnecessary as "insight" into problems suggests the solutions.

BUREAUCRACY AS SOCIETY

Bureaucracy replaces society. This claim may seem farfetched—but only at first. Examine the place of bureaucracy *in* society. At first, bureaucracy is only a tool. It is intended to be the extension of my hand as taxpaying citizen. Through the extension I reach out to other citizens who become the clients of bureaucracy.

Bureaucracy, the Divider

Bureaucracy, initially, is a bridge between citizens as taxpayers and citizens as clients. It links those who have something to give with those who expect to receive—taxpayer with welfare recipient—as distinct individuals. But bureaucracy also links me as taxpayer to myself as car driver in need of a license and license plate, as the victim of crime in need of police protection, as a citizen of a nation needing defense against other nations. The New York State Motor Vehicles Department, the Los Angeles Police Department, and the Defense Department in Washington, D.C.—all are links between me in one role (taxpayer, productive worker, voter) and me in my other roles (driver, crime victim, target for international attack).

When we think about the size of the huge machinery needed, so we are told, to link one part of ourselves to major other parts, a sense of a vast absurdity breaks through into our consciousness: the machinery intended to *link* me with my fellow citizens is also the machinery that separates me *from* them. The bridge has become a chasm.

In the realm of welfare, bureaucracy exists not only to channel funds from me to people whom taxpayers like me have decided are worthy of getting our help. The welfare bureaucracy in its size and complexity puts a vast physical distance between me and the welfare client. The welfare bureaucracy makes certain that I, as taxpayer, will never be confronted face to face with a welfare recipient.

Bureaucracy separates the giver from the taker, the giver from the bureaucrat, and the bureaucrat from the client. All three relationships cease to be personal, emotional, and social and begin to be impersonal, "rational," and machinelike. Here is the practical meaning of Max Weber's original insight that "bureaucracy is *the* means of transforming social action into rationally organized action."

Practical Attitudes Toward and in Bureaucracy

To what practical use can our insights so far be put? We can outline for ourselves as social actor, as citizen, as functionary, and as client—all of whom may be one person in separate roles—the type of attitude natural to each role. Once I can think clearly about the reality of the social interaction in which I must engage, I may hope to extricate myself from various difficulties and perhaps become more successful in my dealings with bureaucracy.

SOCIAL RELATIONSHIPS

If I want the benefits of life as a social actor I must take a specific attitude toward others. In society, the social relationship is the fundamental type of action. It involves at least *two people* who talk with one another about a *shared reality* and who interact with one another to construct or maintain that reality.

In more precise terms, any social relationship requires five elements:

1. Two discrete individuals,
2. each capable of orienting himself or herself to the other as if he or she were that other,
3. who share a common perception of a shared world,
4. who communicate about the world, and
5. who interact mutually to gain or maintain control of that world.[46]

Each of the words used here has a very special meaning in phenomenology. By "two discrete individuals," I mean people capable of social contact. They must be authentic and undamaged individuals, having an existence in their own right and free in a profound sense of such dependency-making forces as bureaucracy.

Graphically, the picture of external human interaction that emerges in society can be drawn as in Figure 1.3

Internally, however, the social relationship requires the existence of a core of values within the individual. To these the individual refers what he or she does. An action referred to values is a meaningful action. Similarly, in trying to understand what the action of another means, the

Figure 1.3: Elements of Social Interaction

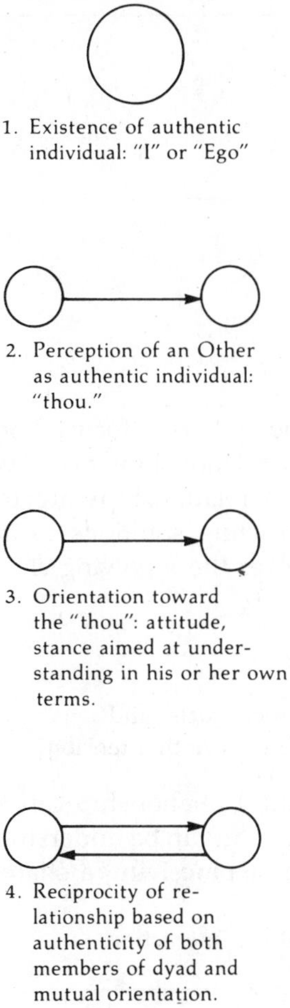

1. Existence of authentic
   individual: "I" or "Ego"

2. Perception of an Other
   as authentic individual:
   "thou."

3. Orientation toward
   the "thou": attitude,
   stance aimed at under-
   standing in his or her own
   terms.

4. Reciprocity of re-
   lationship based on
   authenticity of both
   members of dyad and
   mutual orientation.

Source: Derived from R. P. Hummel, "Are There Groups in Organizations?," paper
presented to the fifth scientific meeting of the A. K. Rice Institute, Washington, D.C., April
2–4, 1981.

individual perceiving the action first refers that action to his or her own
values, and if the result is not satisfactory, begins checking what the
action might mean in terms of the values of the other.[47] Social interactions
require the drawing of a more complex picture than that in Figure 1.3.
Figure 1.4 reflects the fact that the social actor must be adept at coming to
terms with his or her own inner values and with those of another.

Figure 1.4: Inner Referents of Social Action

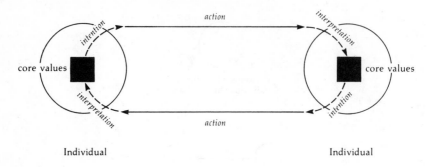

POLITICAL RELATIONSHIPS

The political attitude is more sharply focused on the ability to recognize human tensions. Political relationships are a variant of social relationships. In general, political relationships are those social relationships having to do with constructing solutions to acute social problems. A political relationship involves the following elements:

At least two people
who perceive and communicate
shared tension
between human needs and social facts, and
who initiate a relationship to resolve that tension.

Graphically, the political relationship can be depicted as in Figure 1.5. Any truly political situation can be understood in terms of at least two individuals, each capable of perceiving a shared tension and orienting

Figure 1.5: Elements of Political Interaction

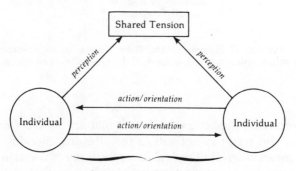

Interaction to Satisfy Need

Source: From Ralph P. Hummel and Robert A. Isaak, *Politics for Human Beings*, 2nd ed. (Monterey, Calif.: Brooks/Cole Publishing Co. Duxbury Press, 1980), p. 17

action toward the other to satisfy needs expressed in that tension. A political tension is not necessarily a tension between individuals but arises from the perception of a gap between existing solutions to human needs (social facts*) and new human needs. Political consciousness is the formulation of that tension in terms that can be communicated.

BUREAUCRATIC RELATIONSHIPS

The bureaucratic attitude is neither primarily social nor political but physical. Thus would things treat things, if they had any consciousness at all. In contrast to full social and political relationships, bureaucratic relationships are truncated. A bureaucratic relationship, or the bureaucratic field of action, consists of these minimal elements:

1. An individual (the manager) and a pseudo-being (the functionary),
2. the first orienting himself to the second as if it were the exclusive task of the latter to orient himself to the first,
3. both lacking a common perception of a shared reality but organizationally restricted to living in worlds apart,
4. the first speaking a language at the second that is totally instructional and one-directional and that does not allow mutual redefinition of the relationship, and
5. both prohibited from reciprocal interaction for constructing a shared reality, the first retaining a monopoly on initiating reality construction for the second.[48]

One-sided though the bureaucratic relationship is, its very one-sidedness is demanded by what people expect from bureaucracy. We do not want functionaries to act on their own volition and from a position of independence. We want managers, whom we empower with authority, to be able to define tasks, to possess or control superior technical knowledge of what the tasks are all about, to be able to give orders one way and see them carried out. All of this seems, from the point of view of the bureaucratic solution to such expectations, to require the subordinate to tune in to the manager, to attempt to understand the manager's intentions and language rather than impose his or her own intentions and terms, to be passive rather than active in an initiating sense.

But not even this much activity is required of the functionary. Tuning in, understanding, even acceptance are necessities of social action, not of bureaucratic action. The functionary simply learns proper responses to specific orders. The functionary refers to the rule book. In exceptional instances, the functionary seeks authoritative interpretation of an order from above. Lacking is the effort involved in voluntary and intentional acts of interpretation and understanding. It is not required that function-

*Whether objectivations or reifications.

aries understand either their orders or their actions, but merely that the latter reflect the former.

That the major social and political powers of the functionary are not utilized but are, rather, suppressed is both the strength of bureaucracy and its greatest handicap. A future form of organization that can both enforce socially legitimate policies through organizational structure *and* mobilize the social and political power of those working in such structure will overwhelm modern bureaucratic organization.

SUMMARY

What is the immediate practical use of being able to recognize one's own location in different types of relationships—social, political, and bureaucratic?

First, our ability to do well in life or in situations depends on bringing our expectations into congruence with realities. If I identify my situation to be a bureaucratic one, I will not make the mistake of expecting to be treated as a fully contributing social equal or of expecting that my sensitivity to human tensions will be rewarded by the bureaucratic structure. I can even ask myself the very practical question: Does my personality best fit roles of social, political, or bureaucratic action? If I am mainly concerned with understanding others, a social role might be advised. If my sensitivity is toward the recognition of tensions between human needs and social facts, a political role might be best. If I am by nature a truncated human being, limited in understanding and consciousness of political tension, but enabled by nature or training to perceive human behaviors in the same cold light as I see the behavior of things, a career in purely bureaucratic functions of modern organizations promises success.

Second, however, the ability to place myself in the kind of reality that surrounds me—social, political, or bureaucratic—and to tailor my expectations and actions accordingly does not automatically lead to passive acceptance of what is. Recognition of the limits of human satisfaction that a truncated relationship such as the bureaucratic one offers not only the functionary but also the manager may encourage the political activist to appeal to the suppressed dimensions of bureaucracy—the social and political potential of its members—to work his will, whether for good or evil. A form of organization that suppresses two-thirds of the human capacity for interaction with other human beings is forever vulnerable to new social and political formations.

Third, from the viewpoint of the bureaucrat defending bureaucracy, there may indeed be in all this the message that he or she must stand constant guard over the possibility of independent social and political relations arising within the iron cage of tough one-sided rules and relationships. But the bureaucrat, also, will be aware that to stick to bureaucratic relations alone is to deprive himself or herself of immense power to mobilize the work of subordinates and to accomplish things that are difficult or almost impossible within the one-sided, top-down bureaucratic relation.

Finally, there is here at least the hint that, even in the bureaucratic relationship, there is a residue of political and social relations that mobilize the willingness of subordinates to fit themselves and their work into the organization. It may well be that, if any work gets done in bureaucracy, it gets done not because of the force that structure imposes from above but because of the social and political capacities that human beings bring to their jobs—the capacity to initiate understanding, the capacity to communicate in such a way that a piece of work is defined for mutual co-laboration, the ability, in other words, to do what all humans do: to construct a work reality out of one's own capabilities.

WHAT PEOPLE CAN DO:
Managing Despite the Organization

*Michael M. Harmon**

What can the manager do to manage despite the organization?

Hierarchy seems to lock the manager into a "me against them" relationship with subordinates. Hierarchy enables me as manager to tell them what to do. Along with other practices of bureaucracy—including the division of labor, specialization of tasks and impersonality in work—hierarchy serves to promote and support top management's claim to the rational and efficient exercise of control. Organization becomes intendedly rational activity structured into social relations for the purpose of using resources to achieve goals efficiently and effectively. Some managers may then work under the illusion that all they have to do is to seize the levers and handles of the organization they find when they go on the job and organized work by subordinates will result.

Successful managers do not operate under the illusion that the organization enables work. Instead they approach work situations involving subordinates, in their long-term planning and in their everyday relations, with the question: "What are *we* trying to do?" If people were totally rational, of course, they would *know* what they are trying to do. Then their only problems would be instrumental ones of deciding *how* best to do it. In fact, most theories about managing and organizing take for granted that it is the manager who must know *what* to do. In

*Prof. Michael M. Harmon is professor of public administration, George Washington University. He is the author of *Action Theory for Public Administration* and coauthor of *Organization Theory for Public Administration*.

traditional bureaucratic organizations, the manager who admits he or she doesn't know what to do is criticized for displaying either a human failing or even managerial ineptitude.

Successful managers, however, know that their subordinates already have their own idea as to *what* they are doing. The problem, then, for the successful manager becomes to shift from an attitude that assumes he or she knows what the employees are *supposed* to be doing to an attitude that tries to share in their knowledge of what they *are* doing and convert this collegially into a knowledge of "what *we* are doing."

Like organizing in general, managing then becomes a process of *collective sense-making about what people have been doing, what they might want to do in the future, and how they might want to do it.*

How do successful managers get the knowledge that enables them to make sense of a situation together with employees?

The first step for the manager is to *give up* knowledge. As some of the purer application of Management by Objectives, for example, have shown: unless the manager shares with his or her subordinates the goals whether qualitative or quantitative of the manager, the employee cannot know whether he or she is helping the manager reach those goals by what he or she does. Similarly, the manager has no idea what it is that employees "are up to," as many suspicious hierarchical managers complain, until it is too late: that is, until the product of a work relationship is already produced or the deadline for producing it or a part of it is passed.[1]

What tools are available to the manager to engage in management as a joint knowledge enterprise with employees?

Despite the fact that formally the manager is locked into the top-down way of determining what shall be going on in organizations—hierarchy—he or she has a great deal of latitude in applying other rules for making such decisions in his or her relations with subordinates. Such rules are called decision rules.[2] To change a decision rule is to change in the most fundamental way an organization's structure.

Within the discretion of the manager, four decision rules alternate to hierarchy are often available:

1. *voting*, usually conducted as majority rule.
2. *contract*, in which both or all parties voluntarily agree to a decision, which is subsequently binding.
3. *bargaining*, a marketlike rule in which participants trade with one another or use an impersonal medium of exchange to reach noncoercive decisions.
4. *consensus*, in which people synthesize differing points of view, including different knowledge of a situation, in an attempt to reach a mutually acceptable (or at least tolerable) decision in which all interests or perceptions are served.

Of these four alternate decision rules, consensus is the most open to allowing mutual knowledge of a situation to emerge, thereby opening up the situation to mutual definition.

Voting is seldom used as a formal decision rule within public organizations, although voting is the rule most commonly employed by legislative bodies, higher courts, and the public.[3]

Contract has long been used by public organization in the procurement of products from private suppliers—such as weapons by the Department of Defense.[4] Managers at all levels will increasingly have to learn how to use contract as the privatization of public services involves them more and more with private contractors. However, contracts of a sort have also been used between managers and employees within organizations in such productivity-enhancing and innovation-stimulating programs as Management by Objectives.

Bargaining has informally dominated relations between public service agencies, private interest groups, including corporations, and the legislative branches of local, state, and federal governments for many decades: such relationships have been characterized as "iron triangles."[5] Bargaining is also recommended as a more rational way of making decisions than hierarchy by public choice theorists.[6] Voucher systems have been proposed as a market-exchange system between agencies and clients, for example, where scarce housing is to be allocated or in school systems in which parents might want to use vouchers to "buy" education for their children at a school they select.[7] Within organizations, vouchers have been used in the management of children in the classroom, in a process in which students collect credits for work done, which they then can trade in for rewards. Profit-sharing systems in private bureaucracies may be considered deferred voucher systems: the bargain is that the company will put money in a fund to be collected upon retirement, or departure, in return for each unit of profit added by the work of employees.

Consensus rules are increasingly used in private bureaucracies under systems of management/worker participation (for example, Japanese management and Theory Z) and are gaining a formal foothold in public management. By 1984 eight states had introduced quality circles into state bureaucracies: Indiana, Louisiana, Minnesota, Missouri, North Carolina, Oregon, Pennsylvania, and Utah.[8] Under pressure of the drive for excellence coming from such private-sector-dominated study groups as the Grace Commission and under the model held up by private industry of successes in worker/management participation programs, public service managers can increasingly expect to be required to learn consensus rules. This is quite apart from and in addition to the informal use of such rules by managers.

Consensus is valued because it discourages forms of conversation in which some may exercise domination by unilaterally imposing their meanings on others. To make consensus binding, unanimity is required: conscious agreement in the absence of domination. Consensus discussions not only enable one person to discover what others have been doing or intend on doing, but they enable that person to discover what he or she has been doing. Such open discussions elicit not only knowledge about others but self-reflection. When actions no longer have to be justified, as they do in hierarchy, then it becomes possible to discover meanings hidden within actions and to evoke possibilities for future action that such meanings might reveal.

As a process, consensus involves individuals, usually in face-to-face discussion, in an attempt to reach agreement with one another through synthesizing their initially held and divergent positions into a qualitatively different (and presumably better) solution than any of those initially proffered.

As a product, consensus quality is determined by the quality of the process; that is, by the extent to which definitions of the problem are shared and understood, mutual trust is developed, solutions are arrived at free of coercion or domination, and all those with a stake in the outcome are included in the process.

One method of engaging others in a consensus process is to ask them how they define the assumptions at bottom of a particular situation and then ask them how they believe other people define them.[9] By purposefully bringing up into open discussion conflicting definitions of the situation, participants have at least a fighting chance of negotiating a mutually agreeable definition of reality on the basis of which cooperative action may then proceed.

The consensus process can also include a negotiation of roles. In this process, participants ask each other, "What would you like to be doing more of?" and "What would you like to do different?" and "What would you like *them* to do more of, do different, or stop doing?"

While consensus operations are often introduced by outside consultants, who have no axe to grind of their own and can moderate power relationships, there is no reason why the reflective manager cannot introduce such questions into his or her daily dialogue with employees, especially when new tasks and programs are about to be launched. While it is important to engage all stakeholders, and while the manager himself or herself is admittedly locked into the formal hierarchy of the organization, it is possible to use that room for discretion that every manager has to launch consensus operations.

Managers may even discover that by "surrendering" authority to such participative practices they may actually gain in authority.

In the words of one supervisor who went far beyond consensus operations in teaching employees to take over his functions, "Since I started giving it away, I've never had so much authority."[10]

NOTES

1. Max Weber, *Economy and Society: An Outline of Interpretive Sociology*, 3 vols., eds. Guenther Roth and Claus Wittich, trans. Ephraim Fischoff et al. (New York: Bedminster Press, 1968), p. 987.
2. Interview conducted by the author. All such interviews in this chapter were conducted in the period 1974–1976, except where noted.
3. Ibid.
4. Weber, *Economy and Society*, p. 975.
5. A social worker in New York City, anonymity requested. Interview conducted by the author.
6. Written report to the author, May 1974.
7. All data presented in this case from State of New York, Office of the State Comptroller, Office of the Special Deputy Comptroller for the City of New York, "Trends in Public Assistance Caseload and Expenditures in New York City with Comparisons to Selected Counties in New York State," Report No. 36-85, Nov. 27, 1984, submitted to the Financial Control Board of the City of New York. My thanks to Norman Gertner, chief analyst for economic and revenue forecasting, Office of the New York State Special Deputy Comptroller for New York City, for explaining the methods used in forecasting public assistance caseload.
8. Weber, *Economy and Society*, p. 1401.
9. Ibid., p. 1393.
10. Henry Jacoby, *The Bureaucratization of the World* (Berkeley: University of California Press, 1973). Originally published in German in 1969. My thanks to Dwight Waldo for calling this work to my attention.
11. Contrast the victory of modernization in China today with Weber's own description of the antimodern cultural barriers of traditional China at the turn of the century. See Max Weber, *Gesammelte Aufsätze zur Religionssoziologie*, 3 vols. (Tübingen: J.C.B. Mohr, 1920–21), vol. I, pp. 308–309 ff.
12. I have taken the translation of this passage directly from Max Weber, *Gesammelte Politische Schriften*, 2nd ed., ed. Johannes Winckelmann (Tübingen: J.C.B. Mohr, 1958), p. 310. In the English translation, in *Economy and Society* cited above, the translators use the term "public ownership" instead of Weber's " 'socialization.' " While his use of the term "socialization" undoubtedly signified "public ownership," the translators took an unjustified liberty. Weber meant socialization, with direct reference to Russia and socialism. His use of quotation marks always indicates that he means to use a term ironically or not in the sense in which it is routinely used. Here the use is ironic. Weber meant to indicate that what was taking place in Russia in terms of "socialization" was not socialistic in Marx's sense but was a case of conversion to state capitalism. See also *Gesammelte Politische Schriften*, p. 505.
13. Written report to the author, June 1975.
14. Here the regular print contains the demand for logic; the italicized part, the demand for visibility. Talcott Parsons, *The Structure of Social Action* (New York: McGraw-Hill, 1937), p. 58.
15. Personal conversation with author.
16. Official rules become so structurally embedded in everyday regulation of performance that the functionary spends more time looking over his or her shoulder at the rules than looking forward at the product. The assumption that visible work constitutes the totality of what goes on in modern organizations is, however, an illusion. The manager who succumbs to that illusion simply blocks out part of the reality, which is, at least in part, coconstructed by his subordinates. As one commentator writes: "The organization is what members make of uncertainty and the formal organization."—Stewart Clegg, *Power, Rule and Domination: A Critical and Empirical Understanding of Power in Sociological Theory and Organizational Life* (London: Routledge & Kegan Paul, 1975), p. 130.
17. Michael P. Smith, "Alienation and Bureaucracy: The Role of Participatory Administration," *Public Administration Review* (November/December 1971), p. 660. For further research into the bureaucratization of the teacher, begin with the older but still valid analysis

by Willard Waller of what teaching does to teachers in *The Sociology of Teaching* (New York: Wiley, 1932), pp. 375–409.

18. A report on Eliott Eisner et al., "What High Schools Are Like: Views from the Inside" reported in Fred M. Hechinger, "An Inside Look at High Schools," *New York Times*, Sept. 9, 1985, pp. C1 and C7; citation from p. C1.

19. Eliott Eisner in Hechinger, op. cit., p. C7.

20. Charlotte Kerpismann in Hechinger, op. cit., p. C7.

21. David Schuman, *Policy Analysis, Education, and Everyday Life: An Empirical Reevaluation of Higher Education in America* (Lexington, Mass.: Heath, 1982).

22. For the motivations of police, see my "Teaching Human Beings: A Socio-Psychological Role Model of Relationships with the New Student," paper presented at the 1976 annual meeting of the New York State Political Science Association, Albany, N.Y., March 26–27.

23. Personal interview with the author, August 1975.

24. For numerous reasons the cop on the beat exercises immense discretion, and the costs of supervision to limit that discretion are usually considered too high. On patrol officers' discretion, see James Q. Wilson, *Varieties of Police Behavior: The Management of Law and Order in Eight Communities* (Cambridge, Mass.: Harvard University Press, 1968), especially Chapter 2.

25. Weber, *Economy and Society*, p. 4.

26. Ibid., p. 26.

27. Max Weber, "Ueber einige Kategorien der verstehenden Soziologie," in *Gesammelte Aufsätze zur Wissenschaftslehre*, ed. Johannes Winckelmann (Tübingen: J. C. B. Mohr, 1968), p. 471. The fact that Weber here defines social action in the same way he defines social relationship in *Economy and Society*, and thereby vitiates the distinction between the two, should not be held against him. Great men are allowed to be inconsistent, and besides it is difficult to engage in social action without waiting to hear a signal from a partner and thus engaging in a social relationship.

28. Ibid., p. 441 especially; also pp. 452–64.

29. Ibid., p. 467.

30. Ibid., pp. 465–466.

31. The tone for this acceptance was set in Parsons's own classic, *The Social System* (New York: Macmillan, 1951).

32. Perhaps the fundamental essay in which Habermas develops these implications is "Technology and Science as Ideology," in Jürgen Habermas, *Toward a Rational Society: Student Protest, Science and Politics* (Boston: Beacon Press, 1970).

33. This distinction is further developed in Ralph P. Hummel and Robert A. Isaak, *Politics for Human Beings*, 2nd ed. (Monterey, Calif.: Brooks/Cole Publishing Co.-Duxbury Press, 1980), especially chapters 2, 3, and 12. See also the more recent recovery of the "action" concept as the essential creative attribute of human beings in social and organizational relationships as developed by phenomenologists in public administration, policy study, and planning: Michael M. Harmon, *Action Theory for Public Administration* (New York: Longman, 1981); Robert B. Denhardt, *In the Shadow of Organizations* (Lawrence: Regents Press of Kansas, 1981); Bayard Catron, *Theoretical Aspects of Social Action* (Ph.D. dissertation, University of California—Berkeley, 1975); Frank Fischer, *Politics, Values and Public Policy: The Problem of Methodology* (Boulder, Colo.: Westview Press, 1980); David Schuman, *Policy Analysis, Education, and Everyday Life* (Lexington, Mass.: Heath, 1982); and the work of John Forester and Howell Baum in Pierre Clavel, John Forester, and William Goldsmith, eds., *Urban and Regional Planning in an Age of Austerity* (New York: Pergamon, 1980). For general surveys of the phenomenological movement that began in the early 1970s in political science and public administration and in the mid-1970s in planning and public policy study, see R. P. Hummel, "Doing Phenomenology in the Social Sciences: The Rise of Intentionalism," *Policy Perspectives*. Fall 1981, pp. 111–123, as well as R. P. Hummel, "Phenomenology in Planning, Policy, and Administration," book review, *Polity*, vol. 15, no. 2 (Winter 1982), pp. 305–14.

34. Alfred Schutz, *The Phenomenology of the Social World* (Evanston, Ill.: Northwestern University Press, 1967), p. 205.

35. Ibid., . 202.

36. Ibid., 204.

37. Ibid.

38. Ibid.

39. Ibid.

40. Ibid.

41. Ibid.

42. Ibid.

43. Michael M. Harmon, *Action Theory for Public Administration* (New York: Longman, 1981), pp. 5, 9, 93, 95–96, 101 ff.

44. The following discussion is based on running discussions between members of the Institute for Applied Phenomenology, including Michael M. Harmon, Sandra Fish, and Ralph P. Hummel, though only the present author should be held responsible for the final interpretation presented in this understanding of Harmon's decision rules.

45. Personal communication with Michael M. Harmon, Feb. 6, 1986.

46. This summary and the subsequent discussion are based on Hummel and Isaak, *Politics for Human Beings*, especially chapters 2 and 14.

47. This section is based on the work of Max Weber and the phenomenological philsopher Edmund Husserl. Weber defined meaning in terms of action referred to values *(Wertbeziehung)*. Husserl set out to show that for every type of object in the outer world the individual would need to have recourse to a specific inner attitude suitable for understanding that object; the term "intentionally," used by Husserl, refers to that attitude. For the relation between Husserl and Weber, who cites Husserl, see R. P. Hummel, "Max Weber as Phenomenologist," paper presented at the sixth annual meeting of political science departments of the City University of New York, New York City, Fall 1980.

48. Adapted from the description of the bureaucrat-client relationship ("bureaucrat" can be substituted for "manager" and "client" for "functionary") in R. P. Hummel, "Toward a Human Cost Audit of Modern Organizations," paper presented to the Conference on the Phenomenological Analysis of Asymmetrical Relations, Wright State University and Ohio University, Dayton, Ohio, May 20–22, 1977. See also Hummel and Isaak, *Politics for Human Beings*, pp. 329–31.

Michael M. Harmon: Managing Despite the Organization

1. See also Michael M. Harmon, "Applied Phenomenology and Organizing," *Public Administration Quarterly* Symposium on Applied Phenomenology, forthcoming.

2. Decision rules are essential elements in the structuring of relationships. Decision rules not only define authority relationships within organizations, but also "between them and elements of their domain (e. g., legislatures, constituencies, the courts)." "Decision rules as they apply *within* organizational boundaries specify who makes decisions and the means by which those toward whom the decisions are directed (the 'implementors') may be held accountable." Michael M. Harmon, *Action Theory for Public Administration* (New York: Longman, 1981), p. 561. See also above, "What the Experts Say."

3. For difficulties with the use of voting, see Harmon, *Action Theory in Public Administration*, pp. 100–101.

4. On contract, ibid., p. 101.

5. Theodore J. Lowi, *Incomplete Conquest: Governing America* (New York: Holt, Rinehart & Winston, 1981), p. 134.

6. Harmon, *Action Theory for Public Administration*, pp. 98–99.

7. See Milton Friedman, *Capitalism and Freedom* (Chicago: University of Chicago Press, 1962); for a critical view: Henry M. Levin, "The Failure of the Public Schools and the Free Market Remedy," *Urban Review* 2 (June 1968), pp. 32–37.

8. Stanley B. Botner, "The Use of Budgeting/Management Tools by State Governments," *Public Administration Review*, vol. 45, no. 5 (September/October 1985), pp. 616–20; data from p. 617.

9. Long before the current popularity of such processes in Organization Development, asking participants in budget discussions at the old Bureau of the Budget to define their assumptions was a standard procedure. "If we couldn't agree on our basic assumptions, we might as well forget about it," said one participant. Source: Public comment by public administration scholar Harold Seidman at the panel "Is There a Need for Theory or

Theorists in ASPA or the Profession?", 1986 annual meeting of the American Society for Public Administration, Anaheim, California, April 13–16.

10. Paul Reaves, a foreman at the Harman auto parts factory in Bolivar, Tennessee, quoted in Michael Maccoby, *The Leader—A New Face for American Management* (New York: Ballantine Books, 1983), p. 75.

2
Bureaucracy as the New Culture

Since bureaucracy has a "rational" character, with rules, means-ends calculus, and matter-of-factness predominating, its rise and expansion has everywhere had "revolutionary" results . . . as had the advance of rationalism in general.

—Max Weber[1]

The world of modern organization today is rent asunder by a culture conflict.[2]

Human beings entering private or public bureaucracy from the world of social life once more reassert human demands against systems demands:

Society/Bureaucracy Conflict

Important in Society[3]	*Important in Bureaucracy*[4]
justice	stability
freedom	discipline
violence	reliability
oppression	calculability
happiness	of results
gratification	formal rationality
poverty	formalistic impersonality
illness	formal equality of
love and hate	treatment
salvation and	victory and defeat
damnation	

Can bureaucracy's inner values help us deal with the concerns of general human life?

Second, the society/bureaucracy conflict today seems to cut right through organizations themselves. Responding to market forces flowing from society at large, vanguard corporations in search of survival raise new values under the banner of excellence against traditional corporate values under the flag of control:

Control/Excellence Conflict in Corporations

Important to Control Corporations[5]	Important to "Excellence" Corporations[6]
Bigness . . . because it gives economies of scale.	Belief in being the best.
Low-cost emphasis . . . because survivors make it cheaper.	Belief in the importance of the details of execution, the nuts and bolts of doing the job well (emphasis on the actual work well done).
Analysis as the solution to everything . . . because if you can take it apart into numbers you know what's going on.	Belief in the importance of people as individuals.
Peace at all costs . . . because keeping trouble makers down ensures following the plan.	Belief in superior quality and service (emphasis on putting things together).
Decision-making as more important than follow-through . . . because, if you make the right decisions, things will fall into place.	Belief that most members of the organization should be innovators, and its corollary, the willingness to support failure.
Control over everything . . . because things and people out of control introduce the unpredictable.	Belief in the importance of informality to enhance communication.
Growth as a hedge against insecurity, even in industries one knows nothing about.	Belief in and recognition of the importance of economic growth and profits (in industries known to managers).

The conflict between the two sets of corporate values is not made any easier by the fact that some control values explicitly or implicitly are still present among the excellence values. For example, growth and profits are values shared by both corporate cultures, though perhaps growth is a hedge against the insecurity for one and an opportunity for the other. Also, it is hard to believe that those working on excellence will be left so unorganized as not to be able to perform according to the general goals of the company. The conflict of corporate cultures is left to cut right through the minds of individuals. They must use their own judgment on which value to pursue when in what mix. And yet the new excellence values represent the biggest turnabout in coporate values since the invention of scientific management at the turn of the century.

A similar turnabout in actual *values in practice* can be observed in public bureaucracy. Bureaucratic *values in practice* increasingly confront bureaucratic *values of structure*. The result is a developing, though often subtle and silenced conflict in public bureaucratic culture:

Structure/Practice Conflict in Public Bureaucracy

Structure requires[7]:	*Practice requires*[8]:
Hierarchy . . . orders and rewards flow from the top down.	Collaboration . . . managers and workers working together on a project.
Division of labor . . . makes clear who does what and solves problems of fights over power and collusion among employees that might lead to corruption.	Teamwork . . . employees freely communicate with one another to get the work done.[9]

Similar growth of work practices as well as in consulting and training challenge Max Weber's other traditional characteristics of strict bureaucratic structure. Written communication, while retained for record keeping, is challenged by the nurturing of dialogue. Tight control over the full working capacity of the official is challenged by flexible hours and appraisal based on accomplishment, not hours put in. Even the requirement of thorough and expert training before entry into a position is giving way to expectations of recurrent retraining programs and four career changes in an individual's life. Most crucially, the assumption that all work can be organized by a single set of universally applicable general rules has given way—beginning with the studies of Joan Woodward. First came contingency theory suiting organization structure to organization task and lately contingency practice: letting the individual determine on the basis of bottom-up knowledge how work is to be done.[10]

Changes such as these not only provide the newcomer to modern organization in our day with a shock but put the individual before terrifying choices of selecting the value most applicable in any given situation from sets that are often contradictory. How can such choice be simplified?

One critic of modern culture, the philosopher Martin Heidegger, suggests we can cut through all complexities of modern life if we realize this: causing all the confusion is a battle between one culture that believes what is real are things that are measurable and another culture that believes that it is the quality of life that matters, not its measurement. The overall conflict in current culture is between quantity and quality. We can think of any organization today as split between these two views of reality[11]:

Quantity/Quality Conflict in Contemporary Organizations[12]

Quantity Culture	Quality Culture
What is real is things that can be measured: *quantity*: emphasis on external measurement of things and derivation of general laws applicable to all things.	What is real is the internal nature of things: what a thing is: *quality*: emphasis on determining the inner nature of individual things and approaching all things uniquely in their own terms.

Here lies the crisis of modern organization. It is the split between job and work. Jobs are designed from the top down, according to quantitative standards, the more modern an organization. Work has to be performed in contact with reality: whether it is a physical reality like testing a space shuttle or a social reality like caring for welfare clients. When pure quantitative design of jobs takes over, decisions as to the ability of the space shuttle to fly are made by computer jockeys not by the engineers who have their hands on the seals that hold the booster together. When pure quantitative measures are applied to serving clients, more clients may get welfare and the list of those ineligible may dwindle, but no client may fare well (as the welfare caseworker on the line will know when he or she applies human standards in contrast to case rules to her or his clients). The task for the bureaucrat is to strike a balance between quantitative and qualitative standards—between the fact that *something* must be delivered that has physical or social reality to the recipient and concern about how much is delivered or how it correlates with other variables such as cost.

The difficulties for the bureaucrat, however, do not end with recognizing the split sets of values encountered when entering or running the institution. In addition, especially in America, the bureaucrat must be politically astute. He or she must balance what can technically be done inside bureaucracy and according to bureaucratic standards against what is politically feasible in the political environment. But there too, the bureaucrat encounters a split culture. America's political culture is divided between concerns of social conscience and concerns of the individual—"Let us care for others" and "Where's mine?"*

Both survey research and philosophical analysis have exposed the values of the dual political culture.[13] They may be summarized as follows:

Political Culture[14]

Values of Social Conscience	Values of Individualism
Equality	Individualism
Social justice	Competition
Community	Hard work
Great leadership	Property

Alternating between social conscience in taking care of the other guy and the individualism of making it oneself, Americans will vary in their support for bureaucratic values depending on which of the two subsets is dominant in political discourse at a given time. Specific political values can support or oppose bureaucratic ones. The social conscience subset says it is legitimate to pursue the ideals of social justice and equality as the American community progresses ever onward and upward morally under the leadership of great presidents. The individualist subset says it is legitimate for any individual to compete hard against any other individual to acquire property through hard work and defend it against all comers.

It is easy to see that bureaucracy may be perceived at one time as lining up against individualism in treating all people alike. Similarly, the ends values of social conscience, though they deal with a collectivity as does bureaucracy, may be used to criticize purely instrumental bureaucratic translations of such demands as those for equality or social justice. Pure modern bureaucracy, in short, is not likely to have an easy time in America.

WHAT PEOPLE VALUE

People experience conflict in social, bureaucratic, and political culture. Social values are opposed by bureaucratic values as bureaucracy, once a part of society, grows and becomes a cancer that opposes society. But bureaucratic values themselves are becoming increasingly split as Amer-

*My thanks to Dr. Conrad P. Rutkowski, political scientist and then Dean of Continuing Education, Fordham University, for first formulating the concept of *quid mihi*, a Latin approximation summarizing the pure individualist attitude in American political culture. Traditionally, when conscience and individualism are balanced, the "where's mine" attitude is modified into an attitude of *quid pro quo*, or you scratch my back and I'll scratch yours, when Americans try to get the goods of their political system. However, when the inclusion of others implied by the *quid pro quo* weakens, as in times of extreme narcissism, extreme selfishness sets in.

icans proceed from the belief that quantity is good enough to the recognition that the products and services of modern organizations must have a qualitative base: that there has to be a "what" (qua) at the bottom of "how much" (quanta). Cars that are mass produced and available to everyone but can't get you there. Airlines that fly you cheaply and efficiently but have no standby planes, so that their effective ability to deliver passengers to their destination is undermined. Defense departments that produce "permanent prehostility" as the quantitative surrogate for peace. These are examples of the inexorable onward march of the belief in quantity; numbers become so removed from reality that organizations lose their base in the quality of real life. The question "what is life all about?" is replaced by the question, "How much can we produce?" In the end a lot is produced but little of human value. Postmodern critics and bottom-line analysts have laid out the specific ways in which the quantity/quality conflict manifests itself in both private and public organizations. Finally, the bureaucracy/society split and the bureaucracy/bureaucracy split has to be digested by citizens, bureaucrats, and clients alike in the context of a split political culture in which selfish individualism competes with an ethic of social caring.

Here is how citizens, bureaucrats, and clients deal with what is a civilization-wide crisis that results when classic bureaucratic beliefs about the nature of the world encounter social, political, and physical reality. Three types of culture conflict are shown: (1) society/bureaucracy conflict, (2) bureaucracy/bureaucracy conflict (the quantity/quality conflict within modern organizations); and (3) bureaucracy/politics conflict.

Society/Bureaucracy Conflict

Society/bureaucracy conflict results from the encounter between a society's ends values—what a society thinks life is all about—and bureaucracy's instrumental values: the methods by which we are promised satisfaction of our ends values. When methods become as important and powerful as ends, conflict results.

The gap between social values and bureaucratic values can best be seen when the existence of either set is up for grabs: When bureaucracy is born, new organizational values challenge old social ones. When bureaucracy dies, its own values are attacked by a rebirth of social ones. And, in daily skirmishes of everyday life, all of us engage as individuals in the struggle to get the goods from bureaucracy.

When Bureaucracy Is Born

JUDGES

"I love the work, but I hate the job," laments a New York state supreme court justice caught not long ago in a change-over from a judicial system run by judges to a system run by court administrators. What we see is a conflict between personal gratification and the changing value-concerns of bureaucracy—efficiency, formal rationality, discipline, and calculability of results. These concerns become apparent in the following article in *The New York Times:*

There was a time when conversation in the judges' lunchroom atop the State Supreme Court Building in Manhattan centered on fine legal points—the handling of a motion, say, or the implications of a decision.

Now, discouraged by cuts in their budgets, distracted by charges of corruption in the courts, and vexed by an administrative struggle that they contend threatens their independence and dignity, judges are exchanging notes on the lack of morale.

"I love the work," one judge commented recently over lunch, "but I hate the job."

After frequent informal discussions of the problem, the 120 State Supreme Court justices in New York City were invited to join a committee last week to "act as one voice in a time of crisis."

The committee's acting president, Justice Edward J. Greenfield, said that the justices' first worry was how they would be able to function without their confidential aides, who were scheduled to lose their jobs today for budgetary reasons. The aides type decisions, answer phones, and perform other clerical functions for the justices.

More generally, Justice Greenfield said his colleagues were concerned about their reputations and credibility, which they maintained have been damaged by the charges being made by Maurice H. Hadjari, the special state prosecutor investigating corruption in the criminal-justice system.

But the issue that has preoccupied the judges, according to Justice Greenfield, is how to fight domination by the state's Office of Court Administration under the direction of Justice Richard J. Bartlett.

"We want the right to give the orders," said Justice Moses M. Weinstein, deputy administrative judge in charge of Queens, who is also a member of the committee. "Who knows the courts better than a judge right on the scene?"

At issue is who should oversee the nonjudicial matters of the State Supreme Court: the Office of Court Administration or deputy borough administrators under the direction of Justice David Ross.

Up until last November Justice Ross and his deputies were responsible for the management of nonjudicial personnel: court officers, secretaries, stenographers, and so on. In November this authority was signed over to Justice Bartlett's office. The justices' fight is to regain this responsibility. They view the matter as crucial to maintaining the judiciary's independence.

Justice Bartlett, a Glens Falls judge who was appointed state administrator in January 1974 by Chief Judge Charles D. Breitel of the State Court of Appeals in a move to spur statewide improvements in the judicial system, said he viewed the matter in terms of efficiency.

"There are many advantages," said Justice Bartlett, commenting on centrally managed personnel. "Nonjudicial needs could be viewed from a citywide perspective, the city court system could be viewed as a single budgetary entity and costs could be handled on a uniform basis."

The justices contend that they are not opposed to centralization as such but rather are concerned about taking directions from a central administrator who is not a judge. Peter Preiser, Justice Bartlett's deputy administrator in charge of the city's courts, is not a judge. The judges maintain that Mr. Preiser's appointment is a first step to taking judicial power away from the judiciary.[15]

In terms of the conflict between bureaucracy and society, the crucial sections of this report are those that expose the changing situation of the judges as a clear-cut example of bureaucratization.

Until November 1975 administration over nonjudicial personnel had been in the hands of one of the New York City justices—Justice David Ross. This meant that management of nonjudicial personnel, ranging from court officers to stenographers and secretaries, was, in contradiction to bureaucratic principles,[16] in the hands of a judicial office, not of a manager. The rationalization for this is, "Who knows the courts better than a judge right on the scene?" It is the same complaint that people in practical work always make against those charged with the administrative coordination and control of that work.* What they are asserting is a principle—their right to personal mastery over a piece of work. The judge's statement, "I love the work," is directly related to that sense of mastery.

But what are the bureaucratic values being asserted against that sense of personal gratification? And are they in some sense valid?

"There are many advantages" to centrally managed personnel, says the judge who became the new central state administrator under bureaucratization. Specifically he mentions:

1. Nonjudicial needs could be viewed from a citywide perspective.
2. The city court system could be viewed as a single budgetary entity.
3. Costs could be handled on a uniform basis.

*See the distinction between "visible" and "invisible" work made in Chapter 1. This is also the distinction between *work*, perceived by the worker as actions that are suitable means to achieve a given end or task, and *labor*, defined by accountants as units of measurable activity whether task-related or not. Managers, of course, tend to equate efficiency with visible work. Efficiency to them refers to the degree of integration between *visible* segments of work seen as elements in a means-ends chain. In contrast, workers ultimately relate all work done—whether visible or invisible to higher authority—to energy expenditure and psychologically to personal or professional judgment about the relevance of a work action to a work goal.

When managers speak of efficiency, they therefore mean work done in such a way as to become visible to them and to enhance their control. When workers speak of efficiency, they refer to the appropriateness of an action to work being done.

Failure to understand managerial appeals to efficiency as attempts to assert control leads to confusion over exactly what the basic values of bureaucracy are. Examples may be found in James D. Thompson, *Organizations in Action* (New York: McGraw-Hill, 1967), pp. 5–6.

And ultimately all these advantages are justified in terms of "efficiency." Here, then, we have a typical society-bureaucracy conflict—personal *gratification*, based on mastery over judicial work, versus *efficiency*, as seen from a central managerial perspective.

Where social values are being succeeded by bureaucratic values, bureaucracy is being born. That bureaucracy is just recently penetrating the New York State Supreme Court indicates the lack of modern organization in the court's administrative system. This points up the widespread fallacy that large organizations are necessarily modern organizations. A simple way to test whether an organization is modern or premodern—whether it has the coordinated power of bureaucracy or is a fragmented shadow of what it could be—is to match its major activities with the values of bureaucracy and society as listed at the beginning of this chapter.

There is a postscript. After the case was first reported, a state supreme court justice, preferring to remain anonymous, gave us the following insight:

The press are having a field-day with this. And so is the Mayor [of New York City]. Every time somebody gets a short sentence or somebody convicted does it again or somebody gets probation, the press and the Mayor yell and scream that the judicial system needs to be better organized. This plays right into the hands of the administrative judge, who does things like transfer upstate judges down to the City to "solve" these kinds of problems and make us more "efficient."

The point is these kinds of issues are judicial issues that have got to be handled by judges, and they're not management issues at all. So you've got the public going after us to turn us into something it isn't good for the public to have us be: managers instead of judges.[17]

As others have pointed out, bureaucratic values are widespread in society.* Bureaucrats know this, and it is possible to gain public political support for increased bureaucratization by appealing to the citizen's interest in "efficiency" and "control" precisely because people interpret these in terms of social needs like "lower taxes" or "fewer crooks on the streets." That the control and efficiency values enhance the power of managers to the detriment of citizen power is not immediately apparent.

However, as time passes, the effects of blindly putting instrumental before social values may become apparent, and there will be a second round and more in the struggle. The ultimate outcome is determined by how many people believe how strongly in instrumental values—and how much political clout they have.

*See David Nachmias and David Rosenbloom, *Bureaucratic Government USA* (New York: St. Martin's Press, 1980), especially Chapter 9, "The Bureaucratic Citizen." See also Nachmias and Rosenbloom, *Bureaucratic Culture: Citizens and Administrators in Israel* (New York: St. Martin's Press, 1978), Chapter I, "A Theory of Bureaucratic Culture."

Take, for example, the entry of a new chief judge into the court system of New York State. After taking over this top judicial position, in January 1985, Chief Judge Sol Wachtler told the New York City Bar Association that his first move would be to assign cases to the same judge from beginning to end.[18] This approach, known as "individual calendaring" and beginning in 1986, would, of course, enable judges to get a sense of what a case was all about by reducing the fragmenting effects of a cherished bureaucratic institution: the division of labor. The division of labor, applied in a calculated way, might, of course, be used to take a case already started off the back of a judge already burdened with too many cases and assign it to a less burdened judge. This would increase utilization of judges and gain time and space efficiencies. More time of judges would actually be filled more evenly, more courtroom space utilized on a planned basis. But the grasp of a case would also elude a judge.

FIREFIGHTERS

I once had the challenge and opportunity to orient fifty battalion chiefs in the Fire Department of the City of New York to a new management system—management by objectives (MBO).[19] Because management by objectives places emphasis on translating work activities into measurable objectives, its introduction into the fire department constituted, to some extent, the imposition of modern managerial norms.

Conversations with firefighters I had taught earlier at John Jay College of Criminal Justice, and with each group of battalion chiefs, indicated that this department, admittedly one of the most effective in the city, was still being run on the basis of traditional, social, if not communal, norms. One example may suffice. Battalion chiefs were given a choice between two descriptions of systems of authority and asked to pick the one that more closely described their own command experience.

The first description delineated a system of authority involving leaders and followers. Orders from above were couched in terms of command, and obedience from below was described as based on trust. Motivation for work on the part of followers was described in terms of inner motivation based on a sense of duty to peers and commanders and a sense of vocation, or calling.

The second description delineated a system involving managers and employees. The giving of orders from above was labeled by the term "management" in contrast to command. Obedience from below was described as based on clearly defined rewards and promotional opportunities. Motivation was described as based on legal commitment to observe a contract specifying duties, hours, and pay. Employees were said to work on the basis of having sold their labor for a specific time in return for which they would be reimbursed. In other words, motivation was described as based on external incentives, not internal obligations.

In each group of ten battalion chiefs, only one or two felt the fire department operated primarily on the basis of the manager-employee system. All the battalion chiefs involved agreed that authority was shifting more and more from the leader-follower to the manager-employee model. There was at least tentative evidence here that the fire department of the City of New York, with a history of effective fire fighting for more than 200 years, had only recently (in the 1970s) entered the bureaucratic era. And there was evidence not only of considerable hostility but also of considerable pain at the change-over. Again and again during the introduction of the new management system the question was raised: "Why us? The city admits we're the most effective department. Why us?" Or, in the theme repeated over and over by old-timers in command and expressed most poignantly by one commander: "My men used to go into fires to save lives because they knew it was right. They risked their lives, and they died for the city. No more. When morale goes, what can I put in its place? I can't order the guy to get himself killed. He'll either want to take that risk because he feels he has to, or he won't. More and more, he won't."[20]

"Victory and defeat, love and hate, salvation and damnation" have been, as Habermas said, the categories of human life and work for millennia. To break the values and emotions involved is both the power and the agony of modernization. Perhaps at some future date the cost in human terms may be deemed too high. For the present, all we can do is begin to understand the cultural difference between the two opposing worlds, bureaucracy and society.

When Bureaucracy Dies

A POSTMASTER GENERAL

"I don't give a damn what politicians say," said the postmaster general to the senator. The time was 1973, and the Post Office Department of the United States had just died and been reincarnated as the United States Postal Service. What provoked the outburst? What does it mean in our discussion? The following article in the *New York Times* sets the context:

Postmaster General E. T. Klassen was told at a Senate hearing today that, despite a major reorganization, the mail delivery service has deteriorated to the point where it was a national joke.

"Postal Service jokes have become a national pastime," said Senator Alan Cranston, Democrat of California, in asserting that the reorganization of the Post Office Department into the United States Postal Service had failed to speed service or to slow down rate increases.

Mr. Klassen, meanwhile, apologized to the Senate Post Office Committee for remarks that he made to a reporter before the opening of the hearings yesterday when he said, "I don't give a damn what politicians say."

"I want to apologize for it," he said today. "It was not my intent now, nor has it been my intent, to show disrespect for Congress."[21]

One reason that the Post Office Department yielded to the government-chartered but management-run Postal Service was that delivery of the mails had declined to levels where at one point it was slower than in the days of the pony express. The Postal Service, less politically dependent, promised to be more efficient. Efficiency is an internal characteristic of bureaucracy. Cost and service are external expectations of society. A common misunderstanding of bureaucracy on the part of outsiders is that the chain of efficiencies inside a bureaucracy will necessarily relate to social inputs (costs) or social outputs (services). In this sense it is entirely possible to explain the postmaster general's outrage at senators. As the chief bureaucrat of his service he knows of specific efficiencies he has instituted through modern management techniques. He is also aware of the constraints put on him in instituting these efficiencies by a cost-conscious Congress and by policies that require the agency to handle mail of a type that doesn't pay (third-class mail, for example). The degree to which he can modernize his agency, then, is limited by political considerations imposed by society.

On the other hand, citizens and politicians—the amateurs of social life in contrast to the experts of bureaucracy—have little interest in how the process of mail delivery is organized as long as the mails are delivered and stamps are cheap. This concern is expressed in Senator Cranston's complaint that the new Postal Service had failed to speed service or to slow down rate increases.

Whether or not the bureaucratic value of internal efficiency can ever catch up with the societal demand for cheaper and faster mail service—that is, low input and higher output—cannot be determined here. What can be observed is this: when an institution, like the original Post Office Department, declined to such an extent that the service it was intended to perform is no longer performed, society judges such institutions not according to their internal standards but according to its own external standards. Is the mail delivered? Are stamp prices within reach?

A GOVERNOR AND A TOP ADMINISTRATOR

Managers who do not adhere to bureaucracy's basic control imperative, aimed at keeping bureaucracy alive, are severely called to task. Sometimes, so are their bosses—the politicians. The death and resurrection of New York State's Urban Development Corporation (UDC) is an example.

The UDC was created in 1968, charged with building low-income housing and engaging in urban renewal. It defaulted in February 1975, having collapsed financially in an environment of shrinking fiscal resources. It finally required a $258 million loan and a direct state appropriation of $200 million in the spring of 1975 to resurrect the agency, which had been intended to be self-financing.

The chief financial officer of the corporation, which financed its operations by selling securities, had warned its director, Edward J. Logue, in 1971 that UDC might be spending money faster than it had a chance of raising it. To this warning the top administrator responded in a letter in December of 1971:

I do not believe there is any evidence to support your conclusion, and I do not propose to go looking for any. We are going to build as much as we can. The need is here now. When, having managed our affairs, we have gone as far as we can go, and we can't borrow any more, that is another day.[22]

A key characteristic attacked by various sources, including the report of the commission that investigated the collapse, was the lack of control exercised by the governor as chief state administrator over the agency and the degree to which legislative control was made impossible by the way the governor insulated the agency from legislative oversight. The Moreland Commission in charge of the investigation concluded, "The relationship between UDC and the executive chamber was one of cooperation and partnership, rather than one of control."[23]

Asked to testify about the collapse, the man who was governor when the UDC was created, Nelson A Rockefeller, clearly asserted the primacy of service over control in the operations of the agency:

We were not running a bank, not running a corporation for profit. We were trying to build housing for people who need it.

Sure there was some risk, but I was always willing to err on the side of achieving social objectives.[24]

Given an agency head who admittedly shared the governor's concern for service, those concerned with control were clearly shunted aside:

Mr. Rockefeller brushed off testimony by previous witnesses cited to him by Mr. [Sheldon H.] Elsen [counsel to the Moreland Commission]. Of budgetary officials who complained that they could not get his ear, he said their job was to carry out his orders, not dictate policy.[25]

Here the normative conflict between the survival needs of a bureaucracy and its mission of public service is clearly spelled out. As a representative of the political will of the people of New York, Rockefeller was, of course, on defensible grounds: a politician's prime legitimate task is to provide public service, in this case the achievement of "social objectives." But as chief executive of the state's bureaucracy, a responsibility he clearly accepted when he told complaining budgetary officials to carry out orders, Rockefeller was nevertheless called to task.

Unlike politicians and the rich, typical managers cannot so easily escape responsibility—and they know it. They therefore recognize and respect the fundamental imperative of the bureaucratic enterprise, which is to keep its activities, no matter how purely and socially motivated, within such bounds that the bureaucracy will survive them. From that survival orientation they derive their cost consciousness. And from that cost consciousness they derive their need for tight control over their subordinates and for ever-continuing drives for efficiency. Efficiency is a measure of managerial control internal to a bureaucracy*—that is, to what extent managers are able to join one link to another in the long chain of administrative means that converts public expenditures into public services. The more control they exercise over this process, the more easily they can bring their organization's action into accord with the demands for accountability made by legislators and executives in the political institutions above them. Efficiency in this sense means the managers have their organization well in hand. As the case of UDC proved, not only are having an organization in hand and delivering public service not the same thing, they may on occasion be antithetical goals. Managers who allow the service goal to impair the control goal risk both their jobs and their organization's capacity to survive into the future.

All of the norms of bureaucracy listed at the beginning of this chapter favor inner stability and the survival of the bureaucracy, whereas the norms of society are external expectations that become pressures capable of eventually draining the capacity of the bureaucracy to survive. Power once expended is no longer power. Service once expended is no longer power. It is in the interest of every bureaucrat to hoard such power.

AUDITORS AND SEMI-INDEPENDENT BUREAUCRATS

There is a postscript to the UDC story. It points to a third set of values that is neither political nor bureaucratic. This third set becomes effective in all situations in which politics creates semi-independent entities whose day-to-day functioning is not integrated into the functioning of either politics or society. New York's Urban Development Corporation is such an entity. Able to issue its own bonds, it may be accountable to the bond market—if it acts too irresponsibly, bond buyers may shy away—but it may be able to resist demands that it adhere either to general political

---

*Efficiency is here distinguished from effectiveness. Efficiency denotes the process internal to bureaucracy of logically connecting means to means with the least cost. Effectiveness denotes joining the internal processes of bureaucracy (means) to external products or services (ends). A bureaucracy can be highly efficient in all or part of its processes, and yet there can be a breakdown at the boundary it shares with society; the result is that, while there is efficiency, there is little or no effectiveness. For evidence of confusion on these concepts and an attempt to reach consensus on efficiency, effectiveness, productivity, etc., see Charles R. Wise and Eugene B. McGregor, Jr., "Government Productivity and Program Evaluation Issues," *Public Productivity Review*, 1 (March 1976), 5–19.

values or to standard bureaucratic ones. In fact, the continuing case of the UDC demonstrates just how much bureaucratic values themselves are dependent on the ability of the parent government to enforce political power.

The third set of values emerges exactly when an agency develops its own power base. Of course, all bureaucracies develop their own power base merely out of the fact of their own existence. They control the internal use of time and space allocated to them. Since external demands must flow through their time and space they can slow or speed up, fast-track, or side-track external demands. One of the most powerful resistances to outside demands is that of bureaucratic inertia, usually put in terms of the saying, "We're working on it."

At the end of 1985, the comptroller of the State of New York, Edward V. Regan, issued a press release and summary audit report[26] of the UDC indicating to what extent the 1970s culture of political nonaccountability and internal lack of control still persisted into the 1980s.

Citing an original UDC policy goal, economic development, the comptroller pointed out that, despite auditors' recommendations of a year earlier, the UDC still had no way of knowing what impact its activities were having on economic development: "UDC still does not maintain basic records that would enable it to determine and evaluate the total cost of public support provided UDC projects and the related economic benefits to be derived from the projects." The audit report went on to warn that "If UDC cannot document measurable benefits, supported by cost benefit determinations, public support of economic development projects could be severely undermined.[27]

Since its economic power base continued to rest in its ability to issue bonds to borrow money from the private sector, however, the UDC understandably might be less concerned with short-term public legitimacy than the state comptroller. Was the UDC actually achieving its public service goals? The question could be reduced to: Who has a right to ask? and, if someone does, Can we do without them? Through June 30, 1983, the comptroller's auditors estimated that the UDC had received $882 million in public support by way of $60.3 million in UDC-issued bonds, $22.2 million in State appropriations, and an estimated $800 million in real estate tax abatements.[28] In terms of its economic power, UDC might conclude it could do without state appropriations and that the tax abatements could be taken for granted since no community would oppose projects that were assumed to lead to economic benefits. Having its own power base might well explain an emerging culture of resistance to both political (human) goals and to bureaucratic standards such as evidenced in the following behaviors. The state comptroller's auditors found:

1. In 1984 that the UDC "had not formally and comprehensively evaluated the actual accomplishments and necessity of its economic development programs, or how the benefits realized compared with program costs." By September 1984, an interdepartmental staff working group was reported by UDC to be working on the problem. The state's follow-up study found a year later that a project information management system was being set up but that this would not provide the information demanded in the prior audit report.
2. In 1985 that, while UDC "had not rejected the concept," it had done nothing to calculate tax abatements or interest subsidies.
3. That UDC blamed extensive turnover among senior management and priority of other concerns for its inability to produce a uniform reporting mechanism of its impact on employment levels in project impact areas.
4. That, despite efforts to reach potential customers for its financing, UDC had to return to state coffers $5.6 million out of an original $9.5 million appropriated in fiscal 1982-1983 because of inability to find users.
5. That the UDC first rejected preparing an up-to-date policy and procedures manual in 1984, then slowly went ahead on beginning to commit to writing its organizational structure and project processing cycle, and as recently as the 1985 issue date of the follow-up report "stated that they will investigate further" a previous demand for formalizing criteria for project acceptance.[29]

In short, ordinary human beings might be justified in concluding that the UDC is unable to learn. A decade after its fiscal crisis those in charge still had little idea how much it was accomplishing. This was reflected by the lack of quantitative data on borrowings and outlays and on impact of such policy goals as improving employment figures or physical impact of projects as reflected by absence of completion standards. This "bureaucracy" was unable to measure up to ordinary bureaucratic standards of internal control and efficiency, which would not be possible without having input/output figures. Insulated in great part from political demands, the UDC might well be on the way to competing in arrogance with such great independent authorities as the Port Authority of New York and New Jersey, which, formed by Congress to assure interstate transportation within 25 miles of the Statue of Liberty, did almost nothing in the area of mass transportation, claiming that the interests of its bond holders forbad expenditure of funds in that area.[30]

Collision Between Bureaucratic and Social Life

The conflict between the culture of bureaucracy and the culture of society arises not only in times of crisis. It pervades everyday life. Human needs collide with systems needs, and the individual suffers.

A Corrections Officer

Consider the story of a California corrections officer who was forced to make a choice between his survival in the job and the survival of his mother:

I was at work. My mother called me and expressed a desire to be taken to the hospital. (My mother is 73 years old and lives alone.)

At this time I made application to the personnel office for time off. Why did I do that? It was as though I had asked for his right arm. He immediately responded in the negative, giving no consideration to the seriousness of the problem.

All he was interested in was: by letting me go, it would cause a shortage of personnel.

His inability to react to me in a humanistic manner turned me off completely. It was all I could do not to react violently.[31]

Here one functionary of a bureaucratic system makes a decision that puts the needs of the system before those of another functionary. The possible death of a functionary's mother was not a problem with which the bureaucracy could be ultimately concerned. In addition, we can be almost certain that the personnel manager was protected from censure, should the woman die, by a system of personnel rules that took absolutely no account of an employee's external family obligations.

We are assuming here that the manager did not act arbitrarily. We are assuming that he acted according to the work rules. But if the objection is raised that such work rules, which did not cover the case of illness in a functionary's family, were insufficient and should be amended in a "good" bureaucracy, we have to protest.

Ultimately, conflicts between individual human needs* and systems needs are unavoidable no matter how many adjustments are made. Managers must always make their decisions within the constraints of the

*The term "human needs" used throughout my argument refers to a concept of essential characteristics that make human beings human in all times regardless of civilizations or cultures. In a modified sense, I distinguish human needs in a social context from systems needs. Through the process of socialization, human needs in society are modified into needs adaptive to society as a whole just as social values are modified to meet human imperatives. When systems theorists, like James D. Thompson, for example, speak in a laudatory manner of the advantages of "open systems," they are speaking, without realizing it, of society. Society is an open system toward its environment in that it must adapt to environmental challenges to survive. It is also an open system toward its inner biological components—the human beings that comprise it—shaping them and being shaped by them. Society, when it is successful, is the mediating tool between humans and their natural environment. The human needs it shapes are nevertheless affirmed by it; otherwise society fails as an adaptive device.

No such saving grace can be ascribed to bureaucracy. Because of its immense power, and often immense size, it can conquer or at least hold in abeyance the power of its environment—as happened with industrial pollution—until the environmental reality strikes back with an iron hand. Bureaucracy, therefore, may temporarily look like an adaptive device expressing human needs only to be exposed long-term as the best possible device to negate human needs, whether these are conceived as essential and fundamentally unchangeable or as socially modified needs. The reason for this is that bureaucracy has so much power that, as an instrument, it can afford to lack the corrective processes built into society. We thus have no assurance that what bureaucracy makes any one of us do at any time has any relationship whatsoever to human needs—individual and essential or social.

situation—given rules and suddenly arising demands for deviation. When such conflict arises, the tendency built into the system is to put the system first. This means internal security and survival needs—expressed in demands for efficiency, reliability, and so on—predominate. For no bureaucracy will decree its own death to assure the fulfillment of its functionaries' needs when these contradict its own.

In summary, people high or low experience the confrontation of bureaucracy and society in terms of incompatible values and needs. Bureaucracy was instituted to allow people to achieve social goals and to achieve them better, more quickly, more cheaply, and most of all on a larger scale. Yet the managers of such a modern organization may be forced to make a decision to have their bureaucracy survive rather than provide services. The governor of a state, aware of this proclivity toward protecting self-interest, may make a conscious decision to set up a bureaucracy in a way that will put service first, even at the risk of having the organization die. Functionaries on the line—firefighters and their battalion chiefs, for example—struggle between the work they see has to be done, such as a fire that has to be put out, and the pressure for control from above, which demands not simple but measurable performance. How to put a measure on a firefighter's willingness to risk his life for another human being? Like the firefighters, judges in New York State, and very likely elsewhere, struggle between the personal gratification work can give and the need to subordinate that gratification to account-ability, efficiency, cost consciousness, and productivity—all related to a largely unseen system and beyond to unseen taxpayers and citizens.

Between all these poles stand the managers as guardians of the new culture of bureaucracy. But they are guardians who are themselves imprisoned. How can that imprisonment be explained, not only for the managers but for all the rest of us?

Bureaucracy/Bureaucracy Conflict

The emerging values of those who manage business and government institutions *successfully* in response to the qualitative challenge of the 1980s often challenge traditional bureaucratic values in turn. Yet it seems this internal conflict moves toward resolution or, at least, a balancing only when there is public *failure*.

The battle of engineers who still deal with physical things and bureaucrats who run the National Aeronautics and Space Administration could not come to public attention until the failure of the space shuttle Challenger on January 28, 1986.

When Bureaucracy Meets Physics

ENGINEERS AND ADMINISTRATORS: THE DEATH OF A SPACE SHUTTLE

Listen to the different words that engineers and administrators use in discussing the explosion of the space shuttle Challenger in 1986. They split into words of different kinds: physical terms for engineers and numbers terms for administrators. The bureaucratic perception of reality is mediated by numbers.[32]

Physical terms. Analysts in touch with engineers still use physical terms. In a memorandum by Richard C. Cook to Michael Mann, head of the resources analysis branch of NASA, Cook warns of the danger of leaky seals that hold segments of a booster rocket together: "The *charring* of seals" poses "a potential problem affecting flight safety and program costs." In a previous rocket, in the joint between the nozzle section and the adjoining segment, "not only has the first O ring been destroyed, but the second had been partially *eaten away.*" (The joint was the one nearest the spot where a plume of flame was first seen emerging from the Challenger rocket just before the explosion.) Similarly 1982 "critical items list" for the booster warned that, if seals should fail, the result could be "loss of vehicle, mission, and crew due to *metal erosion, burnthrough,* and probable *case burst* resulting in *fire* and deflagration (rapid and intense burning)."

Quantitative terms. Ultimately, physical terms are translated into higher-level abstractions and finally into numbers. Charring of the rings, reported as early as 1982, becomes one of the "budget threats" at an August 21, 1985, budget briefing for top-level NASA officials. Introducing a typical bureaucratic concern, the deputy manager of shuttle projects at Marshall Space Flight Center in Huntsville, Alabama, assured the press that evidence of soot between the joints of the seal had been "completely *documented.*" (See Max Weber's list of characteristics of bureaucracy under the "Experts" section of this chapter.) The individual experiences with charring—12 in-flight instances were reported by one engineer's study— are captured at a September 10, 1985, status report and briefing by NASA's propulsion division under the general category "solid rocket booster issues." As the mathematization of experience progresses, warnings are put into numbers: a consultant to NASA estimates in December 1983 that the chance of a catastrophic accident involving the booster rockets is 1 in 35.

Because of typical bureaucratic secrecy,[33] it is impossible to tell to what extent NASA administrators had access to either the physical reality or the numbers reports, but ultimately top management of the booster supplier let the shuttle fly because engineers were unable to translate their feel for O-ring fragility into numbers.

It is clear, of course, that any bureaucracy, aside from accomplishing its physical and social mission of delivering a product or a service—and in NASA's case, the space shuttle was a product designed to deliver exploration, research, and commercial services—must be responsive to political, social, economic, and general cultural pressures.

The danger for the top administrators, however, is that, in the interest of developing their organizations and seeing them survive in the larger political, social, economic, and cultural environment, they will have political skills honed to the neglect of quantitative, scientific skills to say nothing of qualitative, hands-on skills. Beyond a certain size of project, while quantitative and even social knowledge can grow to permit the sense of having a grasp on the project in its totality, qualitative hands-on feel for a project is reduced below a level of tolerable optimality. In short, at some point the physical reality takes its revenge on quantification that looses touch with it and on socially enacted actuality. Or, at some point, as quantitative control over a product or service increases, quality decreases below the level where the product is still the product and the service a service.

Bureaucratization as the abstraction of work ultimately begins to fail when its framework of rationalistic, nonhuman thinking begins to become palpably detached not only from morality, emotion, relationships, politics, and human language and thought but from the physical reality it is designed to control.

Most managers know their difficult function: to translate physical world into numbers and back again. They have sustained for a long time the bureaucratic experience of tension between physics and numbers. They have long known this: there comes a time when you push the numbers so hard you reduce to a below-tolerance level the time and space available for knowing what the work is all about. The bureaucracy/bureaucracy conflict arises when bureaucratic organizations pursue their values of formalization and mathematization to such an extent that less, rather than more control, results the more forms are imposed and numbers pushed. With the resulting loss of quality—loss of touch with *what* is produced—the numbers also become meaningless.

Bureaucracy/Politics Conflict

Bureaucracy/politics conflict is experienced in America as a tension that people suffer from being pulled in three directions at the same time: we are torn between the mechanical collective values of bureaucracy, the organic collective values of political conscience, and the organic individual values of the individual trying to make it.*

A POLICE COMMISSIONER: DUTY ETHOS VERSUS INTEREST ETHOS

A former police commissioner had this to say of one of the country's largest forces:

The guys are out on the street all day. They do pretty much what we trained them to do, and they do it pretty well. But all around them they see people on the take. Not just crooks but all the ordinary business people too, everybody grabbing what he can. So it's pretty hard for the guys not to think that there's not much harm in their taking a little too when it comes their way.[34]

It is easy to think—from a moralist view based on the social conscience part of America's political culture—that this is a story about corruption and specifically police corruption at that. It is not about corruption; it is about *the way public service is provided in America*. It is not a story that applies only to police officers. As one of the leading theorists of American public administration, Vincent Ostrom, has suggested, adjusting how one provides public service to the particular needs and special clout of clients is *the* American way of running bureaucracy.[35] In a country where the claims of the community are always operationally expressed as individual or group interests, this means the bureaucrat is culturally required to tune in to the needs of each individual and group he or she serves. If that is corruption, make the most of it!

So do groups approach bureaucracy, always with the ultimate clout that if they can't get what they want now they might get it later through group influence on legislatures that approve bureaucracy's budget. An administrator would be suicidal were he or she not to be "sensitive" to the needs of such groups.

WHISTLEBLOWERS: BUREAUCRATIC ETHOS VERSUS SOCIAL ETHOS

The bureaucratic tendency to treat all people collectively is modified not only by Americans' individualism but by their social conscience.

When presidential administrations go through their cyclical security paroxysms of plugging information leaks, the attempt is experienced by government bureaucrats as a denial of their God-given right—and duty—

*This is not *the* fundamental tension between bureaucracy and politics generically. That tension is between an administrative way and an evocative way of dealing with the world (see Chapter 5). But the tension here described is the kind with which most Americans are most immediately familiar: that between bureaucratic values and the cultural values of their specific political system (see Section II of this chapter for the theory underlying the bureaucracy/politics conflict, specifically, H. Mark Roelofs: American Political Culture).

to leak information to the public. For example, in 1986, the Department of Energy instructed its employees to tell their superiors immediately about any outside requests for "illegal or unauthorized access to classified or otherwise sensitive information."[36] This was immediately greeted with cries of outrage. Not only did the press complain, but bureaucrats argued that failure to report even the most innocent inquiry from reporters would subject them to severe penalties.

There are, of course, dual reasons for this. Restrictions would interfere with bureaucrats' ability to try individually to improve their status with and through the press and ultimately the public and legislators. Restrictions also would interfere with Americans' sense of social conscience. Say something happens on your job that you judge would be bad for society, groups, or individuals. You don't just complain to your superior and then carry out the order. You leak information favorable to your cause and conscience to the press. Such an attitude may even be constitutionally protected. In the words of an attorney for the American Civil Liberties Union in Washington, "I think the Department of Energy regulation violates the First Amendment right of government employees to freedom of association."[37] Nevertheless, the individual bureaucrat walks a tightrope between his or her conscience and the orders of a superior. The tightrope spans the gap between democracy and bureaucracy. In democracy, citizens have a public obligation to respect and protect other citizens. In bureaucracy, in Max Weber's words:

The honor of the official is the ability to carry out an order on the responsibility of the commanding officer conscientiously and exactly in such a way as if it accorded with his own conviction, [even] when the higher authority insists, despite his protests, on an order that appears wrong to him.[38]

"Without such ethical discipline in the highest sense and self-denial," Weber warns, "the entire apparatus would disintegrate."[39] The extent to which this has not happened in America and the extent to which Americans have not as yet been visited by Germanic bureaucratic excesses are testimony to the extent to which individual bureaucrats modify bureaucracy every day by reference to a democratic culture of conscience and operational realism.

In short, the bureaucratic experience in the American political culture is one of being pulled back and forth between bureaucracy's values and the political values of social conscience and individual interest. No bureaucrat interested in survival can ignore any one of these three sets of values.

WHAT THE EXPERTS SAY

The use of studying culture is to find out what people value. Values give meaning to people's actions. Meaningful actions we can deal with. When a man rushes at me with a sharpened axe, it helps me to know whether I am on the New York City subway or at a reenactment of medieval battle scenes. In the one case, the act is likely to be deadly in intent because I know that I live in a culture in which it is possible for a police series to run on television under the motto, "Let's do it to them before they do it to us!" In the other case, the act's meaning—and its consequences—are likely to be shaped by what is valued by people playfully reenacting violence, not reproducing it.

Modern organizations are human relationships organized according to rational principles. If we know these principles, we can predict what people are likely to do. In the words of public administration theorist Jay D. White, "The greatest force for ensuring predictability is the establishment of the norms, values, and rules that make up the formal and informal structure of our organizations. The bureaucratized model of organizations is the classic example of an idealized system of explicit values, consistent norms, and formally stated rules.[40] This means those of us working in or with bureaucracy spend most of our time *interpreting*[41] what actions are required of us and what actions are addressed at us according to our understanding of a few underlying values that give meaning to norms and rules. It *pays* to know (1) the bureaucratic culture, in both its private and public versions; (2) the general culture of modernity with its emphasis on the value of science and rationality that underlies bureaucracy; and (3) the political culture that encompasses and limits the rationalism of bureaucratic culture.

In all these worlds, the individual needs to find out *what* is going on. But what is going on can be understood only by discovering the values according to which typical individuals in a situation understand the facts of their world. Take this scenario:

A middle manager is called upon to "do something, quick" by her executive assistant who bursts into her office announcing: "Your people are killing each other on the fifth floor."

The manager rushes into the elevator, takes it down to the fifth floor, flings open the door to the claims bureau and finds a fistfight in progress among ten of her employees.

What is the first thing the manager says? Take your pick:

a. "Get me a consultant to do a scientific study to explain what happened here!"

b. "Get the operations research department to do a trend projection on how long this is going to go on!"

c. "What the hell is going on here?!"[42]

The manager concerned with understanding what it is that is going on—is it a rehearsal for the medieval battle reenactment? Is it a fight over the new compensation system? Is it a fight over who gets to succeed her if she doesn't settle the fight?—will seek to get a grasp on the reality before her by trying to get at its meaning. But understanding meaning is neither an explanatory or predictive scientific enterprise; it is a question of interpretation. Interpretation is possible when we understand the underlying motivations, beliefs or norms, and values that people try to achieve or defend. These may be highly particular to a given situation—for example, the fifth-floor battle scene—but there are general values according to which all people in a given culture act. And the fact is that most of us have never consciously tried to discover the values that are the means to answering the question that arises in our daily lives: What is going on here? What follows aims to give us the basic points of reference for such interpretation. Those points of reference apply whether we work for a corporation or for a public bureaucracy, whether we deal with general questions that arise as to the meaning of modern life, or are forced—as bureaucrats so typically are—to balance economic, bureaucratic, and general modern values with the values of politics.

Max Weber: The Culture of Private and Public Bureaucracy

The method of understanding what people do by digging down to their basic values was first and foremost developed by the sociologist Max Weber. Weber asked: Without which assumptions does the behavior of people in a given culture make no sense? He applied this question to modern capitalist enterprises. He found a specific set of values according to which modern capitalists—as distinct, for example, from ancient Roman capitalists—guided their actions and made sense of their world. Similarly, he discovered a basic set of bureaucratic values in general according to which those in bureaucracies, private or public, guided their behavior. Entrepreneurs, of course, use bureaucratic organization for some of the same purposes as do governments. Out of this research emerge imperatives of capitalism and imperatives of bureaucracy without which capitalist and bureaucratic life, complementary parts of modern culture, make no sense.

Max Weber: The Imperative of Capitalism

Those of us interested in understanding the conflict between bureaucratic and human values can learn something from the fact that bureaucratic norms surround us everywhere—not only in public service but in the bureaucratic components of private enterprise.

All business people at all times have always wanted to make money. But there is only one way to succeed in business today, and that is to recognize that modern capitalism is a specific way of making money superior to previous forms of doing business. The proof of the pudding lies in the fact that an entrepreneur not using modern business practices simply cannot compete against one who does. There seems to be a central set of rules—a modern capitalist imperative—which, if followed, puts the modern business person at an advantage over the more traditional predecessor.

The owners of my favorite doughnut shop on Manhattan's 14th Street understand this imperative of modern business perfectly. If the doughnut shop is to stay in business and overcome slow days when income is low, the enterprise needs to accumulate money to increase its margin of security. This money can then be directed into two channels: it can be put away as a cushion against bad times, and it can be invested in another doughnut machine to increase sales and further profits. Growth and security are intimately related.

But to know how much of a cushion is needed or how much profit can be reinvested, operating costs (rent, labor, materials, depreciation of machines) must be calculated. In addition, the owners have to determine how many doughnuts must be sold to break even. How many customers have to go in and out of the shop each hour, on the average, to let them reach their break-even point?

The owners of the shop, in other words, are highly modern business people. They understand that profits are not just to be spent, but are a guarantee for the stability and growth of the shop. And they understand that sound use of investment and reinvestment can be achieved only through calculating everything—not only materials, machines, and labor, but also customers and consumption.

They have understood the imperative of modern capitalism: capital stability and growth through sound reinvestment achieved by the calculation of everything. This imperative can be analytically divided into two parts, the goal and the means. The goal is growth of capital. The means is calculation—or, to use a term with which we are already familiar from our discussion of bureaucracy, rationalization. In other words, bureaucratization of business practices becomes the means through which capital growth as the imperative of modern capitalism is achieved. The private bureaucracy of the accounting office is the first pillar supporting capital enterprise.

This is an important point for understanding the imperative of public as well as private bureaucracy. The imperative of bureaucracy, from the first, has always been control. It was through the bureaucratization of his accounting methods, personnel selection and use, and market calculations that the first modern capitalist became truly modern and therefore superior to his less calculating predecessors.

Max Weber contributed mightily to this understanding of both modern capitalism, with bureaucracy as its control instrument, and modern public bureaucracy as the control instrument of the political system. Bureaucracy in both cases is the outgrowth of a unique Western belief that everything in the world could be calculated and thereby be brought under human control. This attempt to bring the world under the command of calculating reason—rationalization—becomes not only an inner tool for capitalism but an outward condition. Weber reminds us of the rationalistic control component of the overall bureaucratic imperative, for example, in his definition of the manufacturing type of modern capitalism as "orientation to the profit possibilities in continuous production of goods in enterprises with *capital accounting*."[43]

So much for the internal norms of capital enterprise. To the extent that accounting spells control, they are entirely within the range of the list of bureaucratic norms drawn up at the beginning of this chapter.

But elsewhere Weber's extensive research[44] also establishes that modern capitalism can exist only in an environment in which general rationalized norms, including bureaucratic ones, become the external conditions of existence.

In drawing up his summary of the conditions under which modern capitalism can develop, Weber includes these three points:

1. Complete calculability of the technical conditions of the production process, that is, a mechanically rational technology.
2. Complete calculability of the functioning of public administration and the legal order and a reliable purely formal guarantee of all contracts by the political authority.
3. The most complete separation possible of the enterprise and its conditions of success and failure from the household or private budgetary unit and its property interests.[45]

These points summarize the dependence of the capitalist imperative— profit-making through capital reinvestment—on the concurrent development of modern technology, modern bureaucracy, and modern economics.

Max Weber: The Imperative of Bureaucracy

The imperative of bureaucracy is control. This is true, for historical reasons, whether bureaucracy is master or tool.

CONTROL THROUGH RATIONALISM

In capital enterprises, the first office to be bureaucratized was the accounting office. Rationalistic methods of accounting, embedded in regularized procedures and office structures, which are themselves susceptible to rational oversight, allow entrepreneurs to "account for" any and all operations of their enterprises and how each affects the other. The final measure of such accounting is "the bottom line"—the profit-loss statement. The bureaucratization of accounting is the starting point for bringing financing, raw-material supply, machine and labor operations, and sales into a tight relationship with profit outcome. By demanding the rationalization of the labor process—that is, its description and organization in quantifiable terms—the accounting office could adjust the labor process as a means to maximize profit as an end. The logical and effective linking of means and ends in this way constitutes the very definition of the concept of modern rationality.* Bureaucracy becomes the practical carrier of the rationalization process inherent in Western civilization.

But what makes this emphasis on rationalistic control the imperative of bureaucracy when applied to public service? The answer seems to be that modern bureaucracy was specifically conceived as a control instrument to be applied to public service from the very beginning. In this sense, it has always been more master than tool.

One of Weber's contributions is that he calls attention to the need that capitalism, as an economic enterprise, has for the bureaucratization of the social and legal world. The outstanding value that bureaucracy offers to capitalism is that it makes the behavior of labor, fellow capitalists, and consumers predictable. Especially in law, bureaucracy freezes into relative permanence behaviors that are in the interest of capitalist entrepreneurs to have permanent. The previous types of capitalists, with their innate tendency to play for high risks and take their money and run, come to an end when not only the methods of production but also the stabilization of the external environment make reinvestment of capital for ever-expanding growth a good risk. On the behalf of this growing class of entrepreneurs, state bureaucracies set norms of contract among entrepreneurs and marshaled the power to enforce them. They also regulated the ways in which workers could and could not sell their labor and began regulating markets to protect entrepreneurs from foreign and domestic fluctuations.

The central value that public bureaucracy offers private enterprise is stability against the tendency, found in previous types of administration, to allow flux through the arbitrary and unpredictable application and enforcement of policy. Such previous policy was, of course, the policy of kings, nobles, and landholders. Thus from the very beginning, bureaucracy served the purpose of limiting and regulating the exercise of political power by providing conditions of stability favorable to the exercise of economic power.†

Bureaucracy ensured this relative permanence in contractual, labor, and market conditions through its structure. Instead of being left to the

---

*For some amusing and not-so-amusing deviations from this rationality, especially in contemporary business, see William J. Haga and Nicholas Acocella, *Haga's Law* (New York: Morrow, 1980).

†The ultimate replacement of politics by administration was in this sense a tendency built into bureaucracy from its inception. See also Chapter 5.

good will of individuals, policies became embedded in offices or more accurately, became the operating procedures of permanent offices which, if followed, guaranteed the income, status, and institutional identity of their temporary occupants.* By making the structure of administration inflexible, bureaucracy made an ever-changing world permanent. To accuse later bureaucracies of inflexibility is therefore to ignore the origin and nature of bureaucracy as an administrative concept.

When Max Weber first analyzed the central characteristics of modern bureaucracy, he also isolated its central values by a comparison. But his comparison was with the dominant system of administration that preceded it. Weber's famous six characteristics of bureaucracy (which are discussed below) mean little and reveal none of their value biases if they are read out of context—that is, without comparison with the preceding forms of patriarchal and patrimonial rule.

An overall view of Weber's six points shows that his theme was to contrast a new form of administration, moving toward permanence of control, against the occasional, haphazard, and often unpredictable form of arbitration associated with feudal kings and ancient empires. Each of the six points describes conditions that will prevail if a permanent and predictable administration of control is achieved. To bring out this emphasis on control through comparison more strongly, I have below taken the central ideas of each paragraph, explained them in terms of the control aim, and related them to comparisons against older forms of administration that stem mainly from Weber himself. The full text is available in a number of reprinted versions.[46]

CHARACTERISTICS OF MODERN BUREAUCRACY

1. Bureaucracy is characterized by "fixed official jurisdictional areas."[47] *Jurisdiction* literally means to speak the law. Jurisdictional areas become areas of the exercise of law. These are clearly defined, systematically differentiated within a system of legal-rational legitimacy, and assigned to specific offices. They are the beginning of a rationalistic *division of labor*.

In its own internal structure, bureaucracy is initially a rationalistic model of patterns of behavior that it is designed to impose on the outside world. Once the world itself has become ordered, bureaucracy is intended to reflect that order in its internal structure.

In contrast, the precursors of modern bureaucracy are patriarchal and patrimonial systems—rule by the father. Premodern organizations that survive today include the family, especially the extended family of some ethnic groups, political machines, and the Mafia. In such premodern organizations, the law is what the father-ruler says it is, within the confines of tradition.[48] Areas of responsibility may be delegated, but not

*On identity as the ultimate reward for bureaucrats, see Chapter 3.

systematically, and they are subject to the arbitrary will of the father as sovereign. The vague and overlapping boundaries of jurisdiction reflect the lack of clear social organization. This is frustrating, especially to the rising classes of modern entrepreneurs, merchants, and industrialists who require stable laws and administration regarding labor, raw materials, markets, and contracts binding one another.

1.a. Bureaucracy is characterized by "official duties."[49] Duty is defined by law and by superiors in their capacity of office holders. A favorite saying of functionaries is, "I just did my duty; nothing personal." The psychologically compelling source of duty is an external one. Functionaries are obedient to rationally traceable, external command.

In contrast, work in premodern organization is done out of a sense of personal obligation. The source of the sense of obligation is conscience; that is, it is *internal*. A favorite saying of subordinates is, "I owed it to him; I couldn't live with myself if I didn't pay my debt to him." Subordinates act as if they obeyed an inner voice. In premodern organization, the reasons why someone is obeyed cannot be traced rationally by comparing actions to a list of prescribed duties; they become a matter for depth psychology.

1.b. In modern bureaucracy, authority is "distributed in a *stable* way."[50] Here Weber elaborates on Point 1: the emphasis on stability favors predictability and control. To the bureaucrats it means they can expect to see different types of orders always come from different places: the payroll department orders you to submit timecards; personnel rules on your fitness for the job; line supervisors give task commands. In a different sense, the bureaucrat learns to associate distinct forms of behavior with occupancy of distinct offices. Authority is clearly structured into permanent offices.

A further subpoint is that "authority . . . is strictly *delimited* by *rules* concerning coercive means."[51] Rules, in other words, are in existence and are published before administrative behavior takes place. The range of sanctions is strictly limited and assigned to specific offices.

In contrast, under premodern rules, authority is centralized in the paternal ruler and either not clearly distributed, if delegated, or not distributed at all. A contemporary example is the unstable fate of a White House staffer whose authority not only may overlap with that of others, but who has no permanence since the president may relieve him at any time; nor are his functions usually clearly delineated or clearly understood by others. Contrast this with authority distribution in any of the permanent cabinet departments.

In contrast to the delimitation of authority by rules, consider the family as a leftover of premodern organization. Here rules may not exist until a child engages in behavior not approved by the parent. Rules are often *ex post facto*. Notably, the purpose of administration in the family is not primarily control but growth. The range of coercion is infinite to provide for a vast range of possible behaviors and family needs: the Roman head of household could kill the child; the parent today can torture the child psychologically to develop control mechanisms of guilt and shame even as the child grows through individuation to material independence. Any member of the family can apply psychological torture to any other member; there is no official office of torturer, though there tends to be a chief executioner. In traditional families, it is the father.

Similarly, in the political machine, rules regarding reward and punishment for graft collection or political payoffs are never published. They change with the recipient, though an ethic related to them is understood.

1.c. Bureaucracy is characterized by "continuous fulfillment of . . . duties."[52] Such an arrangement favors the client's expectation that the administration of rules and behaviors in a functional area is permanent.

In contrast, premodern organization offers no such reliability, fulfillment of duties being dependent on the whim of part-time administrators whose interests in administration and assigned authority are ever changing. Such lack of continuity makes it impossible to develop expectations of finding the same market conditions, the same enforcement of contracts, the same administration of freedom of commerce, or a labor supply from one day to the next. This in turn makes impossible the rational calculation of means and ends for entrepreneurs or, for that matter, the rational planning of state tax levies to continue to support the administration without interruption.

Second, permanent assignment and fulfillment of duties gives rise to "corresponding rights."[53] Rights are habituated expectations on the part of people that they will be rewarded in exactly the same way for an exact repetition in their performance of assigned duties. Without clear definition of duties and guarantees of the continuous application of sanctions and rewards to ensure their fulfillment, there can be no development of rights for either the functionary or the citizen.

In contrast, in patrimonial and patriarchal systems, exactly because they lack administrative structures to continually exercise duties, there are no "rights," only privileges bestowed by the ruler and left to the holders to assert as best they can.

Third, those employed to carry out duties must "qualify under general rules."[54] Again this provision enhances both the orderliness of administrative structure and the orderliness of administrative behavior in the environment. Functionaries picked according to their qualifications by standard rules can be expected to behave in an orderly and standardized fashion. Further, such standards can now be task-related rather than remaining ruler-related. In summary, in bureaucracy: (1) there are qualifications related to the task; (2) these qualifications are established in regulations; and (3) they are universally applied.

In contrast, in premodern organization: (1) there may not be task-related qualifications, loyalty to the ruler taking precedence; (2) there are no official regulations, only ad hoc rules stemming from the ruler's temporary will; and (3) the ruler's will varies from case to case. No way to run a railroad.

2. Bureaucracy is governed by the "principle of office hier-archy . . . levels of graded authority . . . a firmly ordered system of super- and subordination."[55] Again orderliness favoring control is fostered. Whereas jurisdictional areas provide a vertical division of labor hierarchy provides a horizontal division between levels of administration concerned with matters of different scope and importance. It is also the control mechanism that holds the vertical division of labor together. This latter point is of great importance to bureaucratic control: the division of labor weakens the possibility of anyone acting successfully on his or her own, especially in situations where the division has been carried to such an extent that one functionary's action completes only a fraction of an authorized administrative act. At this point the individual functionary becomes dependent on guidance from the next higher office as to when and how to perform his or her action in such a way as to integrate with the actions of other functionaries. It is this dependence, based on the division of labor, and the management of that dependence by ever higher offices in the hierarchy that constitutes a law of causality for the immense power of modern bureaucracy. Functionaries are forced to look upward for the ultimate norms and rewards governing their actions. In doing so they must provide a higher office with information on which sanctions can be based; they thereby surrender the management of their actions. The structuring of offices into a pyramidal hierarchy in which the highest office is the ultimate judge and manager guarantees central control over all offices.

In summary, hierarchy means the clear delegation of authority descending through a series of less and less powerful offices, the clear status knowledge of where you are located in hierarchy, and the principle of supervision by the office next higher up.

In contrast, premodern organizations show an overlapping delega-tion of authority, with the higher office not necessarily more powerful, responsible, or authoritative. There is also uncertainty about what one's own place and authority and responsibility are from case to case. And there is a continuing struggle for power as a normal condition of office-holding, a continuous circumvention of higher-ups. Politics remains a fact of everyday work life.

Dependence on hierarchy for guidance and reward in one's own actions, and therefore dependence as a style of survival, cannot develop in premodern organization. Without the dependence, premodern organization fails to develop a means of control that is reliable over a long period of time and can encompass the immense vastnesses of geographical or demographic space covered by bureaucracy.*

The interaction between the division of labor on rational grounds and the management of divided labor by hierarchy is the basis for the scope, intensity, and controlability of modern bureaucracy as the power instrument without compare.

3. In bureaucracy, management is "based on written documents."[56] Written records make visible both what bureaucrats are ordered to do and what they actually do. Rationally organized administration, suiting means to ends—including the correction of such administration based on written reports from below—thus becomes possible. In private business, written methods of accounting are an example, as are computer methods, which are equally visible because they are retrievable. Examples in public service include records and reports. Administration activities are recorded and survive personal willfulness, incompetence, dishonesty, and the departure or death of functionaries. Activities are at least potentially *open to supervision* from above—the hierarchy—and ultimately from outside—the public. There is here the promise of administration as a politically controllable enforcer of orderliness in those areas of human activity assigned to it.

In contrast, in premodern organization, communication and command tend to be by word of mouth and by humanly fallible memory. Personal control over bias of perceptions and understanding, personal determination to put personal interests aside—these guarantee reliability. Where such honesty is absent, administration breaks down.

Without permanent records, activities are difficult to inspect and analyze for the purposes of future correction and control. Control from one center becomes doubtful given the lack of formal regulation, evaluation, and feedback.

4. Bureaucracy's office management requires "thorough and expert training."[57] Here Weber not only repeats his earlier observation that modern bureaucracy requires employees who qualify under general

---

*Charismatic authority, for example, can be more intense than bureaucratic legal-rational authority, but it is usually short-lived and yields to eventual rationalization. Traditional authority may encompass vast areas, but it is subject to fragmentation as office-holders develop their own power base on a psychology of independence from higher-ups ultimately demonstrated by force—knights versus the emperor, feudal lords versus their liege lord, and so on.

rules, but emphasizes that office management as an activity itself becomes specialized and rationalized.

In contrast, in premodern organization, the qualifications of employees are mainly the confidence and trust of the ruler—e.g., the boss, the machine. The question is not so much "Can you do the job?" but primarily, "Can you be trusted?" This does not mean that a political boss, for example, will purposely hire incompetent people; rather, he or she will seek out competent people but make sure that, first of all, they can be trusted. The myth of the hack is just that—a myth—often perpetrated by professionals.

5. Bureaucracy requires the "full working capacity of the official."[58] Weber contrasts bureaucracy with the previous, premodern state of affairs in which the reverse was true: "Official business was discharged as a secondary activity."

Here Weber reemphasizes implicitly the primacy and continuity of administration over other personal interests. Officials discharge administrative duties as their primary effort in life. This effort not only excludes time for personal or other interests, but suggests the development of an inner loyalty to and therefore inner dependence on the institution: bureaucracy becomes a way of life.

In contrast, in premodern organizations, the available work capacity of the individual is given primarily to private endeavors. The office is second, at best. Officialdom is a source of private or social honor and income, not of institutional status and identity. Given such orientations, we can hardly expect officials to favor the rationalistic ordering of society according to general rather than individual interests.

6. In bureaucracy, management of the office follows "general rules."[59] General rules are rules codified in the interests of all or of those in whose general interest a bureaucracy is set up. Specifically avoided are rules favoring some as against others. Thus management itself becomes predictable; expectations of functionaries become regular; and a general atmosphere of orderliness and predictability is fostered—even within the structure of bureaucracy itself—with an aim toward projecting this onto the outer world.

In contrast, in premodern administration, management tends to be ad hoc, guidance occasional and spotty, the expectations of functionaries uncertain, leading them to look outside of the office for security and support. A classic example of this is the type of administration that leads to corrupt police departments.

In summary, a restudy of Weber's brilliant analysis of modern bureaucracy should place the characteristics he cited in the light of the past and the light of the purpose for which this form of administration was created. The ultimate imperative of control is reflected in each of the characteristics of structure, behavior, and implicit psychology he cites.

Martin Heidegger: Science as the Culture of Modernity

As early as 1903–1906, Max Weber warned against the tendency of the growing scientific culture to consider those things more real that could be measured and placed under a rule or law showing things occur in patterns or with some regularity. Especially when you or I are engaged in trying to *interpret* what other people mean when they act out toward us, knowledge of laws and human behavior "mean nothing to us."[60] Even social science's ability to show that a certain behavior is distributed uniformly throughout the world doesn't get us "one step closer to the interpretation" of that behavior.[61]

At the same time, the mathematician and philosopher Edmund Husserl, whom Weber read,[62] issued a related warning. Given natural science's increasing reliance on mathematics—bringing physical phenomena under mathematical rules—modern culture was getting out of touch with things physical.[63]

Nowhere have the warnings that science gets us out of touch with things human and things physical been more fulfilled than in the current crisis of industrial production in the United States. Parallel to this crisis, we experience a crisis in the delivery of physical products and human services by government agencies—a crisis more subtle, but a crisis nevertheless.[64]

The industrial crisis of modern organizations cannot be denied. Ironically, mathematics as the study of the bottom line helped us recognize it. Product market share decreases as the "scientific management" of American production lines steadily increased management control over workers' time and space.

By the late 1970s, after American consumers revolted against American automotive and other products by turning to the Japanese, quantitative studies showed each American car had 3 to 5 defects against a Japanese car's 0.7 to 1.5 defects; American air conditioners were 63 times as defective as Japanese products.[65]

American industry's response? Companies raced for survival. They left behind the idea that all human beings and all things could be managed from the top down according to general rules or laws. They fixed their eye on a new knowledge: one based on individual interpretation from below of what was going on between people and between people and things. Copying the Japanese model, American managers started listening to workers in worker-management participation programs. In 1982, 41 percent of companies having more than five hundred employees reported having worker-management participation programs. By 1984, 2.3 million workers were said to take a part in such programs.[66]

Similarly, in the social protest movements of the late 1960s government encountered protests from the political left against the way government was delivering controls and services. By the 1970s, political controls over bureaucratic mechanisms and procedures had been institutionalized: there were community school boards, and there was popular participation in the shaping of environmental impact statements required for government planning. These tended to favor the well-organized among the under classes and the middle class. Finally, in the 1980s, the ideological right, convinced that many of bureaucracy's values were a threat to conservative human values, attacked the budget lifeline of much of social service bureaucracy.[67]

Across the board, modern organizations, while praised for doing well in the delivery of quantity, were judged for doing badly in tuning in to qualitative needs of human life.

How could this happen? A few voices had warned against the culture of quantity for many years. One such voice has been that of the philosopher Martin Heidegger, who took great pains to explain the hidden values of science and to juxtapose values of human life equally hidden in and by modern culture.

The Scientific Imperative

Assume that all we know can be got by listening to general laws of nature.[68] This is not how you and I experience getting to know things. We, as ordinary human beings, get to know things in their individuality: my friend Jay here and my friend Michael there; this car door, which slams differently from that of my other car. But, if it were true that all human knowledge can be got from general laws, this would greatly simplify things. Then all friends, all cars, all things living and dead could be, if not understood, then explained—perhaps controlled?—by reference to a few natural laws, like the law of gravity or the law of self-preservation.

Modern science promises exactly such knowledge by reference to laws. And, at least in physical matters, science seems to have delivered. So that you and I, who don't know much about how to discover general laws, would be well advised to surrender our knowledge enterprise to an elite of scientists. From this it follows that there should be an elite of politicians, of legislators, of entrepreneurs, of bureaucrats, certainly of the clergy—of all those who have developed special methods of gaining access to general laws, whether "given" by nature, by the body politic, or by God. There have, of course, always been elites. Elites are those few who rule by claiming special access to knowledge of what is right and wrong and how to impose it on others. But, once science infests a culture, the necessity for such elites—knowledge elites—becomes obvious to all.

It is the achievement of Martin Heidegger to have shown us that human beings have not always assumed that their lives could be understood and regulated by general laws and to have shown us what orienting ourselves toward general laws makes us miss in the quality of human life.[69]

TWO ASSUMPTIONS OF MODERN KNOWLEDGE

Since Galileo, Heidegger found in an examination of science as the underlying assumption of modern culture, we have assumed that:

1. Knowledge of individual things comes from general laws *outside and above* the things instead of from *qualities inside* the things.[70]
2. Only that can be known which responds to ideas about reality that can be *preconceived*. This notion that reality has to be approached in terms of preconceived hypotheses the Greeks called *mathesis*. It is in this sense that all knowledge of modern science is *mathematical*: the knowledge is obtained by testing or challenging reality to respond (or not) to preconceived ideas about it.[71] Both before modern times and in today's postmodern beginnings, the alternate approach is to let nature—and human beings—speak for themselves in their own terms.

Assumption 1: Top-down Rules Outweigh Bottom-up Knowledge. The organizational consequences of assumption number 1 is scientific management, which organizes work from the top down according to general rules or laws about production generated by scientists and engineers. Today this type of organization is being challenged by the reality that overorganization of workers' time and space from the top down denies them a sense of the quality of the items that pass by on the production line. Without time and space to develop a bottom-up knowledge of *what* passes by on the line, there is no opportunity to judge what is appropriate behavior toward these objects. The result is a loss of quality in production. In public bureaucracies, of course, acceptance of the procedures of production ordered from the top down has produced the key strength of modern bureaucracy: top-down control. But there also, it has long been questioned by street-level functionaries whether their work can really be done simply by following the rules and without tuning in to the needs of the clients at hand.[72]

Assumption 2: Reality Is That Which Responds to the "Mathematical" Approach. The organizational consequence of assumption number 2 is hierarchy. We believe there is no other form of knowledge but the kind reflected in the elite of scientific management: engineers and bosses know best. It is assumed that all that can be known and done is already *pre–figured* in the hypotheses that science and management can make.

Figure 2.1: Scientific Assumptions in Bureaucracy

Assumption 1

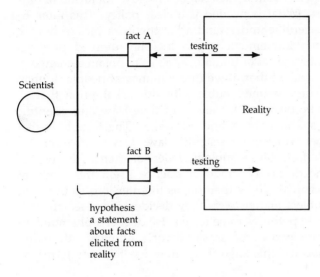

Knowledge is
outside and above
and before things:
hypothesis.

Assumption 2

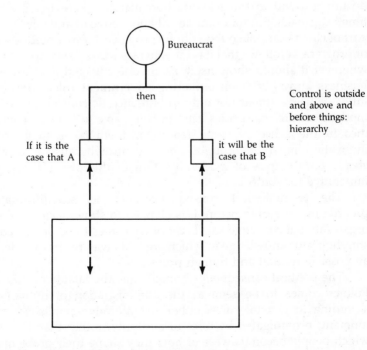

Control is outside
and above and
before things:
hierarchy

Reality is determined by testing and shaping its behavior according to such pre–figured hypotheses. In bureaucracy, this assumption of science supports the belief that all eventualities can be provided for ahead of time in the design of work. What is needed is a clear policy. This must be founded on a solid, scientific understanding of the principles of human behavior. This is then implemented in a logically derived program designed to manipulate one set of human variables to obtain a change in another set. So it is assumed that, if we throw money at people, human welfare will set in. There is one trouble with this assumption that all human behavior can be provided for ahead of time by sound scientific laws translated into sound policies and programs. The trouble is that putting all human behavior under scientific laws leaves no room for human innovation. (In fact, this technological view of science [the logic of technique] denies the discovery mode of science itself: the mode of thinking that great scientists allow themselves to enter into so they can get a feel for their subject matter *before* they decide on a research path expressed in terms of hypotheses to be tested. Heidegger's phenomeno-logical perspective emphasizes processes of getting in touch with nature in its own terms *before* we challenge it to show itself in our terms by testing it.)

The bureaucratic consequence of accepting science as the underlying determinant of what is real in modern culture is to neglect all realities that do not respond to the scientific/bureaucratic "knowing it all ahead of time" approach. So, for example, all knowledge of any new action on the part of clients can, of course, not be provided for in a predesigned policy or program. It follows that it is bureaucracy's task to stamp out new action wherever it should show itself: as anyone engaged in launching a new business knows after encountering government rules. *Any* unplanned innovation is a threat not only to bureaucratic control but to the entire modern culture that prides itself in being able to anticipate *all* eventual-ities in the sense of being ready for them *before* they occur. Such innovation must be brought under control because it threatens the steady-state empire of modernity. Out of this grows the bureaucratic imperative for control.

The technological consequence of the scientific/mathematical preordering of reality before it is allowed to show itself is similar to the organizational consequence. Technology comes to be perceived as a vast storehouse of knowledge in which are laid away recipes for dealing with all possible natural and human problems.[73]

The political consequence brings home the fatality of this approach. Politics comes to be seen as the administration of human problems according to general rules, either scientifically established or, for the moment, promulgated by force or authority, rather than the process by which people become aware of how they shape their problems to begin with. (See the discussion of politics as administration versus politics as evocation in Chapter 5.)

CONTEMPORARY JUSTIFICATION OF QUALITY

Martin Heidegger's questioning of whether all of human experience and all of reality can truly be brought under general laws that preconceive the knowable ahead of time has recently been validated in the experience of crafts people, industrial production and public bureaucracy, and most recently in science itself.

In 1986, the *New York Times* reported that natural scientists had found it was not really longer possible to predict the behavior of falling objects according to the law of gravity alone.[74] Since Galileo's legendary experiments atop the Leaning Tower of Pisa, it had been assumed that a feather and a coin would fall at the same speed in a vacuum—following the external "law" of gravity. New calculations found that *inner* qualities of the objects—a function of mass and atomic composition—would vary the rate of fall.

Heidegger has given us a picture of a culture that would look at the inner qualities of things rather than hope to have all knowledge of things guided by external principles. In such a culture I would recognize you for what you are as an individual. Top managers and staff would recognize the validity of the production worker's knowledge that each fender on a car production line is experienced in its individuality. They would admit that there must be time and space given to the worker to tune in to the reality of *that* fender *now* before him if quality work—work done with knowledge of *what* [qua] is being done (rather than *how much*)—is to be accomplished.

In such a culture individual experience that we have of each other as human beings would take precedence over general knowledge. And methods for coming in touch with and appreciating such experience—whether in the group session of organization development or the encounter groups associated with California pop culture—would come to be valued. Finally, methods for appreciating the knowledge to be obtained in approaching things in their own terms would come to be valued—whether it is in the form of Japanese management, American worker-management participation programs, or any other process that teaches us to recognize the worth of knowledge possessed by those people who still lay their hands on people and things.

To the extent that such a culture is rapidly developing, we may speak of a fundamental cultural revolution occurring in our own times. This cultural revolution, because it questions the monopoly of science on knowledge by juxtaposing the knowledge of hands-on experience, questions the monopoly of all those who now are granted the power and

Figure 2.2: A Culture Paradigm Shift: From General Laws to Individual Objects

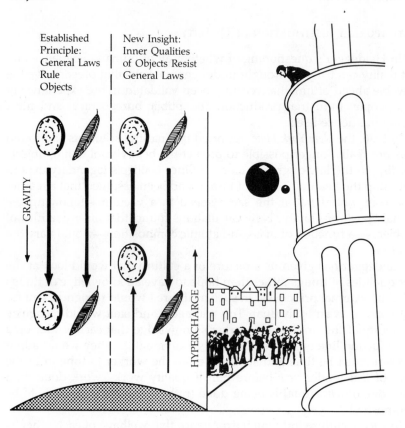

Source: based on data from *Physical Review Letters*, Jan. 6, 1986; and John Noble Wilford, "Hints of Fifth Force in Universe Challenge Galileo's Findings," The *New York Times*, Jan. 8, 1986, pp. A1 and B7. New analyses of early twentieth-century experiments with falling bodies show that the function of the mass and the atomic composition of individual objects must be considered in calculating their rate of fall under the law of gravity. Force resisting gravity (hypercharge) is greater for a copper coin than for a feather; the feather dropped through a vacuum would actually fall faster than the coin. This contradicts the principle established by Galileo at the Leaning Tower of Pisa arguing that general laws external to objects govern their behavior: for example, the law of gravity. As Heidegger would point out, the discovery reasserts the principle of classical Greek physics that objects behave according to inner qualities. The Greeks had assumed that heavy objects tend earthward because of an inner quality of "heaviness," while light objects tended heavenward because of an inner quality of "lightness." While the new findings contradict the Greek prediction that a heavy coin would arrive on earth before the light feather, they nevertheless shift the attention of researchers to inner qualities of objects and away from external laws. The author argues that, along with other shifts in focus from general laws to the particular experience of things, such scientific findings may be used to shift the focus of an entire culture from assumptions that we can control all according to general laws to a focus on the limits to such control emanating from individual objects: such as human beings and their needs and potentials.

authority to tell us what to do because they are located at the top of society, politics, or bureaucracy.

In the meanwhile, the bureaucrat especially will find himself or herself caught up in an increasingly intolerable tension between people's demands for quantity in products and human services and these very same people's demand that the mass of such products satisfy the qualitative needs of human life. Such tension will be reflected in politics.

H. Mark Roelofs: American Political Culture

Any modern society defines the qualitative needs of its members through politics. Bureaucrats are supposed to be the instruments of politics to carry out the political will of the society. When bureaucrats turn to politics what can they expect?[75]

But should a bureaucrat ever turn to politics at all? Isn't there a myth that bureaucracy and politics don't mix? Max Weber himself seems to indicate this when he says that it is "the honor of the official," his "ethical discipline in the highest sense," to carry out the order of the commanding officials exactly as if they accorded with his own conviction. But Weber adds a condition: this is so only if "the higher authority insists, despite his protests, on an order that appears wrong to him."[76] To what values could a bureaucrat, then, appeal even in his own mind? If bureaucracy is instrumental, these must be political values—ends values. The bureaucrat's ultimate measure is the public interest.

When Archibald Cox, special prosecuting attorney appointed to investigate the Watergate accusations against President Richard M. Nixon, came too close to presidential wrongdoing, he was fired by the president. But before that could happen, the president had to find himself a new attorney general, superior to Cox, because the old attorney general refused, out of conscience, to carry out the order to fire Cox. Whistleblowers appeal to such higher values consistently: political values of the public interest. Interestingly enough, however, there are in America very few resignations by top officials because of conscience and very few whistleblowers—especially whistleblowers who survive.[77] This should ring a warning bell in American bureaucrats' minds.

THE POLITICAL IMPERATIVE

Survey researchers for some time have observed a deep-seated split in what Americans want politically. On the one hand, politicians were able to mobilize Americans in favor of broadly generous and deeply caring policies to help their fellow man, woman, and child. On the other hand, these same Americans could be turned possessively selfish and into exhibiting an "others be damned attitude" on these very same social policy proposals—such as, for example, President Lyndon B. Johnson's Great Society program. A switch was easy. Politicians opposing social programs simply raised the issue of whether those on the receiving end deserved the help. They asked whether recipients had really "worked hard" as "individuals" for what they aimed to get or were willing to "work hard" to acquire "property." Or they asked whether sharing with others was not in itself betrayal of "property" that one had "worked hard" as an "individual" to acquire. Do-gooders might be accused of attacking "property" itself as well as the "work ethic" and "individual responsibility." During the Johnson years, the eight or nine out of ten Americans favoring social programs could be turned eight or nine against them if the specter of an attack on individualism, responsibility, the work ethic, or property were raised.[78]

H. Mark Roelofs explains such wildly oscillating behavior by pointing to a long historical development reaching back to the times of religious leaders John Calvin and Martin Luther and political philosopher Thomas Hobbes. The American Founding Fathers compounded the American political culture out of ideas current in those days and crystallized by such religious and philosophical leaders on behalf of the rising Protestant sects and merchant classes. Given its dual religious and secular origins, the American culture was split right down the middle into two subsets of values. One subset, the social conscience one, rested squarely on the Protestant tradition. It suggested that America as a community would march onward and upward toward social justice and equality under the inspired leadership of great presidents. The other subset, the individualistic one, rested for the most part on the early experience of the bourgeoisie rising in England in the sixteenth and seventeenth centuries. It held that if you worked hard for what you got, by the sweat of your brow, you owned it—an attack on inherited feudal rights. Essentially untarnished by inroads from alien ideologies, the American political culture today still presents this dual picture:

Social Conscience Values	Individualistic Values
Equality	Individualism
Social justice	Competition
Community	Hard work
Great leadership	Property

It is Roelofs' achievement to have shown that America's *effective* political institutions, the reservoirs where power lies, are so organized as to support and make effective the individualistic subset on a day-to-day basis. America's ineffective institutions, on the other hand, have been designed to support and uphold the myth that social conscience values can be made powerful. Dispute still rages over this analysis in the academic halls of political science. No one experienced in actual everyday politics, however, is crazy enough to give up working through interest groups and start working through the platforms of political parties. No politico will forego a personal power base with personal hangers-on owing fealty for the voluntary backers of a good "cause," to be the first to reject corporate donations through Political Action Committees in favor of accepting only one-dollar bills from small donors that expect nothing personal in return. The occasional great cause can sometimes succeed; in the meanwhile, day-to-day politics goes on using the effective machinery enshrining the practical individual-interest values of politics.

The effective *political imperative* in America therefore is: follow your own interest, and the public be damned.

This makes it very hard on the civil servant, trying to find support in the *public* interest for what he or she does. The *public* interest is hard to find. Instead, he or she must look to those *individualist* or *group* interests that happen to coincide with the survival interests and mission of his or her agency or bureau. This is why political scientists like Theodore J. Lowi can point to the reality of "iron triangles"—coalitions of legislative committees, corporations, and bureaucracies—as the real centers of policy making in America.[79] From the viewpoint of the pure rational professional in the civil service such "dirty" politicking must seem "corrupt." But such "corruption" may be the only game in town where there is no identifiable public interest or no public interest enforceable except by politicking to get together the power of several individuals and groups. The trick is to play with private interests without running up against the law.

Pure bureaucrats usually reject the need to be political for their own survival suggested in this section. In teaching the connection between bureaucracy and politics, I use the following scenario:

You are the head of a small section or division in the civil service of your town. A town councillor calls you and asks you to meet him for lunch. He has "a few matters of concern to my constituents" to discuss.

Do you:

(a) Tell him you're busy.
(b) Tell him to speak to your immediate superior.
(c) Tell him you'd be happy to meet him for lunch.

Oh, yes, a complicating factor: your section's or division's budget comes up before the town council next Wednesday.

This is not a test question. Your answer merely determines your chances for political survival as a bureaucrat.

BUREAUCRATIC CULTURE

As demands for quality of life and the products and services that support quality have soared over the last ten years, a host of pressures— economic, social, and political—have been placed on the bureaucratic corporation and government agency. For the individual this means there are today more "good" companies to work for—and perhaps even a number of "better" programs or agencies in the government bureaucracy. However, it is as crucial to recognize that the surface phenomena of "corporate cultures" or "bureaucratic cultures," whose tone and style appear so easily changed by a change in top leadership, management procedures, and work processes, *are* surface phenomena at this time. They *may* become prototypes of a future in which not only the products and services but working life will be qualitatively more in tune either with general human values or with the experience of bottom-up knowledge on which contact with reality depends. There is, however, no indication that anyone in Western civilization, is willing to give up the quantitative benefits of that civilization. These quantitative benefits are achieved by those individuals who are willing to put duty to organization above human values, even above the kind of knowledge that puts all human beings in contact with reality; actuality remains subject to enactment by empowered elites: scientific, technological, bureaucratic.

Two possibilities arise:

1. We are either engaged in a universal transformation of bureaucratic culture of which there is an early indication in the broadening variety of organizational cultures; or
2. We are engaged in one of the recurrent paroxysmic encounters of modern rationalism with human forces beyond its control, forces to which, however, rationalism not only remains fundamentally immune but which it is able to absorb by translating them into rationalistic terms.

All talk of creating organizational cultures that may make life easy or more human, or both, may be recognized as a fraud a few years from now, when the rationalistic bias of modernity has reasserted itself—as it did after its confrontation with the cultural revolution of the 1960s. Those concerned with the future of bureaucratic culture in general will therefore look at two things. First, there are the surface phenomena of new organizational cultures. Then there are the deep values contained in the underlying currents of modern civilization. These contain contradictions between bureaucratic life and human life and between quantity and quality that we have seen running as a long-suppressed tow and undertow throughout modernity.

Possibility One: A Multiplicity of Organizational Cultures

In 1963, Thomas J. Watson, then chairman of International Business Machines, said:

The basic philosophy, spirit, and drive of an organization have far more to do with its relative achievements than do technological or economic resources, organizational structure, innovation and timing. All these things weigh heavily on success, but they are transcended by how the people in the organization believe in its basic premises and how faithfully they carry them out.[80]

Watson certainly understood the importance of shared values to corporate identity and coherence. In recent years, much has been written about how the change of chief executive officer (CEO) in a private company or of a cabinet officer or government agency head can revolutionize the experience of working either in a private or public organization. The bureaucratic imperative no longer seems to be inexorably tied to the economic imperative. In fact, studies like *In Search of Excellence* indicate that the bureaucratic imperative may, under certain conditions of worldwide competition—that is, where bureaucratic stabilization of markets has not been imposed—actually sabotage the economic imperative of survival. As a result, it may appear that organization chiefs may today have great creative latitude in determining the exact mix of qualitative (that is, discovery-oriented or work-oriented) organizational characteristics. In fact, the range of possible combinations is infinite when we lay out qualitative characteristics on one level of an imaginary slide rule and quantitative characteristics on another level:

Table 2.1:   A Slide-Rule for Mixing Organizational Culture

Quantitative Traits of Organization	*Qualitative Traits of Organization*
Bigness ———	——Bestness
Hands-off, head-analytical Numbers-oriented ———	——People-oriented
Quantity-oriented ———	Quality emphasis on product and service
Control from top ———	——Innovation by all
Information controlled ———	——Informal communication
Back-protecting growth ——— ↓ ↑	——Forward-looking growth

Source: Values based on Thomas J. Peters and Robert H. Waterman, Jr., *In Search of Excellence: Lessons from America's Best-Run Companies* (New York: Harper & Row, 1982), pp. 42–44.

Depending on whether a CEO slides the qualitative traits left or right over the quantitative traits, a different mix of culture results.

Combinations of personal entrepreneurship with bureaucratic structure are now possible that a few years ago would have torn a company apart. Two examples:

The chief executive officer of an insurance-related firm offers a prayer to God before hiring any employee and seeks God's guidance for the decision. This procedure does not impinge on the computerized operations of the firm at all, but it gives the CEO a sense of who it is that is working for him. Personnel relations are marked by a good deal of trust.[81]

Traditional modern organization would have predicted serious operational conflicts between the CEO's religious view of the world and the firm's highly rationalized operations.

A leading editor of college texts leaksves a large publishing house he has helped develop and sets up his own house in the shape of an electronic cottage industry. He is enabled by computer typesetting technology [rationalized production] and telephone networking with the disciplines he serves [combination of rational technology and personal communication] to exert both the most refined hands-on control over his products technically as well as take advantage of the organizational structure of other firms, such as data processing, warehousing, and manufacturing—all for the purpose of putting his personal values imprint on the type of book he handles.

Publisher: "Now, larger organizations also do this: they network with printing houses, warehouses, etc. But there is one thing I can do. An author can come to me with a book already on a disc on his computer. I can access that disc directly and turn the material into a book for which there is a need. The larger organization has the same technical access but they can't do this. Larger organizations are followers rather than leaders."

Interviewer: "No one in the larger house has the authority to be totally innovative. The tendency is to ask, Does the book fit a need? and, if not, to reject it.

Publisher: "Innovation comes from entrepreneurship, and creativity comes from your smaller organizations, which are trying to become larger organizations. Ten years from now I won't be able to do this."[82]

The ability of those in the electronic cottage industry to combine the advantages of smallness and personal creativity with the advantages of bigness initially gives them an immense competitive advantage. The traditional response to this is for larger industries to swallow up the smaller ones and kill the challenge. However, recently larger industries have spun off smaller units exactly for the purpose of spurring creativity. In the case of one publisher, a smaller unit was created to launch a new line of books separately but with the support services of the large house. In the case of an insurance company, the spun-off investment division was guaranteed the parent company's business for a certain number of years but could now operate unencumbered by bureaucratic rules of the parent, tuning in to market conditions.

In public service, the new recognition of both quality and quantity can give formal recognition to the translating role of middle managers, who always have mediated between workers' hands-on operations and clients (qualitative) and the organization's official rules and mathematical standards for success (quantitative).

For the manager there is opportunity in times in which values oppose one another. They can be made to stand in creative tension. The result: a great deal more leeway in shaping an organization's culture than there was in times dominated by a unitary set of mutually supporting values. For the employee, there also are opportunities for selecting the type of organization that best seems to fit his or her own values. For clients, even in the public arena, there may be a greater variety of organizational services and products to choose from. Demand for quality services aimed at particularistic needs of distinct constituencies begins to become legitimate. It may outweigh concern for one set of products and services aimed at all equally. Examples include the privatization of certain city services or the issuance of education tokens allowing each family to select a school of its choice. Politically, qualitative differentiation in the delivery of government services may run up against the traditional alliance between "liberal" political constituencies and universalistic bureaucratic interests, both demanding large-scale institutions that can deliver "one-size fits all." But the real question is whether *any* qualitative differentiation is possible at all unless its delivery system is at bottom propped up by an underlying system of quantitative controls.

Possibility Two: Increased Bureaucratization as the Basis for "Quality"

The single most striking fact about American industry's turn to quality production methods is that this turn was not spurred by a sudden change of mind on the part of industry executives in which they might have said, "Our customers deserve quality; let's tune in to their needs." Rather the turn to quality was forced upon industry leaders on the basis of bottom-line calculations. Market share decreased below tolerable levels, threatening company growth and security. Only then were programs like the management-worker participation programs introduced—on a large scale and in inordinate haste, which reflected stark naked fear of organizational death. This after industry had ignored for decades the complaints of, for example, automotive production line workers who were saying that all quality had been pushed out of the work as the result of speedups in the production lines.

These are clues that quality may be merely a temporary episode in the continuing bureaucratization of the world. For what brought about the turn was no intrinsic organizational interest in quality. It was a response to one of the few nonrationalized forces left in the world: the relatively free, and therefore irrational, market between Japan and the

United States. While the turn of quality might be an interim solution, to the bureaucratic or generally rationalizing mind a different, long-term solution will seem preferable. The market between Japan and the United States can be stabilized through typical bureaucratic means, such as bringing down the value of the dollar versus that of the Japanese yen; then the nasty Japanese competition of better quality products challenging quantity products can be wiped out. In short, the bureaucratic mind simply tries to overrun the last remnants of such rationally unpredictable behavior as free international markets—for the control of which there are as yet insufficient or inadequate world-bureaucratic institutions.

Success in the bureaucratic stabilization of international markets and the pacification of domestic troublemakers trying to say less is better when large portions of the population still want more—such success would enable the modern culture to sink back into itself in a comfortable assertion of its by now traditional instrumental and quantitative values.

Then we would see not a rebirth of substantive concern for what each of us might be or become as a human being but the reassertion of "a polar night of icy darkness" anticipated by Max Weber.[83] In that night, it is not the moral guidance of human values but a "mechanized petrification, embellished with a sort of convulsive self-importance"[84] that holds us in a cage of our own making. For while we talk of quality, even those who talk of it are not willing to give up any of the rationalization and intellectualization that Weber saw as the characterizing fate of our times. None of us is willing to give up the material benefits that come from the "disenchantment of the world."[85] A reenchantment of the world through the words of poets and liars, the phrase used by Sigmund Freud for those who create culture, is beyond the capability of most of us. We therefore owe it to ourselves to come to terms with the foundation of the culture that we did not create but that pervades our souls and carries us on its shoulders. This means examining the tradition of rationalism.

The Stratification of Meaning

Weber, whose description of the rationalized society is today used less for scientific analysis than for recitation of a ritual wisdom, foresaw that in the rationalized world the masses would function fundamentally not on the basis of reason, but on the basis of faith and tradition.* Except that in this case habitual performance of everyday duties must be based on a faith in the overall rationality of the rationalized society. In exactly the same way, Weber points out, do children have faith in math without ever understanding the rational grounds behind the rules they habitually

*His essay "Ueber einige Kategorien der verstehenden Soziologie" (On Some Categories of a Sociology of Understanding), in Max Weber, *Gesammelte Aufsätze zur Wissenschaftslehre*, 3rd ed. (Tübingen: J.C.B.Mohr, 1968), pp. 469–471.

follow in adding, subtracting, and multiplying: "One determines whether one has calculated correctly, according to custom, not on the basis of rational considerations but on the basis of empirical proofs in which one has been trained (or which have been imposed on us)."[86]

If this means that even in such a rationalistic activity as doing math only a small elite of mathematicians really understand math while the rest of us do it out of habit, this insight applies even more to rationalized society.

Weber in fact proposes that any sense of the overall purpose and meaning of the rational society, of which bureaucracy is the logical successor, is unequally distributed through four levels of social strata: (1) the lawmakers, (2) the interpreters of law, (3) the users of law (those who use law for their own advantage), and (4) the mass of people who obey the law out of habit and simply because it provides comfortable channels for their everyday life. In Weber's words:

The rational institutions of society, be it a compulsory or a voluntary association, are imposed or "suggested" by one group for specific purposes although individuals in the group may already differ on the intent. The institutions are interpreted more or less similarly and applied on a subjective basis by the second group, the "organs" of institutionalization. The third group, in turn, understands these institutions subjectively in so far as adherence to them is absolutely necessary in private dealings; this group converts the institutions into means serving as standards for (legal or illegal) action—because these institutions evoke specific expectations in regard to the behavior of others (the "organs" as well as the fellow members of the compulsory or voluntary association).[†] The fourth group, however, and this is the "mass," simply learns to behave according to "traditional" routines that approximate in some way the meaning of the institutions as it is understood on the average; these routines are maintained most often without any knowledge of the purpose or meaning, even of the existence, of the institutions in question.[87]

If very little of any overall purpose filters down to the "mass" level of rationalized society, bureaucracy's predecessor, then we can expect the filtering out of purpose to be even more serious in the more highly "rationalized" structures of bureaucracy itself.

One of the first to deal with this issue was sociologist Karl Mannheim. In bureaucracies, he wrote, as the rationalization of the overall organization increases, the ability of any given functionary to know the purpose of what he does decreases. Mannheim dealt with this paradox that increasing systems rationality produces decreasing individual rationality by distinguishing between the system's "functional rationalization" and the individual's "substantial rationality."[88]

[†]In other words, "users" adhere to social institutions because they stabilize the behavior of others—individuals or organs of the state—making that behavior more predictable and therefore more manipulable.

Functional rationalization means the logical subdivision of an overall task into ever-smaller units of work, each tightly integrated with the others. Efficiency is the original goal of such rationalization. Substantial rationality refers to the individual's ability to know how his or her small task fits into the overall task. On this knowledge hinges not only individuals' ability to use their own reason to better integrate their work into the overall activity of the system, but also their sense of purposefulness in the aim of work and meaningfulness in the conduct of work.

To the extent that Weber and Mannheim are right, it follows that purposelessness and meaninglessness are unavoidable products, and not accidental ones, of modern organizations constructed on bureaucratic premises.

Is it possible that the functionary's sense of meaninglessness and purposelessness reflects an absence of norms to guide his or her behavior? Weber has already suggested that, even in the rational society, what guides the behavior of the mass is not an understanding of norms but a copying of other behavior.

Rationalism as Mindless Routine

We have thus come to the point at which psychologist B. F. Skinner arrived some time ago. It is not ideas that guide the behavior of people, but other behavior. While this assertion may have been made in too generalized a way by Skinner himself, it certainly describes both the behavior and the experience of meaninglessness of the typical bureaucratic functionary. What functionaries do is not tied to norms as ideas that provide meaning, simply because that is not the way they learn what they are supposed to do. They learn what they are supposed to do by doing it, quite as Skinner suggests. Systemically dysfunctional moves are punished or not supported; systemically functional moves are reinforced. Not ours to know the reason why. . . .

In this sense, the progress of modern bureaucracy from its original collision with the norms of society, to which it counterposes its own inner norms, leads inevitably to the gradual development of the first human organization experienced as being without norms. Bureaucracy becomes an organization without culture.

SUMMARY

Just as the new form of bureaucratic action separates actors from the actions themselves and from those on whom these actions impinge, freeing them of the implications of social ties and social obligations, the bureaucratic culture "frees" them from concern with ultimate values and basic knowledge of reality. Whether an action is "good" or "bad," "real" or "unreal" from the viewpoint of the client or subordinate functionary acted upon, is no longer an issue. The standards against which conduct is now judged are all concerned with means not ends, and knowledge is based on numbers not physics.

The question now becomes: Have I adhered to official rules or numerical standards in performing my duty? Not: Is the effect of my performance in keeping with generally recognized social norms of the type that evolve when human beings face one another as human beings?, or, Is my behavior in tune with physical or social reality?

At the moment, economic, social, and political forces once again seem to knock against the doors of bureaucratic and quantitative standards for human life. But the bureaucratic and quantitative approach is alive and well beneath such surface phenomena as revolutions in organizational culture. Perhaps it is exactly *because* of the underlying systems stability provided by bureaucracy, technology, and science that adjustments to quality—seemingly major from an individual's viewpoint—can be tolerated.

Ultimately, of course, the quantitative standards of reference adhered to by bureaucratic culture become increasingly remote from the practicalities of administrative life in the production of goods and services that can still be recognized by human beings individually as a good or a service. But we are better off in the short term if we doubt that an ultimate reckoning is here, even as we labor toward it.

WHAT PEOPLE CAN DO:
Understanding and Changing an Organization's Culture

*Jay D. White**

A few years ago, the chief of the Columbia Police Department asked me what I thought about management education for his command and supervisory staff. He expressed concern that though his officers knew how to do police work, they did not know how to manage a department. He said he wanted his supervisors and administrative staff to learn to think like managers and not like street cops. Subsequently we developed the Law Enforcement Management Program with my university; this became the major vehicle for cultural change within the department.

Trying to get people to think differently about their work experience is in effect attempting to change their culture. The noted anthropologist Clifford Geertz defines culture as a "web of significance," consisting of the ideas, symbols, meanings, and thinkings shared by social actors. An

*Prof. Jay D. White, organization theorist and management consultant, teaches at the University of Missouri—Columbia. He is a former police officer.

organizational anthropologist would seek to understand the ideas that people in the organization share about the way things are, why they are that way, and the meaning these ideas have for the way in which they live their professional lives. The interventionist who adopts this approach to understanding organizational life is also concerned with how these ideas might be changed. Getting street cops to think like managers is getting them to change their web of significance.

So I set out to study and change the culture of the Columbia Police Department, armed with an education and experience in organization development, and a modest knowledge of the recent literature on organizational cultures. Here I will explain how I went about understanding and changing this culture, discuss some of the things I learned about the culture, and note what difference cultural change has made for the way in which the officers interact with one another. Since I have been involved with them for over two years, I will be selective in addressing significant events.

THE PROGRAM

The original design of the Law Enforcement Management Program consisted of three existing graduate courses in public administration: an introductory scope and theory course, a course on organization theory and behavior, and a course on public personnel administration. In addition, a special course titled "Managing the Modern Police Department" was developed to serve as an integrative learning experience in which the officers could take relevant material from the existing courses and apply it to actual management issues in the police department. Thus the intervention was planned to take place over two years.

Due to some problems, the officers took the introductory course, then the organization theory and behavior course, and the special course. When it came time for them to take the personnel course, events had taken place that suggested a change in the program. In the special course, the officers engaged in a strategic planning exercise, which concluded that the program should be redesigned to help the department achieve accreditation with the International Commission on the Accreditation of Law Enforcement Agencies. A special training course was designed to achieve accreditation. It replaced the personnel course.

Some twenty officers participated in the program. The majority of them were sergeants, although a few captains and patrol officers took part. The primary focus was on the sergeants since the chief delegated much of the management responsibility to them. This was something new. No previous chief had attempted to locate managerial responsibility at this level. Prior chiefs treated sergeants as first-line supervisors. The present chief gave some of the sergeants mid-level management responsibilities and took an active stance in preparing first-line supervisors for mid-level positions.

There was an initial resistance to the program on the part of the sergeants. Even though a strong ethic of education and training prevails in the department, the chief knew that many would not participate. The chief offered a special incentive: each sergeant would receive a 4 percent pay increase while attending the program and would continue to receive the pay increase after completing it. As most of the participants discovered they actually enjoyed the coursework, any residual resistance was overcome.

BUREAUCRATIC STRUCTURE AND SOCIAL ACTION

I taught the first course in the program, which focused on the political and organizational theory of public administration. As part of the course they read Ralph Hummel's *The Bureaucratic Experience*, a devastating critique of the bureaucratic form of organization. The officers referred to their organization as being paramilitary in structure, suggesting that all of the norms of bureaucracy—such as precision, stability, discipline, reliability, impersonalism, and formal rationality—would be highly evident in the department. As it turned out, they are.

I expected the officers to hate Hummel's book. Some of them did. Not because they disagreed with his arguments, but because he portrays an all too real picture of life in a bureaucratic organization and some of the officers did not want to confront that picture in class. They did not like being reminded that they should be functionaries with truncated egos and no superegos (see Chapter 3), and that their interactions among themselves and with their clients should be governed by the norms of bureaucracy (see Chapter 2).

Some of the officers said, "Yes, Hummel's right. But that's not the only way things are done around here." I asked them what they meant by this, and they said that they really do care about such cultural norms as justice, freedom, violence, happiness, poverty, illness, death, love, hate, victory, and defeat. In response I claimed, "Of course. You must encounter these norms every day in the street." They said, "Sure we do. But these things are also important to us in the station." They went on to argue that their department could not function effectively in a strictly bureaucratic fashion and that it was absolutely necessary for them to engage in personal social action, otherwise they would lose their sanity.

After lengthy discussion, we concluded that they live their professional lives in two cultures: bureaucratic and societal. I asked them how they were going to cope with this, and one officer quipped, "We must become social action guerrillas!"

This is the only story from the first course that I will share with you.

The officers had another instructor for the second course, so I cannot comment on that. The rest of this study reports on my experiences with them in the special course on "Managing the Modern Police Department" and their efforts for accreditation.

QUALITY WORK AND QUALITY MANAGEMENT

When one thinks of culture, especially cultural artifacts such as works of art, one also thinks of quality. Yet it is difficult to get a handle on the quality of organizational life. Nevertheless, one of the things I tried to do with the officers in the special course was to get some sense of the quality of their organizational experience. I asked them to write up an example of quality work and an example of quality management. I deliberately left the concept of quality undefined because I wanted to see what they thought about quality. I also believe that quality cannot be usefully defined in any analytical fashion.

They did not play the numbers game with me by defining quality in terms of such measurable outputs as number of case clearances, DWI arrests, reductions in reported rapes, and so forth. Instead, their stories of quality work were about specific instances or events, characterized by a sense of a job well done in which there is some sort of emotional and cognitive exchange between the worker and the work performed. When I asked them why a certain piece of work—for example, a successful investigation or a successful hostage negotiation—was of high quality, they responded with several reasons. The work required persistence, dedication, commitment, ingenuity, creativity, or caring. The last characteristic was the most important to many of them. They truly cared about their work and associated caring with quality. They certainly understood that quality is not quantity.

They had a much more difficult time coming up with examples of quality management. Indeed, many of them concluded that there are no examples of quality management. There are several possible reasons: First, about a third of the officers had been in managerial positions for only a few months to a few years. They complained that they were not familiar enough with management to talk intelligently about its quality. Second, it may be that the nature of management is inherently different from the nature of work, and that a different sense of quality needs to be found for management. Indeed, their descriptions of what they did as managers were very different from their descriptions of police work. Third, perhaps management is all about numbers, and is therefore oriented primarily toward quantity and not quality.

The second reason seems most plausible. Management is different from work, at least in the traditional sense of the term. The best examples of quality management that they could come up with include: recognizing a need, discovering a poor fit, detecting problems, exercising good judgment, having the personal integrity to stand by one's decisions, taking personal responsibility for one's actions, putting proper systems into place, and balancing resources—people, money, and information. Perhaps the best example of what they saw as quality management was expressed by one person when he wrote that knowing you've done a good piece of management is like when that guy on the "A Team" says, "I love it when a plan comes together."

In our discussions, I introduced Sir Geoffrey Vickers's notion that management is the ability to understand, cope with, and change abstract relationships extended in space and time. The task of the manager is the ability to identify, create, modify, and destroy these abstract relationships among people, ideas, and things. This explanation of management was received as being just so much academic mumbo-jumbo. But it helps me, in my academic life, to better understand what they think about quality management.

Symbols, Rituals, and Heroes

In their book *Corporate Cultures*, Terrence E. Deal and Allen A. Kennedy note how symbols, rituals, and heroes convey significant information about an organization's culture. The officers read this book and were asked to write their own stories about the department. The following illustrates how symbols, rituals, and heroes influence behavior in the department.

Symbols. There is a certain police captain who usually does not wear a uniform. He holds an administrative position and often wears a suit. But, as the story goes, whenever he does wear his uniform, he strikes fear in the hearts of the other officers. They know something unpleasant might happen, like a radical shift in organizational policy or the disciplining of a fellow officer.

There's not much to make of this story as it goes so far, but it alerted me to the symbolic meaning of the uniform. Police officers wear uniforms to set them apart from the rest of society and as a symbol of their authority. This is basically true for the officer on the beat or patrol, and for the sergeant in charge of a squad. They have the greatest contact with the public. But when you turn inward and look at the managerial functioning of a department, the symbolism of the uniform becomes less significant. Given the nature of managerial work, there are few occasions in which the uniform means anything. Everyone inside the department fully understands who is in charge.

Managerial personnel in the Columbia Police Department frequently do wear uniforms. I don't have a full understanding of why this is the case, but I have observed the effect that choosing not to wear a uniform has on the socialization of managerial personnel. I once remarked to the chief that one of the best ways to get his staff personnel to start thinking like managers is to order them to wear suits, or at least a sport coat and tie. Nothing ever came of this in any formal way, but I observed that some newly appointed staff personnel were uneasy about hanging up the uniform. They felt doing so would put more distance than they would like between them and the line officers, which of course is what they were before their new appointments. As they grew more comfortable in their new roles, they became more accepting of business attire. Indeed, for some, business attire has become the "uniform" of management that distinguishes them from the line officer.

The tension, reflected in the symbolism of the uniform, between the management of police work and performance of the work itself is reflected in the movie *Beverly Hills Cop*. The character played by Eddie Murphy is constantly butting heads with "three-piece suits" who have lost touch with one of the real purposes of police work, to catch the bad guy. Fortunately, managers in the Columbia Police Department have not substituted bureaucratic rules and regulations for the reality of their mission—law enforcement and crime prevention.

Rituals. Several rituals illustrate the functioning of informal norms. For example, whenever an officer accidentally discharges a weapon in the station, he or she is presented with a piece of floor tile with a bullseye painted on it. This target is hung on the individual's locker door for a few weeks as comical reminder of the error. Similarly, whenever an officer damages a patrol vehicle, he or she is awarded a kamikazi headband. In some cases, the location of the accident is memorialized by naming it after the officer, as in the "officer 'so and so' memorial turn." These little rituals do more to shape an officer's behavior than any written procedure or rule. They also communicate the importance of rule-following behaviors to the other officers.

Heroes. I made an error when I asked the officers to write stories about their organization's heroes. There aren't any, and I assumed there would be many. Instead, I got stories of antiheroes—rogue cops who to accomplish a specific task either severely bent or broke policies, procedures, or the law.

The session in which we discussed the hero stories was particularly difficult for me because I had to overcome my own preconceptions about their experience and to develop a new personal understanding that would accord with theirs. I asked about the present chief: "Is he a hero?" "No," they replied, "He's not been here long enough!" I asked about a previous chief? Their response was, "Hell no! We're glad to get rid of him." Feeling frustrated, I asked, "Isn't there someone who has done something courageous?" Yes, they answered, but courage is expected of all of us. With some dismay I said, "Then everyone is a hero." They replied: Well, yes and no. But what you have to understand is that there can't be any heroes if we are all heroes. To which I replied, "You are right. Maybe that's why the stories you have given me are about antiheroes?" Yes, they said.

We then discussed what the antihero stories meant to them. Most of the stories described actions that the officers would like to take to carry out their job, but which are prohibited by rules and regulations that often protect the rights of citizens. When I asked them why these stories are important, they said that it would be nice to have the freedom to do whatever so and so did, but unfortunately we can't. I then said that these stories let them fantasize about what they would like to do, but they also remind them about how they should act. They agreed that the fantasy was enjoyable, but the reminder about appropriate action was more important. I concluded with them that the antihero stories serve as an outlet for some of their frustrations and remind them of proper action.

ACCREDITATION

The second half of the special course consisted of a strategic planning exercise using a modified nominal group technique. I asked the officers to respond to four nominal questions: What are the greatest weaknesses of the department? What are the greatest strengths of the department? What are the possible external threats to the future of the department? What are the most important future opportunities for the department? Each question was assigned a week apart as homework. The responses were compiled and given back to them anonymously. Each week we discussed the responses, paring away the trivial and duplicate ones. The goal was to arrive at some degree of consensus about the current and future state of the organization, and then develop action plans.

The priority action was to seek accreditation with the International Commission on Accreditation of Law Enforcement Agencies. This will enhance the prestige of the department, lower its liability insurance, and change the way some things are presently done. The latter justification for the priority of accreditation was the most powerful. Accreditation means meeting over nine hundred standard policies, procedures, or rules for the performance and management of police work. Fortunately the department was already in compliance with many of the standards, but in some cases the nature of police work and its management would have to be drastically altered.

All the members of the program are presently in the process of writing the accreditation self-study. This consists in writing policies and procedures to cover virtually every aspect of police work, including its management. The very act of writing policies and procedures is hard work, and, as in most work, one can tell what is of high quality and what is not. The finished policies have something of an aesthetic appeal to them. They are detailed, comprehensive, relevant to the actual work that gets done, and well written. Again, quality is seen in the care that an officer puts into getting the job done well.

Beyond writing quality policies, the officers are learning about management. Policies and procedures spell out in detail the abstract relationships that must be managed on a day-to-day basis. Many of the officers have never taken the time to reflect on the way things are done in the department, the justifications for doing them, and how different parts of the organization fit together.

The intriguing thing about this phase of the program is that the officers are making the organization more bureaucratized. Yet they have not lost their sense of social action or quality work. This is made evident by the frequent outbursts of both anger and joy and the fact that they are willing to openly confront one another as well as their superiors when they are asked to do something they don't believe is appropriate.

NOTES

1. Max Weber, *Economy and Society: An Outline of Interpretive Sociology*, 3 vols., eds., Guenther Roth and Claus Wittich, tr. E. Fischoff et al. (New York: Bedminster Press, 1968), p. 1002. Weber's emphasis

2. See, however, a caution in the third section of this chapter: "Bureaucratic Cultures."

3. Jürgen Habermas, *Toward a Rational Society* (Boston: Beacon Press, 1971), p. 96.

4. Max Weber, *Economy and Society*, pp. 956–958; cf. pp. 224–41.

5. Paraphrased from Thomas J. Peters and Robert H. Waterman, Jr., *In Search of Excellence* (New York: Harper and Row, 1982), pp. 42–44.

6. Quoted, except for material in parentheses, from Peters and Waterman, *In Search of Excellence*, p. 285.

7. See the section on "The Imperative of Bureaucracy," below in Chapter 2.

8. Dail Neugarten points out that today, after the 1978 civil service reform, civil service rewards still flow from the top down to individuals, upholding both hierarchy and the division of labor, while the state of the art of actual practice in the management of work is project management, which reduces hierarchical separation between management and subordinates and cuts across division of labor to produce teamwork.

9. See Footnote 7. The dominant consulting practice both in the private and public sector today is that of breaking down divisions between employees and making possible good communication between them in order to permit them to get work done. This is true whatever the actual approach of the consulting practice. It is true of the psychoanalytic approach to consulting like that of psychoanalyst Michael Maccoby's current consulting work with the U.S. Department of State: Personal Communication. It is true of the major consulting movement that has dominated the country since its origins in 1947 in the field psychology of Kurt Lewin and the phenomenological psychology of Carl Rogers: Organization Development. And it is true of a still-emerging consulting practice connecting people with their work: Technological Development. Technological Development was foreshadowed by worker-management participation programs that by 1982 included 41 percent of companies with more than five hundred employees for a total of an estimated 2.3 million workers involved in all such programs by 1984. (Data on 1982 from New York Stock Exchange survey reported in William Serrin, "Giving Workers a Voice of Their Own," *New York Times Magazine*, Dec. 2, 1984, p. 136. Data for 1984, from Ibid., pp. 125–137. See also R. P. Hummel, "Q-Management Training," paper delivered at the Conference on Training

for a High Technology Future, Pace University, April 19, 1985; and R. P. Hummel, "Good Work/Bad Work: The Silent Psychology of Belaboring the Object—Introduction to Technological Development," paper delivered to the First Cornell Symposium on Psycho-Dynamics of Organizational Behavior and Experience, New York City Center of the New York State School of Industrial and Labor Relations, Oct. 1–2, 1983.

10. See R. P. Hummel, "Bottom-Up Knowledge in Organizations," paper delivered at the Conference on Critical Perspectives in Organization Theory," Baruch College, City University of New York, Sept. 5–7, 1985.

11. See Martin Heidegger, *What Is a Thing?*, W. B. Barton, Jr., and Vera Deutsch, trs. (South Bend, Ind.: Regnery/Gateway, 1967).

12. See R. P. Hummel, "The Two Traditions of Knowledge: Quality Management and the Crisis of Quantity," in Donald J. Calista, ed., *Bureaucratic and Governmental Reform*, vol. 9 of *Public Policy Studies Series: A Multivolume Treatise* (New York: JAI Press, 1986).

13. See the section on "The Political Imperative" below in Chapter 2.

14. Derived from H. Mark Roelofs, *Ideology and Myth in American Politics: Portrait of a Political Mind* (Boston: Little, Brown, 1976).

15. "Morale of Justices in New York is Low," *New York Times*, May 21, 1976, p. 1.

16. Weber: "Office management, at least all specialized office management—and such management is distinctly modern—usually presupposes thorough training in a field of specialization. This, too, holds increasingly for the modern executive and employee of a private enterprise, just as it does for the state officials." (Weber, *Economy and Society*, p. 958).

17. Conversation with the author, spring 1981.

18. Kirk Johnson, "New York Courts Begin One-Case, One-Judge System Today," *New York Times*, Jan. 6, 1986, pp. B1 and B8. Interestingly this attempt to get judges back in contact with whole cases was justified on bureaucratic grounds: more accountability and reduced delays resulting from passing cases from judge to judge.

19. For a picture of the intent and ideal of this management approach, see Peter F. Drucker, *The Practice of Management* (New York: Harper & Row, 1954), and Drucker, *The Effective Executive* (New York: Harper & Row, 1968). The reality of MBO, especially in civil service where it penetrated last, is, of course, nothing like the ideal. It is especially difficult to cut through the morass of regulations to give managers the autonomy of action promised them so they may reach the measurable objectives to which they commit themselves in MBO contracts with their superiors.

20. Conversation with the author, June 1976.

21. "Klassen Told by a Senator That Mail Service Is a Joke," *New York Times*, March 9, 1973, p. 14.

22. Letter from Edward J. Logue to Robert Moss, quoted in "Fiscal Collapse of U.D.C. Was Result of 3 Wrong Moves, Panel Concludes," *New York Times*, May 27, 1976, p. 39. Compare Logue's attitude with that of the bureaucratic type whom Anthony Downs calls the "statesman." The fact that Logue was financially independent of his job may have to be considered in tracing the origins of the statesman type. See Anthony Downs, *Inside Bureaucracy* (Boston: Little, Brown, 1967), pp. 88, 102–103, 110–111.

23. *New York Times*, May 27, 1976, p. 39.

24. "Rockefeller Backs U.D.C.; Says Audit Will Praise It," *New York Times*, Dec. 4, 1975, p. 45.

25. Ibid.

26. State of New York, Office of the State Comptroller, "News for Release" on Report No. 86-S-24 news release, Dec. 30, 1985; and State of New York, Office of the State Comptroller, letter of transmittal dated Aug. 6, 1985, for Report 96-S-24 addressed to Mr. Vincent Teese, Chairman and Chief Executive Officer, Urban Development Corporation, and signed by Edward P. Henderson, Deputy Comptroller, Office of the State Comptroller, State of New York.

27. State of New York, Office of the State Comptroller, letter of transmittal of Aug. 6, 1985, loc. cit., Footnote 26, p. 1.

28. Loc. cit., Footnote 26. "Potentially," the letter of transmittal went on, "$860 million more will be provided for an additional 38 projects in the pipeline. As of April 30, 1985, UDC projects increased to 39 with an additional 56 projects in the pipeline."

29 Ibid., pp. 2–4.

120   The Bureaucratic Experience

30. Cf. Theodore W. Kheel, "Tyranny of a Bureaucracy," *urbia—A Journal for Cities and Their Problems* [Jersey City State College], Vol. 1, no. 1 (Winter 1973–74), pp. 3–7.

31. Interview with the author, June 1975. Anonymity requested.

32. Data in this case was taken from Philip M. Boffey, "NASA Had Warning of a Disaster Risk Posed by Booster," *New York Times*, national edition, Feb. 9, 1986, pp. 1 and 20; and Stuart Diamond, "Study of Rockets by Air Force Said Risks Were 1 in 35," *New York Times*, national edition, Feb. 11, 1986, pp. 1 and 11.

33. See Alex S. Jones, "Journalists Say NASA's Reticence Forced Them to Gather Data Elsewhere," *New York Times*, national edition, Feb. 9, 1986, p. 20.

34. Anonymous police commissioner quoted by H. Mark Roelofs in Roelofs, *Ideology and Myth in American Politics*, p. 225.

35. Vincent Ostrom, *The Intellectual Crisis in Public Administraton*, revised edition (The University of Alabama Press, 1974), pp. 75–76.

36. David Burnham, "Annals of Spies and Information," *New York Times*, national edition, Feb. 11, 1986, p. 8.

37. Ibid.

38. Max Weber, *Staatssoziologie—Soziologie der reinen Staatsanstalt und der modernen politischen Parteien*, 2nd ed., Johannes Winckelmann ed., (Berlin: Duncker & Humblot, 1966), p. 45.

39. Ibid.

40. Jay D. White, "On the Growth of Knowledge in Public Administration," *Public Administration Review*, vol. 46, no. 1 (January/February 1986), pp. 15–24.

41. The methods of interpreting what is going on in life are very specific and they differ from the methods of explaining or predicting events in such lives. See White, op. cit. entire article, for a summary and overview. See also, Linda Smircich, "Implications for Management Theory" in Linda L. Putnam and Michael E. Pacanowsky, eds., *Communication and Organizations: An Interpretive Approach* (Beverly Hills, Calif.: Sage Publications, 1983), pp. 221–241.

42. An early version of this question was first shaped by Jay White in drafts of the article cited in Footnote 40.; it was omitted for space reasons from the final article.

43. Weber, *Economy and Society*, p. 164. My italics for emphasis.

44. Including the three-volume collected essays in the sociology of religion, *Gesammelte Aufsätze zur Religionssoziologie* (Tübingen: J.C.B. Mohr, 1920–21), which actually, in Weber's own words, constitutes "a universal history of culture."

45. Weber, *Economy and Society*, p. 162.

46. The standard source of reference for the essay on bureaucracy is Max Weber, *Economy and Society*, pp. 956–1005. But the essay is reprinted in numerous readers, especially in the areas of sociology, public administration, and management science.

47. Weber, *Economy and Society*, p. 956.

48. For classic cases relevant today, read Mario Puzo, *The Godfather* (Greenwich, Conn.: Fawcett, 1969), for patriarchal rule in the Mafia; and Mike Royko, *Boss: Richard J. Daley of Chicago* (New York: New American Library, 1971), for a thinned-down version of fatherly rule in a contemporary political machine.

49. Weber, *Economy and Society*, p. 956.

50. Loc. cit.

51. Loc. cit.

52. Loc. cit.

53. Loc. cit.

54. Loc. cit.

55. Ibid., p. 957.

56. Loc. cit.

57. Ibid., p. 958.

58. Loc. cit.

59. Loc. cit.

60. Max Weber, "Knies und das Irrationalitätsproblem," part II of "Roscher und Knies und die logischen Probleme der historischen Nationalökonomie," in *Gesammelte Aufsätze zur Wissenschaftslehre*, third ed. Johannes Winckelmann, ed. (Tübingen: J.C.B. Mohr [Paul Siebeck], 1968), pp. 42–105, citation from p. 70.

61. Loc. cit.

62. Loc. cit., pp. 77, 102, 109, 110. See also R. P. Hummel, "Max Weber as Phenomenologist," paper presented at the Fifth Annual Conference of Political Science Departments, City University of New York Graduate Center, New York City, Fall 1980.

63. Edmund Husserl, *The Crisis of European Sciences and Transcendental Phenomenology—An Introduction to Phenomenological Philosophy*, David Carr, tr. (Evanston, Ill.: Northwestern University Press, 1970).

64. See R. P. Hummel, "The Two Traditions of Knowledge: Quality Management and the Crisis of Quantity," cited above, footnote 12.

65. On cars: data from study by James E. Harbour submitted to senior executives of Ford, General Motors, and Chrysler in the fall of 1980; reported in Thomas L. Freidman, "Autos: Studying the Japanese—U.S. Analyst Cites Their Cost Cutting," *New York Times*, Feb. 27, 1982, pp. 29 and 31. On air conditioners: data from David E. Sanger, "Another No. 1 Rating to Japanese: Quality Study is Disputed," *New York Times*, Aug. 25, 1981, pp. D1 and D6.

66. 1982 data: New York Stock Exchange survey; reported in William Serrin, "Giving Workers a Voice of Their Own," *New York Times Magazine*, Dec. 2, 1984, p. 136. 1984 data: William Serrin, "Giving Workers a Voice of Their Own," *New York Times Magazine*, Dec. 2, 1984, pp. 125–137.

67. Ralph P. Hummel and Robert Allan Isaak, *The Real American Politics* (Englewood Cliffs, N.J.: Prentice-Hall, 1986), pp. 230 and 235–239.

68. The entire discussion of the scientific imperative is based in the main on two sources: Martin Heidegger, *What Is a Thing?*, W. B. Barton, Jr., and Vera Deutsch trs.; analysis by Eugene Gendlin (South Bend, Ind.: Regnery/Gateway, 1967); and Heidegger's understanding of Immanuel Kant's *Critique of Pure Reason*, see Kant, *Critique of Pure Reason*, Norman Kemp Smith, tr. (New York: St. Martin's Press, 1965), especially B xi through B xiv.

69. Heidegger's attempts to show us the quality of human life as it extends beyond modernity and technology is a theme throughout his work, but it emanates critically and philosophically from his earlier work and poetically from his later work.

70. This is best expressed in Heidegger's analysis of the meaning of Galileo's experiments in allowing balls of different weight to fall from the Leaning Tower of Pisa; see Heidegger, *What Is a Thing?*, pp. 88–90.

71. Heidegger, op. cit., pp.65–80. To the Greeks, Heidegger writes, "The μαθήματα, the mathematical, is that 'about' things which we already really already know about. Therefore we do not first get it out of things, but, in a certain way, we bring it already with us." Op. cit., p. 74. This is an accusation difficult to understand in regard to our popular impression of how science works: certainly science *tests* its assumptions against things; but the accusation makes sense if we remember Kant's point that science approaches nature like "an appointed judge who compels the witnesses to answer questions which he himself has formulated." Kant, op. cit., B xiii. Nature is asked to respond to those questions, and *only* those questions, preconceived by science. Heidegger's accusation is easier to understand and accept when we look at the cultural impact of the scientific attitude: certainly managers, especially adherents of scientific management, approach things, tools, and us as workers with the idea that they already possess the general principles by which they can successfully manipulate us; it is we who must adjust to the principles, not the principles to us. This might seem a corruption of the true scientific approach; but Heidegger goes on to say that science itself is already corrupt when it does not allow things to show themselves in their own terms.

72. See R. P. Hummel, "Bottom-up Knowledge in Organizations," paper presented at the Conference on Critical Perspectives in Organization Theory, Baruch College, City University of New York, Sept. 5–7, 1985.

73. Martin Heidegger, *The Question Concerning Technology and Other Essays*, William Lovitt, tr. (New York: Harper and Row, Torchbooks, 1977), pp. 15–19 ff.

74. John Noble Wilford, "Hints of 5th Force in Universe Challenge Galileo's Findings," *New York Times*, Jan. 8, 1986, pp. A1 and B7.

75. This section is based on H. Mark Roelofs, *Ideology and Myth in American Politics: A Critique of a National Political Mind* (Boston: Little, Brown, 1976); Roelofs, *The Language of Modern Politics: An Introduction to the Study of Government* (Homewood, Ill.: Dorsey Press, 1967); Roelofs, "Critique of Pure Politics," paper delivered to the 1982 annual meeting of the

American Political Science Association, Denver, Sept. 2–5, 1982; Roelofs, "The Biblical Contribution to Western Political Thought: A Phenomenological Perspective," paper, annual meeting of the Canadian Society for the Study of Religion, Montreal, June, 1985; and other works of H. Mark Roelofs.

76. Weber, *Staatssoziologie*, p. 45.

77. Helen Dudar, "The Price of Blowing the Whistle," *New York Times Magazine*, Oct. 30, 1977, pp. 41 ff; Myron Glazer, "Ten Whistleblowers and How They Fared," The Hastings Center Report, December 1983, pp. 33–41; and U.S. Merit Systems Protection Board, *Whistle Blowing and the Federal Employee* (Washington, D.C.: U.S. Government Printing Office, October 1981). My thanks to Myron Glazer for calling my attention to these works.

78. Lloyd A. Free and Hadley Cantril, *The Political Beliefs of Americans: A Study of Public Opinion* (New Brunswick, N.J.: Rutgers University Press, 1967).

79. Theodore J. Lowi, *Incomplete Conquest: Governing America*, 2nd ed. (New York: Holt, Rinehart & Winston, 1981), pp.138–139.

80. Thomas J. Watson, quoted in Caren Siehl and Joanne Martin, "The Role of Symbolic Management: How Can Managers Effectively Transmit Organizational Culture?" in James G. Hunt, Dian-Marie Hosking, Chester A. Schriesheim, and Rosemary Stewart, eds., *Leaders and Managers: International Perspectives on Managerial Behavior and Leadership* (New York: Pergamon Press, 1984), pp. 227–39. My thanks to Prof. Dail Neugarten of the University of Colorado at Denver for calling this work on organizational cultures to my attention along with other works.

81. From the author's consulting experience; anonymity requested.

82. Based on interviews in 1985 and Feb. 18, 1986, with a publisher of college textbooks; anonymity requested.

83. Max Weber, "Politics as a Vocation," in *From Max Weber: Essays in Sociology*, Hans H. Gerth and C. Wright Mills, trs. and eds. (New York: Oxford University Press/Galaxy Books, 1958), pp. 77–128; quotation from p. 128.

84. Max Weber, *The Protestant Ethic and the Spirit of Capitalism*, Talcott Parsons, tr. (New York: Scribners, 1958), p. 182.

85. Max Weber, "Science as a Vocation," in *From Max Weber: Essays in Sociology*, cited in Footnote 83, pp. 129–156; quotation from p. 155.

86. Max Weber, *Gesammelte Aufsätze zur Wissenschaftslehre*, 3rd ed. (Tübingen: J.C.B. Mohr, 1968), p. 471.

87. Ibid., pp. 472–73. My translation.

88. Karl Mannheim, *Man and Society in an Age of Reconstruction* (New York: Harcourt, Brace, 1940), p. 59.

Jay D. White: Understanding and Changing an Organization's Culture

Deal, Terrence E., and Kennedy, Allen A., *Corporate Cultures*. Reading, Mass.: Addison-Wesley, 1982.

Geertz, Clifford, *The Interpretation of Culture*. New York: Basic Books, 1973.

Hummel, Ralph, *The Bureaucratic Experience*, 2nd ed. New York: St. Martin's, 1982.

Vickers, Sir Geoffrey, *The Art of Judgment*. New York: Basic Books, 1965.

3

The Psychology
of Bureaucracy

The bureaucratization of all domination very strongly furthers the development of . . . the personality type of the professional expert.
—Max Weber[1]

Psychologically, the experience of knowing and feeling—cognition and emotion—is radically different for the bureaucrat from knowing and feeling among people in society. This is so because bureaucracy's structures force bureaucrats into behaviors that alter the psyche's processes by which knowledge is acquired and by which emotions are felt. The individual no longer retains the right to judge what is right and wrong. The individual no longer is accorded the ability to judge when work is done well or done badly. Above all, bureaucracy claims the right to determine who or what we are; no longer are we allowed to work out our personality, we are assigned an organizational identity as we let the organization be our conscience and define what is real. The individual as such disappears and is replaced by a bundle of functions: a role. Emotionally we agree to this dissolution of our conscience, our ego competence, and our personality when we first agree to enter the state of passionless and mind-numbing rationality demanded by bureaucracy's norm of neutrality. When we are asked to give up our personal feelings for the people and things we work on, we surrender the prime human emotions: love and hate.

Yet human beings have great difficulty working without a sense of what they are doing (reality), without a sense that what they do affects others for good or for ill (morality), without an inner sense of who they are (personality), and without feelings for the things they belabor or the people they work with or the work itself (intentionality). Imprisoned in reality structures that can enforce such working conditions from without, people in bureaucracy make up their own reality from within. Fantasy comes to dominate. This is something that the designers of bureaucracy did not foresee in their deep belief that rationalism could conquer all. A psychology of work rises up against the psychology of organization. The psychology of organizations over-all focuses on the dilemma that different, and at times antagonistic, psychologies are required for organizing and for actually accomplishing work.

In sum, the psychological experience of bureaucracy is this:

1. Bureaucrats are asked to become people without conscience; judgments as to right and wrong are to be left to the supervisor, the manager, or the organization as a whole. Those who submit become people without heart: not only does their sense of moral judgment atrophy but so do their feelings for others. Those who cannot quite submit suffer from complex convulsions of their psyche, including guilt over doing things of which their conscience does not approve or from shame at doing things of which they know others would not approve.

2. Bureaucrats are asked to become people without a sense of mastery; judgments as to whether they do their work well or badly are to be left to those in the hierarchy or to the organization's rules, not to direct experience with the reality of things itself. Those who submit become people without head: ego function, their sense of knowing what it takes to get a piece of work done, atrophies. Those who cannot quite submit suffer from conflicts: How can they respect themselves when they submit daily to orders and judgments of superiors that contradict their own experience of the world and the work they do? Especially professionals—but also anyone with a strong sense of what works—begin to question who or what they are and face the choice of exit or hanging their head in shame, confusion, and doubt when confronted with doing something right or doing it according to orders or rules.

3. Bureaucrats are asked to leave their emotions at home. Yet all that human beings do—in relating themselves to other people, the objects of their work, the working itself—carries with it feelings. We love our work when we do it well. We feel affection for a boss who enables us to succeed in what we are good at. We have feelings for those we work with—love or hate, like or dislike, envy or good will—and we feel for those who are our clients—compassion or disdain, superiority or inferiority, and so on. The proper bureaucratic response to the injunction against any open display of emotion is to repress emotion to where it cannot be felt. As a result, unconscious feelings silently accompany all our relations with people and things at work—at times distorting, at times supporting our ability to get work done.

4. Finally, bureaucrats experience, in moments of accidental or organizationally planned personal crisis, their dependency on the organization for identity. Who or what I am is at all times dependent on who or what the organization says I am. To the extent that I have already given up moral and mastery judgments along with my true feelings, there does not seem to be much left of me in the face of the organization. My personality is no longer my own; it has been replaced by what I am for the organization: organizational identity comes to replace self-identity. This is more than a psychological problem; I feel myself challenged by modern organization in my total ability to be a human being.

The following sections explore these difficulties. We ask first: What is the typical psychological experience of the bureaucrat? Second: How have experts interpreted, or how would they interpret, this experience? Third: What psychology of bureaucracy can be constructed today?

WHAT PEOPLE KNOW AND FEEL

A functionary:

When I first joined the traffic department, I felt I knew my job. My job was taking out my crew—I had two helpers—go out with the truck, and we'd see a street sign down, and we'd put it back up. We had all kinds of signs in the truck. We'd do maybe 40 signs a day, and when we got tired, we knocked off. Maybe an hour or two early.

Then they said: Put it on paper. So we knocked off maybe three hours, did maybe 35 signs or so, and the rest was paperwork. I guess if it wasn't on paper, they didn't feel it was done.

Then they brought in an efficiency expert. The section boss one morning hands me a piece of paper: "You will put up this and this many signs a day, or we'll know the reason why." I looked at the piece of paper, and took it out in the street to my crew. Then we rolled in the street for 20 minutes, laughing our heads off. Their quota was 20 signs a day. We'd been doing 30, 40 before they started screwing around. Paperwork, reports, efficiency experts. Now we do 20 signs, and knock off.[2]

A manager:

I'm a banker. That is, I work for the ——— bank. We lend money. To big companies, too. When the company doesn't come through on a loan, we go in and take them over. I've fired an entire board of directors and the entire top management in one afternoon.

Anyway, we go into this one company. There's me for my bank, and representatives for four other banks. This outfit really was stretched thin on loans. They hadn't paid off for almost a year. They made computers. We asked: What's your total output for the year? They said: Well, it varies. We asked: What does one of your units sell for? They said it depends on the market. These guys just didn't know what the hell they were doing. We fired them.

One vice-president came in not knowing what was going to happen. He thought he was there to give the plan for the next year. We told him he was fired. He didn't even hear what we told him. He just went on giving his plan for the next year. I don't think it hit him 'til he got home.

The other vice president just put his head down and cried.

It makes you wonder. You feel you are somebody because you've got a lot of power. You've been running the lives of, say, maybe 300, 400, a thousand people. Suddenly you're out. You're a nobody. How could it happen to you? It can happen, though.[3]

These interviews reflect typical bureaucratic experiences with knowing and feeling. But, in their interpretation, the story tellers also illustrate four popular fallacies about bureaucracy. These fallacies are the direct result of failure to understand the distinct psychology of bureaucracy.

The first is the fallacy of the superego. Here the functionary assumes, because he has intimate contact with the work that needs to be done, that he can remain the best judge of whether that work is done properly according to social standards of moral right or wrong.

The second is the fallacy of the ego. This assumes that bureaucracy can and will allow an individual to achieve and maintain full mastery over a piece of work apart from other individuals and judge whether it is done badly or well.

The third is the fallacy of misplaced emotion. This leads the inmate of bureaucracy—public or private—to falsely assume he or she can lead a purely rational work life—until confronted with a situation where emotion becomes overwhelming.

The fourth is the fallacy of identity. This leads bureaucrats—whether public or private—to assume that after they have given their all to the organization they will be permanently granted an identity. This comes from the social experience that the more one exercises one's personality, the more one "has" one's personality. Organizations' needs change, however, and, when the identities constituted by a cluster of previously needed functions are no longer needed, they are dissolved—and the people who carry the identities with them.

The fallacies are held by many. They are uttered in what amounts to typical folksayings among bureaucrats. What are the assumptions of such fallacious sayings? What truths do they nevertheless contain? How does psychology evoke these truths?

The Fallacy of the Superego

In the case of the sign repairman, he presumed he could best judge what constituted an honest day's work. He knew the job. He presumed he could judge the standards for the job: you do as much as you can, and when you get tired you knock off. His motivation was an inner one. So was his measurement of tiredness. His standards reflected a sense of social usefulness of the work to be done and a sense of social fairness: when signs are down, you help motorists by picking them up, and you give an honest day's work for the dollar.

THE DENIAL OF JUDGMENT

Judgment in work situations can be of two kinds: situational and social. Situational judgments have an inner and an outer horizon. Outwardly, the standard for judgment as to how well or how badly one performs is the definition of the job—the way the organization sees the work. The inner horizon and standard for judgment is the work itself—the way a piece of work must be approached in its own terms if it is to yield to human manipulation. In regard to the first standard, the worker assumes, in a typical folksaying, that, "As long as I do my job [as defined by the organization], nobody is going to bother me." In judgments referring to the work itself, the folksaying is, "I know my work, nobody can tell me what to do." The first folksaying is the refuge of the ingrained and successful bureaucrat. The bureaucrat who relies on the second belief as a standard tends to get in trouble with the organization—for work often contradicts the organizational definitions of the job.

There is also social judgment. Despite their implicit surrender to organizational values implied in the job contract, some employees persist in using society's values as the ultimate standards for judging whether they are doing right or wrong on the job. Industrial managers and workers may show qualms over polluting the larger environment beyond the company's gates. Civil service workers may refuse to carry out legal orders of their bureaucracy that they feel are not legitimate—for example, when a public health doctor is ordered to sterilize a welfare mother. During the Watergate affair, some high administrators allowed themselves to be fired or resigned rather than carry out what they perceived as legal but nonlegitimate presidential orders.

On the other hand, the well-integrated organization man or woman will do anything a superior orders, including breaking into the headquarters of an opposing political party, rifling confidential psychiatrist's records, subverting the election process, putting into question the continuity of American democracy itself, and similar trifles. For such people, effectiveness in organizational terms takes precedence over any higher law. Of the Watergate offenders, Judge John J. Sirica wrote, "There seemed to be no limit to the contempt in which the White House men held the legal process. . . . They seemed always concerned about politics, never about whether their actions were right or wrong."[4] The point, however, is that the structure of modern organization and its system of rewards and punishments makes such behavior perfectly normal: a situation is created in which what works is appropriate and moral issues are irrelevant.

What does this mean psychologically? In Freudian terms, standards for behavior in society are stored in a structure of one's psyche called the superego. The superego stores, after some interpretation, society's norms of what is right and wrong. In society, the work you do for and with other individuals is very much tied in with how they will personally feel about you and your worth; consequently, the superego contains standards both for social relations and for work. Modern bureaucracy, however, is specifically a type of organization that intends to separate work from personal relationships.

In bureaucracy the individual functionary is asked to surrender part of the superego to the hierarchy. He or she must not only, as Max Weber says, "subordinate himself to his superior without any will of his own,"[5] but must agree to become subordinate to an external, alien superego.

Functionaries are thus persons with externalized superegos. This term, "externalized superego," expresses two thoughts. Functionaries still act according to the norms and standards of a superego. But, the ultimate location of the superego containing these norms and standards, and possessed of a will to apply them, is not their psyches but the office of their superior.*

The fallacy of the superego is then a carry-over from the previous solid assumption of subordinates that they are best suited to judge their own work, an assumption that is, however, disputed by the bureaucratic context. It divides into two subfallacies—the subfallacy of the individualist and the subfallacy of the professional.

THE SUBFALLACY OF THE INDIVIDUALIST

The subfallacy of the individualist rests on the functionary's carrying over from society a self-concept that has no place in bureaucracy. The self-concept of the individual in society is that of a personality—those unique characteristics that make a person stand out from all others. The self-concept of the functionary in bureaucracy, however, is never allowed to develop in terms of separateness and uniqueness, but only in terms of integration and similarity (or functionality) in relation to the rest of the organization. What the functionary *is* the organization intends to design exclusively from above.

This is especially important to the question of norms and standards contained in the superego. In normal society, I, as an individual, judge myself, often harshly, according to my own standards, which make up the superego. My superego, it might be said, looks at what I do and, when I fail to measure up to its standards, punishes me severely through a variety of psychic pains—guilt, for example. My inner superego constitutes a sense of my own worth: it is a measure of my self-esteem. There is, of course, the esteem of others. They have their norms and standards, and they often try to impose them on the lone individual who deviates. There is, however, a tremendous difference between saying that in society others "occasionally" or even "often" correct the behavior of

---

*It would be a mistake to now see the superego of the subordinate placed in the psyche of the superior. Superiors simply carry out actions dictated to them by the job definition associated with their office. They are not their subordinate's personal superego; they are his or her official superego. Were the managers to be removed, others would carry out the dictates of the organization approximately in the same manner and certainly within the same definition of the function of the superego, which is that it is always the superior office that exercises the legitimate right of imposing and judging standards, not the subordinate within his or her own mind.

individuals and observing that in bureaucracy all correction is ultimately carried out by an agency outside the psyche of the individual.

Consider the individuation process in society. Society exists before we are born into it. We learn, or internalize, its norms. But as we mature into individuals, as we go through the process of individuation, we adjust, change, and overturn much of what we have learned. Our superego, finally, comprises learned norms and norms we ourselves have developed in our own experience with life. The new norms themselves are then passed on or back to society as new generations take their norms from us as parents, teachers, and fellow members of society.

In addition, social norms and individual norms always stand in a relation of reciprocity to one another; there is a chance that in my social relationships I can affect the norms of others.

Now consider what chance I have of doing so in a bureaucracy should my personal work experience lead to new work standards that I want to discuss with my superior in an open social relationship. Here I encounter one of the great shortcomings of managers if not of bureaucracy itself. Managers view a correction of work standards suggested from below as a challenge to their control. This is a human failing. But ultimately there is also an institutional failure built into the bureaucracy concept—though never in terms of that specific bureaucracy looking at itself. The institutional failure becomes apparent when a particular bureaucracy has just recently reviewed its goals and its methods, found them in keeping with its overall purpose, and is then confronted with suggestions from below. If these suggestions contradict the just-reviewed goals and methods, not only must they be rejected, and if necessary suppressed and action stamped out, but the survival of the responsible subordinate is put in question. Functionaries know this well. The possibility of this kind of reaction to suggestions from below is always there. And because they have little experience in judging norms themselves and are subject to having their own work judged by others according to the norms of others, functionaries are likely to avoid the area of norms altogether.

All of which is to say that in pure bureaucracy norms are effectively dictated from above and accepted from below—all the time. There is a difference between the impact on the individual's superego of this situation and the human situation where one is expected to bring to all social relations, and to society at large, the benefit of one's own norms and judgment—the individuated superego. The individualist moral conscience has no place in bureaucracy.

The Subfallacy of the Professional

The subfallacy of the professional is expressed in the folksaying: "I am a professional and must be judged on professional grounds." The hidden assumption here is that the professional, as distinguished from the functionary and the manager, is subject to internal norms, not to an externalized superego.

This assumption is subtly wrong. It expresses a last attempt by a human being to retain both humanity and individuality. But such an attempt is not viable in the bureaucratic world. As a result it causes many difficulties for the professional and those who have to work with him or her.

In the words of Dr. Robert Jarvick, the developer of an artificial heart, commenting on a Food and Drug Administration review of one model, surgeons would have to "sit on their hands while the F.D.A. shuffles paper."[6] Jarvik had already left one hospital, where paperwork delayed his use of the Jarvik heart, to go to another. This might seem to be an example of asserting professional independence on behalf of human concerns over bureaucratic ones; but not necessarily so. The assumption of professional independence is wrong for two reasons. First, professionals need institutions to work in: doctors, for example, the more specialized they are and the more they consider themselves professionals as a result, need a hospital. But institutions are run by bureaucrats—by managers. Therefore managers, responsible for the existence and continuity of the institution, will either have the ultimate word over the professional's worth to the institution, or the institution will be threatened with organizational decay and untimely death. If these are to be avoided, professionals will have to adjust their inner norms to the dictates of the usual bureaucratic superego. Physicians' acceptance of diagnosis related groups (DRGs) is an example.[7]

The professional's assumption of independence and psychological integrity is also wrong because of the existence of hidden superiors. Professionals exist by the tolerance of a crypto-hierarchy of fellow professionals. Without the approval of this hierarchy, professionals can be disbarred as lawyers, expelled from the medical association with likely loss of license as doctors, or defrocked as priests. Professional associations are externalizers of the superego in their own right; they constitute the conscience for individual professionals who go astray and exercise the power of punishment.* Thus the professional has a great psychic affinity to his or her colleagues in bureaucracy.

Lawyers, especially, have always been members of a bureaucracy: they are officers of the court. Over time, bureaucracy has attempted to strengthen its hold over these professionals who, as defense attorneys, are expected to represent the human interests of their clients. Of course, law itself—the practice of law—has nothing to do with human interests

---

*Professionals do present a special case, if only because of their infinite capacity for self-deception.

but is a rationalized model of what human life would be like if it were conducted by lawyers. Yet many lawyers enter their profession with the idea that they can do some human good; they believe that they can not just apply law but obtain justice. As a result, lawyers in general have defended their relations with clients even when these are known to be of dubious character. In 1984 the Comprehensive Crime Control Act and the Tax Reform Act made it possible for the government to seize money paid lawyers if clients had illegally obtained it and required lawyers to report cash payment of $10,000 or more. A survey by the National Association of Defense Lawyers found that in two years most lawyers had undergone challenges to their fees from federal prosecutors; three-quarters of them were subject to litigation over fees or subpoenas, ending up with the lawyers disqualifying themselves from representing the client.[8] Under pressure from health and legal institutions, the bureaucratization of physicians and lawyers was well on its way, raising the specter that no one would stand for the patient or client.

To summarize, in society, the individual must live up to his or her own inner standards, contained in the superego. A typical folksaying would be: "You've got to be able to live with yourself." The expression indicates the limits the individual puts on willingness to accept social standards when these conflict with individual standards.

In bureaucracy, the individual must live up to external standards. If there is a conflict, he or she can be sacrificed—the strength of bureaucracy as a control institution cannot. Inner standards must be left at home before entering the office; office standards become a replacement superego for the human being during the eight hours a day spent as a functionary on the job. Beyond this, the fact is that many functionaries "become" their organization. They are the identity it gives them. They cease being private persons with private personalities. If they internalize bureaucracy's external norms, they never also internalize the right to make normative demands on their surroundings. In their public identity they become dependent on the organization because they internalize a set of norms the actual and only origin of which remains external. Only their superiors can change these norms or have power to maintain them. In the extreme, therefore, the functionary has an externalized superego, while the citizen has an internalized superego. In the case of the functionary, part of the psyche has been removed and placed outside.* Where? Not in superiors, for these may change, but in their offices. Together, these offices up and down the organization constitute what is called "hierarchy." Organizational hierarchy begins to perform for the bureaucrat the

*This is the origin of the psychology of dependency that characterizes the organization man (or woman).

functions of the superego. Hierarchy is the bureaucrat's externalized superego.

The Fallacy of the Ego

The sign repairman in our case study complains about two demands typically made by bureaucracy. The first is for information from below: "Then they said: put it on paper. So we knocked off maybe three hours, did maybe thirty-five signs or so, and the rest was paperwork. I guess if it wasn't on paper, they didn't feel it was done." The second demand is for obedience to control from above: " 'You will put up this and this many signs a day, or we'll know the reason why.' "

Aside from the fact that each demand reduced the amount of work done in the putting-up-signs department, as experienced by this particular repairman, what was the basis for his objections?

The Denial of Mastery

Psychologically, a demand for information and a demand for control mean that an individual surrenders mastery over a piece of work. Someone is saying, "You are no longer master over your fate. Give us the information about the challenge you face. We'll judge what is the proper response, and we'll tell you what to do."

Such instructions are a direct attack on the individual's ego, a structure of the psyche charged with exactly the functions that our sign repairman's superiors now arrogate to themselves. The ego receives information from the individual's environment in the form of a challenge. The ego judges how the challenge relates to the organism's ability to handle it. The ego designs responses that take into account both environmental demands and human needs.[9] Ultimately, the ego is master over the individual's survival within an environment.

How can an attack on such mastery be justified? The fact is that the power of a modern organization to cope with challenges larger than any ever met before rests exactly on its assuming mastery over the actions of all its employees. The organization handles huge tasks; an individual handles limited tasks. The organization has a vast horizon; the functionary has a limited horizon.

The sign repairman's complaint about the denial of mastery stems directly from his limited horizon. Within that limited horizon he sees it as his task to put up signs, as many as he can, as well as he can. Any order from above that reduces his sign output, he sees not only as an attempt to supersede his mastery but as bad mastery. Yet, from the viewpoint of the organization at large, less work from him might actually mean more work overall from all departments of the organization. This is especially true when less work from him means less uncontrolled work.

For example, imagine that our hero presses happily ahead day after day putting up as many signs as his crew's strength will allow. One day, a Friday, they put up forty signs. On "Blue Monday," when the crew is tired and hung over, they put up fifteen and knock off at noon. On Tuesday, stirred by guilt they make it up: they put up a total of sixty-five signs.

Now assume there is a section of signpost painters who scrape and paint signposts from which signs have fallen. To let the paint dry, they are always supposed to be one day ahead of the repair crew.

Various problems can arise if the repairers are allowed to set their own quota. If the painters' quota is smaller, the repair crew will be falling over painters while putting up signs. Signs are likely to get splattered with paint, and so are the repairers. Motorists won't be able to read the paint-covered signs. No one will like it. And the repair crew will put in for an additional uniform-cleaning allowance.

Moreover, such problems will not arise in a predictable fashion. Let us say the quota for painted posts is thirty a day. On Friday collisions between painters and repairers might occur at a maximum of ten posts. On Monday there will be none. By Tuesday the repair crew will have caught up with the painters again and be exactly a day behind. The reader who intends to be a manager can envision further complications, beginning with the day when the repair crew comes into the garage demanding a gallon of cleaning fluid for their clothes and extra wash-up time.

Even at this simple level of coordinating two crews, each crew's horizon, their view of how work is best to be done, does not extend to encompass that of both crews together. Once labor is divided and becomes specialized, it must be coordinated. Such coordination is best done by an office superordinated to both crews. In this way the function of evaluating work to be done—the environmental challenge—is shifted from the level of those actually doing it up to the supervisory level. So is the ultimate decision of striking a balance between organizational capability to respond and the demand of the environment for a response. And so, finally, is the task of designing the response.

Because workers on the scene are intimately involved and acquainted with the nature of the immediate work at hand—which means they have more detailed and close-at-hand knowledge than anyone else can have—they always perceive the removal of the final decision-making power from their egos to the "organizational ego" of a superior office as a psychological insult.* Yet, if bureaucracy survives as the most successful control institution yet invented, it does so exactly because it does not

*I use the term "insult" here in both the popular and the medical sense. In the medical sense it signifies an injury or impairment of an organic function.

leave mastery to each and every individual employed—especially not to the individual on the line.

From the functionary's point of view, this is a major paradox of working in bureaucracy: if I know more about my work than anyone else, why is it that I cannot be allowed to manage my own work? The problem, of course, is that the functionary's definition of the work is circumscribed by a limited horizon. The organization's definition of the job, with its larger horizon, must supersede the individual's if the organization is to remain what it is—an organization.

The individual worker is conditioned by organizational structure to misperceive what life in the organization is all about. It is never about getting the work done. It is always about integrating yourself with the rest of the organization so that the organization can get the job done. When there is a conflict between getting work done individually and the demand for integrating one's self with the organization, the primacy of the latter is and must always be asserted—again, if the organization is to survive as a control instrument.

THE FALLACY OF MISPLACED EMOTION

A vice-president of a computer company invests his work, his hopes, and his emotions in that firm. Bankers judge the results, find them lacking, and coldly—without fear or favor, love or hatred—dismiss the vice-president and his colleagues. Emotion bursts out. The vice-president puts his head down and cries.

Emotion is normally repressed in modern organizations. Yet in social life, our very sense of self rests from the beginning on emotion. Psycho-analysts who deal with the pain reported by inmates of organizations focus on what the individual "takes in" from his or her organizational environment.[10] One major source of pain arises when we are disappointed in other individuals whom we have taken into our psyche and allowed to become part of our self. Relations with bankers are no exception. Loss of relations with fellow managers also evokes emotional pain.

Taking others into our self is a fundamental human tendency. Freud speaks of the child's original experience of being the center of a loving world. This gives the child a sense of cosmic significance. A love of others arises from which the child gets a sense of self; this he labeled "narcissism."[11] Others orient themselves toward the child. This makes possible a mutual chain of love: the child loves these mirroring others and opens itself up to them, permitting it to bask in their love for it. The experience of that love is one of love for oneself.

It is easy to see how, while love for others permits self-love, rejection by others becomes self-rejection. Psychoanalyst Melanie Klein takes up this problem. As we continue to live and work with others, according to Klein, we run into those who have needs other than providing love for us; these, too, are internalized. Their rejection of us becomes internalized as our rejection of ourselves, to form a stable part of our personality. In the words of psychoanalytic organization theorist Howard Schwartz, "It is thus that a permanent wound to our narcissism is created, thus that we cannot permit ourselves to be what we are, that the locus of our identity shifts from who we are to who others will permit us to be. . . ."[12]

Partial self-rejection, then, is a normal wound we all sustain as we grow up, and we learn to live with it. In our adult working life, we encounter people who remind us of internalized others. We work with them. We cannot avoid them. These will reopen wounds of self-rejection.

This is the pain of loss of self that work-oriented psychoanalysts try to deal with and try to alleviate. Modern organization is not accidentally or only occasionally populated by people who have no love for me. Modern organization prides itself on promoting emotional neutrality. Love is one of the most dangerous emotions for a rationalized organization, if not *the* most dangerous. Max Weber pointed this out in his studies of charisma.[13] Love is therefore institutionally driven out of all formal relations in a modern organization. Yet it persists personally—along with other emotions. When the rational cover over the subterranean emotional fabric of organizations is torn off, the fallacy of assuming we can misplace our emotions without personal cost is exposed.

The Fallacy of Identity

The vice-president of an organization is fired. The man who fired him comments: "He thought he was there to give the plan for the next year. We told him he was fired. He didn't even hear what we told him. He just went on giving his plan for the next year." Another vice-president in the same situation "just put his head down and cried." A federal civil servant at the G-16 level discusses with friends the possibility of applying her fifteen years of top management experience to the private sphere. Then she admits she probably will not take the leap: "I am afraid that outside the office I won't have any identity at all."[14]

Psychologically, something very serious is going on in all three instances. In the first case, there is an inability to even admit the reality of the firing; in the second, a breakdown; in the third, a sense of dependency on the institution and fear of other institutions despite a clear display of superb competence within one's institution.* Are these atypical cases?

---

*The résumé of the civil servant in question reads like the life history of an Horatio Alger. Contrary to popular assumptions about civil service bureaucrats, many of them climb to the top through a display of considerable energy, initiative, and even courage within the institutional framework—as was the case in this instance.

In our workaday world we distinguish between who a person is in and of himself or herself (personality) and the role the person plays in an institution (identity). There is a difference between who I am for myself—my personality—and what I have to be for others—my institutional role identity. Furthermore, each one of us knows that I am much more free in determining who I am in society than in bureaucracy.

To the extent that we surrender who we are to what the organization intends us to be, we lose our personality and take up institutional identity. If we do this over the life of a career, when we retire, we suddenly find ourselves without institutional identity and with only an atrophied sense of self to fall back on. In a moment of existential panic, we face the reality that without the institution we are nothing. Only people with considerable strength are able to retain their personality within the outer mask they must put on to display their institutional identity.

To the extent that bureaucrats are typically unconscious of the externalization of their superegos and the fragmentation of their egos—as reflected in the false assumption that they are still possessed of these—they commit the ultimate fallacy of identity. While they are institutionally employed, bureaucrats assume they have personal identities, or personalities, in the same way that they had personalities when still within society. That is the fallacy of identity.

This fallacy is twofold. The first part we commit when we assume that we are independent of bureaucracy. Bureaucracy is what ultimately dictates our norms and assigns us our jobs. We are deprived of self-judgment (superego) and mastery (ego) and we refuse to acknowledge it for the simple reason that it is too painful to do so. The fallacy expresses itself in the folksaying heard again and again at social parties in answer to the question, "Who are you?" Typically, those of us imprisoned in the fallacy of identity reply: "I am a professor at the University of Oklahoma," or "I am an autoworker at the Ford Rouge plant," or "I am the secretary of state." What is wrong with all these statements is that while we may "be" these things when we are in our office or on the assembly line, we are not these things outside our office or away from the line. For without the institutional environment, we cannot know what we are to do or whether what we do is right or not, and worst of all we lack the power that only institutional structures can give us to exercise the quasi mastery that our role entails. The secretary of state vacationing in a mountain cabin and away from a telephone is not the secretary of state.

Second, the fallacy of identity involves a confusion between personal personality—the patterns of behavior we have learned and that remain at our beck and call no matter where we go—and institutional identity—the patterns of norms and behavior that have meaning and can be exercised only within and through cooperating institutional structures. Identity in this sense is not personality. Individuals who surrender their personalities, who they are, to institutional identity, what others make of them, give up something that can never be recovered. To send a well-conditioned functionary out into the world of society, which was originally formed and continues to be formed by the interaction between autonomous individuals, is akin to amputating a man's head and sending him off to fend for himself.

WHAT THE EXPERTS SAY

The bureaucrat's psychology is radically different from that of the man or woman in society. This assertion stands supported by three groups of experts. First, the picture painted of normal people in society by leaders of traditional psychology does not mesh at all with the reality of the bureaucrat's psyche. This point is made below in applications of two traditional psychologies to the bureaucratic reality—Freud's individual psychology and existential psychology. Second, entirely new psychologies have had to be constructed to match the new reality while denying our human experience of it. "Organizational psychology" now treats the institution itself as possessed of a psyche, in which case human beings become mere subcomponents that must be integrated into the organizational psyche. And as bureaucracy penetrates into society, B. F. Skinner's behaviorist psychology tries to explain behaviors inconsistent with earlier models of an integrated psyche standing apart from the conditions that surround it. These new techno-psychologies,* whether of bureaucracy or society, emphasize the two characteristics most striking in our discussion of bureaucrats in the preceding section—their lack of personal psychic integration and their psychic dependence on the environment.[†] The third school explicitly takes the individual psychologies originating in the social context of the nineteenth century and updates them to apply to the context of modern organizations. This movement is affiliated with the

---

*Skinner refers to his psychology as "human engineering" and as a "technology of operant behavior."

[†]Representative examples of these new psychologies, which generally deny that the self has any problem at all in modern organization because they deny either that there is or that there ever was a self, may be found in Edgar H. Schein, *Organizational Psychology* (Englewood Cliffs, N.J.: Prentice-Hall, 1965), and B. F. Skinner, *Beyond Freedom and Dignity* (New York: Bantam/Vintage, 1972) and *Science and Human Behavior* (New York: Free Press, 1965). Critiques of these two approaches, present in the first edition of this book, were omitted in the second edition to make room for new psychologies and are not repeated here.

neo-Freudian social psychiatry of Harry Stack Sullivan, object relations, and a new phenomenological psychoanalysis.

Freud and Individual Psychology

The most striking event of the bureaucratic age is the disappearance of the individual. This becomes clear when we juxtapose Sigmund Freud's image of humans against today's reality.

ELEVATING THE EGO

As Freud saw the history of the psyche, it developed through two stages. In the first, the communal stage, the individual was submerged in the mass. His or her psychic structure, to the extent that separate components could then be considered as already differentiated, consisted of a dominant superego, a weak ego, and a repressed id. Graphically the constellation might be depicted in this way:

Superego

Ego   Id

This constellation asserts the supremacy of communal norms through the superego. The ego, as autonomous integrating center for the individual to adapt to reality, is correspondingly weak: all the allowable patterns of adaptation have already been worked out by the community and are dictated through the superego. Similarly, the superego, at this stage almost entirely congruent in its norms with the will of the community, sharply represses or punishes any asocial attempts by the instinctual drives, death-dealing and life-loving, to assert themselves. The id is repressed. It can gain satisfaction only through tightly circumscribed, culturally approved social channels.

In contrast, we may observe, as Paul Roazen has done, that in applying his psychology to the people of his time, "Freud's whole therapy is aimed at liberation and independence."[15] The concern of Freud's ego-dominant psychology is with the maturing of the individual into an autonomous source of intelligence and power from whom society in turn draws its strength. Gone is the idea of each member's subjection to the community. Here also lies the difference between society and community, the form of social life that preceded it.[16]

In the second stage of development, the social stage, the psychology of the single human being is restructured. The ego rises to the top, pushing the superego aside when its socially derived norms get in the way of individual survival. And the id is freed to express itself in channels approved by the ego in its attempt to mediate between the outer and the inner world. This is not total freedom, as is psychosis in which the id runs wild, but in contrast to the restraint and submission to both the laws of nature and of humans characteristic of the communal stage, individuals in modern society did radically make over the world in their own image. We need think only of the vast destruction wreaked on nature and the vast construction of both material and social empires. The psychological structure of individualist man can be depicted as follows:

Ego

Superego   Id

Here ego is dominant. "The ego has a unifying function, ensuring coherent behavior and conduct. The job of the ego is not just the negative one of avoiding anxiety, but also the positive one of maintaining effective performance."[17] And what Freud did not do for the dominance of the ego, having developed his ego psychology late in life, his successors did.[18] With the ego dominant, society's standards, as enshrined in the superego, were subject to revision and adaptation to the needs of individuals. In contrast to the communal era, the superego now becomes dominated by the ego. The id remains often repressed, but when its needs are fulfilled, they are more likely to be channeled through the ego than through the superego.

Freud considered the growth of the individual not only crucial to the individual himself but essential for society at large:

The liberation of an individual, as he grows up from the authority of his parents, is one of the most necessary though one of the most painful results brought about by the course of his development. It is quite essential that that liberation should occur and it may be presumed that it has been to some extent achieved by everyone who has reached a normal state. Indeed, the whole progress of society rests upon the opposition between successive generations.[19]

Exactly for the reasons that politically Freud was a liberal and that scientifically he made the individual his unit of analysis,[20] his ego-dominant image of humans stands in stark contrast to our age. There, the individual person created himself or herself in the company of other humans. Often the individual would be, in the words of Thomas Hobbes, alone, alive, and afraid. But then freedom was defined in terms of being left alone by others to work out one's own fate. On this definition both the political philosophy and the theology of liberalism met.[21] Today the prevailing political and social reality is that of the corporation. The unit of

analysis now is the disindividualized individual at best, as in the works of
B. F. Skinner, or the organization itself, as in the works of Edgar H. Sc
hein.[22]

Fragmenting the Ego

With the separation of the superego from the rest of the psyche and the
fragmentation of the ego, the possibility of the individual resubmerges
into the mass from which it only recently emerged. The concept of the
individual derives from the Latin word *individuus*—"indivisible." The
individual as such did not exist in the world of community; he or she was
molded too much by the social environment. The individual arose only
with the development of modern society, owing his or her existence to
the idea that humans could grasp hold of their world, including the social
world, and reshape it in the individual's own image. This was the idea of
early modern science, technology, and industry, and it carried over into
the early social sciences.

Freud's psychology, despite its group context (which he did not at all
deny), was an "individual psychology."[23] The task of Freudian psychoanalysis and therapy to this day remains, at least avowedly, the reestab-
lishment of the functioning individual. If analysts or therapists are asked
to whom they owe their direct obligation, they reply that it is to the
individual whom they analyze or attempt to heal.

But man or woman the indivisible is now no longer so. Especially not
in bureaucracy. He or she is man or woman the divisible. Whether or not
he or she is still a human being in some absolute sense need not be asked
here. All we require is an understanding of why the bureaucratic human
looks so inhuman to us as outsiders. He or she looks inhuman from our
perspective to the extent that we still operate under the definition of
"individual" that emerged with the rise of society, the form of social
organization within which we still perceive ourselves to live apart from
working hours. Similarly, the more our own perceptions reveal the
penetration of bureaucracy's human-concept into society at large, the less
surprised we are at the divisible human.

The cutting edge of that penetration is revealed in a television
commercial in which a young woman who feels she is in fact three
women is regarded as perfectly normal—and requires the "normal"
equipment of such a fragmented individual, i.e., three types of watches to
go with her three incarnations. This acceptance of the split personality is
quite new, as reflected in the fact that in the 1950s a young woman was
subjected to considerable psychiatric treatment when she had a similar
experience. The story is told in *The Three Faces of Eve*,[24] which also became
a popular motion picture.

In contrast to both preceding pictures of the structure of the psyche in other eras, perhaps this is the best that can be done for the image of the bureaucratic human:

Externalized Superego

Fragmented Ego

Id
(in the service of the organization)

While this image has a faint resemblance to the communal psyche, under the dominance of a superego, it bears no resemblance at all to the structure of the individualist human. The individual has simply disintegrated under the immense power of bureaucracy and his or her need to make a living in it because one cannot make a living elsewhere in the shrinking arena of society.

THE PROBLEM OF INDIVIDUALIST PSYCHOLOGY

Yet there is a problem with traditional psychoanalysis's focus on the individual. Increasingly, in the doing of work, it is useless to speak of individuals in separation from other individuals. Work today is organized work whether the hierarchically organized work of the modern organization or the teamwork or program management of postmodernity. The corporation in-*corporates;* the organization *organ*-izes. In an echo of medieval times, we are speaking here of bodies [*corpus*] and organs [*organon*]. Nowhere except in psychological analysis does it become more clear that the natural process of in-*corporation* and *organ*-ization is reversed when the center of analysis stops being the individual and becomes the corporation or organization. Traditional psychoanalysts can still talk of the individual incorporating the outer world: internalizing it. But today it is the outer world that incorporates the individual. It takes the individual into its organized body; there it absorbs and redistributes what used to be individual functions. In the face of that reality, how inadequate is an orthodox psychoanalysis founded on the primacy of the individual?

The problem for any individual is not that he or she may feel pain because part of the organization rejects him or her—a rejection that is felt as self-rejection. The problem is that the organization, which incorporates the individual into its functioning whether for profit or control, *systematically denies all love* to the individual. Using orthodox psychoanalysis's own foundation assumption about how individuals find self-love through the love of introjected others, I can only conclude that organization members find themselves in a system that is the absolute enemy of the human need for love that orthodox psychoanalysis stipulates.

THE PROBLEM OF PSYCHOANALYSIS

We can now understand why it is that traditional psychoanalysis, as a human way of dealing with our reality, finds itself on the defensive when it is challenged to explain contemporary life of human beings incorporated by organizations. The conditions of modern organization are so totally and absolutely inimical to the condition for human psychic health presumed by psychoanalysis that traditional psychoanalysis would have to declare itself to be unable to deal with such conditions if it were to be honest with itself. This, however, would mean the end of an individual-centered orthodox psychoanalysis—which those committed to it must, of course, deny.

There are two ways to go. Either the basic assumption of orthodox psychoanalysis must be reexamined. This means a philosophical reexamination of its metatheory—the theory behind psychoanalytic theory. Or, orthodox psychoanalysis must take into itself an additional way of looking at the world: that is, a second basic assumption. Psychoanalysis has, indeed, chosen the latter course as we see in such successor psychologies as object relations theory[25] and social psychiatry.[26]

Individuals, however, cannot wait. The question for the individual is more acute. It is not how a method of knowledge can adapt itself. It is how individuals who have learned to rely on themselves and love themselves can adapt to a world in which they must adapt, officially at least, to the total absence of love. Such a world does not simply question my ability to love myself; it questions my entire being. The experience of life in modern organizations is bigger than, and qualitatively different from, that portion of life that orthodox psychoanalysis can deal with. The basic question of late modernity is not a psychological one but a philosophical one. It is the perennial question of what life is all about. The question is not concerned with the origins of pain but with what it means to be alive today in an organized world that incorporates us into itself.

Between Experts: The Problem of Existence Meets the Problems of the Psyche

The bureaucratic experience is marked not only by pain but by loss. Modern organization does not merely attack our psyche. It puts in question whether we can still have a psyche. Modern organization challenges not simply our psyche, it puts in question what kind of *being* we have: who or what we are. The bureaucratic experience is not most fundamentally the experience of deadened feelings that explode into pain. The pain arises precisely because we face being nothing and nobody. We recognize this in occasional confrontation with that nothingness: on being disciplined, fired—and, more subtly, even on being hired. Our response is to seek deeper and dekseper refuge in exactly that which is able to question our existence: bureaucracy. Once bureaucracy has already incorporated us, once our hand, and minds have constituted it as a voluntary externalization of self, it becomes a necessary externalization of self without which there is no self.[27]

An Employee Deals with a Firing

When a dismissed employee tells us of her attempt to counter the loss of self occasioned by her dismissal, she is not simply recounting a tale of the loss of self-love but a tale of an attempt to reattain *existence*. Take the story of her firing as told by Cynthia Confer[28] and of her attempt to counter not only its psychological but ontological effects: the threat not only to self-love but to having any being at all:

I didn't really mind getting fired. The company had been in trouble for a long time. What I did mind was passing my boss every day in the hallway and his being unable to look me in the eyes, say hello, much less smile. I still had two weeks to go before I'd actually have to leave. He'd see me coming down the hall and he'd turn away.

What did she feel?

Why, it makes you feel like you're nobody—a nonentity!

What did she do about it?

I felt hurt, and angry, and a whole bunch of things. Insulted mostly, mostly insulted. I don't know what precipitated it, but I just lay in bed one night, not sleeping at all, and thinking about it, and getting very excited about going in and talking to him about it. I—you know—I just got feeling really happy about it. Even if—well, what could they do: fire me? [laughter] So I spent almost all night doing that, trying to decide what I was going to do and getting just so excited I couldn't sleep. Happy! You know.

And I just went in the next morning, right the first thing at eight o'clock, and walked in his office and said, "Jack, I'd like to talk to you sometime, when do you have time?"

And he said, "Well, how about right now?"

And so I just sat down and—I remember it was December 14, I remember the day—I said:

"Jack, I want to talk to you about this whole situation. Jack, I don't *care* [I talked just like that, full of emotion] I don't care about being laid off. We *all* have known for years we're going to be laid off, always waiting for the other shoe to drop, and I don't hold that against you at all and nobody here in their right mind does. But! I can't *stand* the way you're treating us. And I remember him just staring at me, like, "What?"

How did the manager react?

The first minute or two, he didn't have any reaction. I had to keep on going under my own steam. He finally said, "What do you mean?" And I told him about his avoiding us in the hall and that stuff.

"We don't exist anymore," I said, "after you've given us our notice. . . . Maybe the rest of the people here don't mind but it bothers me. We've always had a good relationship for six years now, and it makes me angry when you treat me like this, and all of a sudden you won't speak to me, etc. etc." I was very emotional.

How did the manager respond?

He *relaxed*! He leaned back in his chair, put his feet up on the desk, heh, and smiled. And so I knew at least he wasn't going to say: Get the hell out of there! [Laughter.] And he said, "Cindy, that's the *only* way I know how to deal with it. Do you know what hell I've been going through here? This place is . . ." He swore and said everything and he was the classiest guy you'd ever want to meet. He said, "This has been putting me through hell." I can't remember what swear words he used. He said, "Coming in here just drives me into little pieces; I have to go to a shrink, because I'm so screwed up over this. The only way I can deal with what I have to do is, after I lay people off, I can't—I act as if they don't exist any more. I can't handle it." And I said, "But that's just *exactly* the wrong thing." We went on and on about that. It was incredible. He talked to me like I was his sister or his mother or something. I couldn't believe it.

How was it all resolved?

Finally he said, "Is this what you want out of life?" And I said, "No!" I said, "I'm going to move to Maine and live in the country, and have the simple life. That's all I ever wanted." And he said, "Me, too. This is just b---s--t! You know what I'm going to do? As soon as I get *my* walking papers—which, of course, are coming after yours—I'm going to go to California and sell Mercedes!" And you know, he went and he did!

The narrative is full of a number of psychological and organizational points. The manager's *numbing of his senses*—to the extent not only of not looking at others but not seeing them anymore—fits the purposes of emotional neutrality of any bureaucracy. The manager's example leads, even on the firing line. The modern organization "wants" the manager to set this emotionally neutral example; as long as emotions can be repressed at the dying of an organization, employees can be expected to go through their routines.

The *pain* of the firing experience arises only when the fired employee faces up to what the deadening of experience will ultimately do to her. Rather than perpetuating the bureaucratic routines through emotionless following of the daily tasks, she feels compelled to face up to the change that the organization has forced her into. Her strong emotions reflect both pain and hope.

But, most important, the employee's decision to stand up for herself—and to do this by confronting her boss and saving him also from the inhumanity forced upon him—is not an issue of psychology at all. It is an issue of *basic humanity*.[29] Cynthia Confer undertakes the rescue of her being. And she undertakes that rescue by accomplishing it in the company of others. She speaks on behalf of her coworkers and she enables her manager to speak the unspeakable: to damn the company and plan to save himself.

In no better way than through the words of human beings confronting annihilation by the bureaucratic machine can we express the quiet daily heroism of men and women living in the modern age.

However, the analysis of the problem of *existence* requires an approach beyond the analysis of the individual psyche.

Ernest Keen: Existential Psychology

The crisis of the individual penetrates all traditional psychologies—that is, those psychologies that either have not sold out to organizational masters and distorted themselves or those that recognize the new organizational reality and voluntarily abandon the concept of the individual.* While it is not possible here to survey the scope of that crisis, it is possible to examine specific problems of individualistic psychologies in the face of the bureaucratization of the world.

PRESENTING A FALSE SELF

Existential psychology is concerned overall with what existential psychologist Ernest Keen termed the three faces of being[30]—the faces an individual turns onto his existence. A very conscious concern of existential psychologists is that at least one of these faces of being is so overemphasized by the pressures of the modern world that the individual's essential integrity is permanently challenged. The three faces of being are as follows:

1. Being-in-the-world. This is the way I experience myself as actively engaged in the world. It is my direct experience of the world through my involvement in it. I am the active subject working my way out in the world. Maslow might say that this is the me that is actualizing itself in the world. What is important is that my experience in the world is, in this state of being, direct, not reflective. I am not looking back at myself in action from a detached distance. I *am* in action.

---

*The psychology of Abraham Maslow is of the first type, although its distortion was accomplished by others. For an outline of Maslovian "third force" psychology, see Abraham Maslow, *Motivation and Personality* (New York: Harper & Row, 1954). For examples of the second type, see the behaviorism of B. F. Skinner and the organizational psychology of Edgar H. Schein.

2. Being-for-oneself. This is the way I see myself by doing what I did not do in the state of "being-in-the-world"—through reflectively looking at myself as an object. "Out of this experience of oneself 'as object' comes the notion of 'self-concept' and the casting of oneself into substantive terms so that there is some kind of solid 'me' or definition which one can use to make decisions about what to do, how to act, etc."[31]

3. Being-for-others. This actually means how others see me as an object. But since I can never directly experience how others actually perceive me, being-for-others means presenting myself to others in terms I expect will be acceptable to them. "Oneself is experienced through the eyes of others, and one becomes the object of 'the other.' "[32]

In a well-integrated individual, there is a balance between these three states of being. But life in bureaucracy forces me to overemphasize an aspect of myself that others—specifically coworkers and superiors in the hierarchy—will like. When this presentation of a face to others is in conscious conflict with what I know myself to be, I am said to be "lying-for-others." The first experience of lying-for-others occurs when I, as a child, discover that I can present myself to my parents in a way that differs radically from what I perceive I am. This is an important stage in growth because I previously believed, as Jean Piaget among others has pointed out,* that my parents could read my thoughts. The problem becomes serious because "there comes a time in the life and lying of the child when he comes to believe his own lies."[33] It is this problem that modern man faces in bureaucracy: he must so much be what others expect him to be that he loses his own self. Keen gives a specific example:

Suppose, for example, that a salesman is encouraged by his company to be aggressive. His supervisor is aggressive and this supplies a model for the salesman. Because of the power structure, satellization around the supervisor occurs and the individual internalizes the value "aggression = good" as a criterion against which to measure himself. He comes, then, to see himself as aggressive (whatever that might mean to him) and to feel that he is not being the "real him" when he is not. Idealization of one's self around this concept and guilt for not living up to the idealized image grow together in the vicious circle of lying-for-oneself. The guiltier one feels, the more adamant is the affirmation of the standard, and vice versa. Soon the salesman has identified with the role to such an extent that his immediate perception of the world is changed. Neutral persons become potential sales targets; relationships are subordinate to the goal of sales.[34]

It is easily understood how an organization might be very happy

---

*Jean Piaget is best known for his cognitive psychology emphasizing child development. Typical examples among a large array of works are *The Language and Thought of the Child* (Cleveland: World Publishing, Meridian Books, 1955) and *The Construction of Reality in the Child* (New York: Basic Books, 1954). For an introduction to Piaget's concepts, see Barry J. Wadsworth, *Piaget's Theory of Cognitive Development* (New York: David McKay, 1971).

with such an employee, but anyone concerned with what might happen to him in his journey from society into the world of bureaucracy can only shudder. Keen here asserts what within Freudian analysis we have understood as a loss of integrated self—through the absorption of external superego standards—and foreshadows what below we describe as the dynamic of the bureaucratic psychology. That is, he answers the question: Why do bureaucrats, though they suffer in bureaucracy, feel forced to return again and again? Keen's answer is that once I have absorbed for my state of being the external standard set by bureaucracy, I cease to have a state of "being-for-myself"—cease not only to "be" myself, but cease even to "have" a self. For this reason, the bureaucrat cited in the preceding section expresses the constant fear: "I am afraid that outside the office I won't have any identity at all."

THE BUREAUCRATIC PERSONALITY

What drives people to continue to work in bureaucracy? Bureaucracy tears from them their conscience. It fragments their ego. It satisfies and punishes them at their lowest level by titillating the id's craving for power, by threatening psychic identity, and by challenging even existence itself. In contrast to the integrated personality of the nineteenth-century individual in the center of Sigmund Freud's psychology—with the ego as the mediating center between organism and environment, dominating superego and id—the bureaucrat's personality is devastated. It is no longer possible to speak easily of the individual's personality as "belonging" to him. It is more accurate to say that instead of a personality, which the individual carries along wherever he or she goes, there is a role identity. The individual slips into a role identity on entering the office—and desperately tries not to let this cloak slip on leaving at the end of the day.

To an outsider, who can understand such clinging to office because of the status and class position it brings, the bureaucrat's intense devotion to office and duty is incomprehensible. To us it must seem clear that the bureaucrat's office is a prison; the bureaucrat's duty, chains. As Max Weber mourned in a related work: "But fate decreed that the cloak should become an iron cage."[35]

To what fundamental human need could the cold machine of bureaucracy possibly appeal to find perennial recruits to scrape and paint the rusting structure, to grease the cogs, to put their shoulders to the very same wheels destined to run over them?

From experience and experts we must conclude that the bureaucratic psyche is not internally integrated but rather is externally integrated into the organization. This applies in all modern bureaucratic structures, whether private or public. An American Management Association survey of 1,408 corporate managers reports that three characteristics mark managers in large private organizations:

1. Conforming to certain role expectations.
2. Keeping one's nose clean and not violating bureaucratic role norms.
3. Demonstrating strong personal loyalty to the individual superior and to the organizational authority structure.[36]

This is exactly what experiential and psychological analysis led us to expect. Naturally, the individual who surrenders superego and ego to bureaucratic role expectations and role norms has no other choice, in order to keep on existing, but to place strong personal loyalty in those structures and their occupants who have usurped the individual's superego-norming and ego-mastery functions.

The bureaucratic personality is superego-less and ego-less. It is not internally integrated. It is dependent on—more accurately, interdependent with—personality functions of norming and mastery exercised by superiors. The id, the remaining psychic structure, is open to manipulation by superiors or by organizational structures such as hierarchy and division of labor. In this sense, structure pressures the bureaucrat to be or pretend to be an inhuman being without conscience, without brains, and without a self. The bureaucrat is forced to be soulless and headless and, in an autonomy-denying way, selfless. If these are harsh words, they are not meant to be pejorative; they describe a harsh and dehumanizing reality. Best of all, they are words that work. To the extent that we assume bureaucrats to be as described, they can present us with no surprises.

Yet there is also this: bureaucracy has variety. Some inmates are relatively powerful; others are powerless. Some submit; others command. Some adapt to and seem to enjoy bureaucratic life; others just play the game; while still others are destroyed by it. Place in structure shapes identity: the organizational structures closest to an individual seem to exercise the greatest influence in reshaping his personality into job-related role identity.

Innumerable questions confront the researcher. Three can be addressed here:

1. What keeps the functionary in bureaucracy? If a wholesale attack is launched on the psyche, causing intense pain, why not escape? The answer seems to lie in the success of that attack. A disintegrated self, which has large portions of its psyche ripped out of it, cannot easily confront or live in the outside world. The functionary and manager unite in a work bond.[37]
2. What accounts for the great variety of bureaucratic personalities? If organizational structures shape the psyche, then we can expect those structures closest to a functionary's role position to shape him or her most intensely. Personnel

at the top *are* the hierarchy and can be expected to exercise more mastery functions than those below (though it would be wrong to think those at the top escape organizational strictures altogether). Personnel in the records departments (payroll, accounting, personnel, computer section, etc.) and also staff versus line people can be expected to be affected by the lessened demand on personal memory afforded by written and retrievable records. And so on.

3. What motivates people who stay in the organization? What is the prime job or work motivator of inmates? Drawing on the work of the phenomenologist Martin Heidegger and the psychiatrist Harry Stack Sullivan, we will argue that the main everyday motivator is not fear of losing institutional identity but existential *Angst*, or profound anxiety.

These assertions derive logically from work showing that the integrated individualist psyche is not viable under the pressures of bureaucracy's day-to-day demands. They need to be developed further, conceptually and through research, but for now they can briefly be explained.

The Work Bond

Take any human being. Now remove his or her ability to judge what is socially responsible. The result is a sociopath. Then remove the ability to master challenges from the environment. He or she does not survive. Yet modern organization strips the human being of control over both these abilities. How does the functionary so deprived nevertheless survive?

The functionary survives, socially and physically, exactly because bureaucracy exercises the functions of superego and ego activity on the person's behalf. As long as the individual remains inside, the same agency that takes away the use of certain individual psychological capabilities also exercises them *for* him or her.

The functionary exists as long as he or she establishes strong bonds with managers or offices, into whose hands two-thirds of the original individual psyche has been placed. This may be represented as in Figure 3.1.

After the externalization of superego and ego, the functionary must identify or bond with the hierarchy and division of labor or their representatives: the functionary's superiors. If not, he or she ceases to exist. Since the manager is the closest representative of the powers of hierarchy and the division of labor-externalized superego and ego functions—the manager becomes the object for such bonding. Identification and projection establish the bond.

Bonding also derives from the organization's need to get work done. Under the imperative that only the responsible manager shall judge the propriety of a piece of work and the methods and tools to be used, which leaves functionaries with little more than their id energy, the organization itself welds the manager and functionary into one work unit. The

Figure 3.1: Externalization of Superego and Ego

I. PSYCHE IN SOCIETY

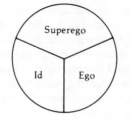

Superego = Moral judgment

Ego = Mastery

Id = Energy

II. PSYCHE IN ORGANIZATIONS

A. Superego Externalization

Test Question: What happens to an employe who brings personal values (conscience, judgments of right and wrong) to work?

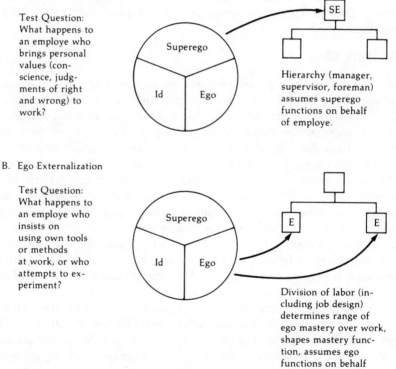

Hierarchy (manager, supervisor, foreman) assumes superego functions on behalf of employe.

B. Ego Externalization

Test Question: What happens to an employe who insists on using own tools or methods at work, or who attempts to experiment?

Division of labor (including job design) determines range of ego mastery over work, shapes mastery function, assumes ego functions on behalf of employe.

functionary cannot work without the manager, and the manager is similarly dependent on subordinates: without their energy the work cannot get done.*

*The manager who insists on working along with subordinates is generally considered a "bad" manager from the organization's point of view. The "good" manager is expected to

Figure 3.2: The Work Bond

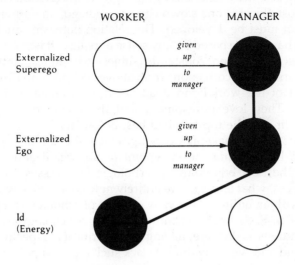

WORKER   MANAGER

Externalized
Superego
given
up
to
manager

Externalized
Ego
given
up
to
manager

Id
(Energy)

The new unit of analysis comprises both the manager and the functionary in a work setting. Psychologically, I have called this the "work bond." The work bond refers to the structure that is the simplest unit of the modern organization that can get work done. This structure is welded together not merely by external reinforcements but actively by a psychological bond between manager and subordinate. The bond stems from the positions of mutual dependence into which the manager and functionary have been placed by the organization. The bond is the very human attempt to salvage lost personal integrity by placing portions of what was lost in one other person and identifying that person as part of one's self.[38] The manager and the functionary in the work bond become, together, a reconstructed self. What does human nature in bureaucracy look like? Investigate the work bond. Pictorially, the work bond can be depicted as in Figure 3.2

Workers who do not integrate themselves into the work bond may engage in a misplaced narcissism: the desperate search for a lost self conducted in the wrong place—within the self. But from the viewpoint of individualistic psychology, the psychic activities necessary to maintain the work bond are similarly pathological. Identification with the manager is regressive, reawakening early childhood ways of bonding before the capacity for loving existed. Projection is the attempt to bridge the gap

---

make judgments designing the work and then leave the actual expenditure of energy to those below.

between the self and a lost object in one great subconscious leap of faith; when the lost object is one's own ego or superego, an entirely new form of projection must be developed. The relation between functionary and manager is hardly one based on any sense of reality. It is, from the bottom up, a projected relation constantly subject to sudden, unforetellable, apparently irrational* corrections from above. People who fit well into the bottom half of the work-bond dyad are those trained in society to be masochists. They love punishment and the power of the punishers. Those who fit into the top half had best be sadists.

Visions of the snakepit open up when the lid of organizational structure is lifted. From the viewpoint of an organization psychology looking at the new bonds and psychological processes with cold and "neutral" eyes, what emerges are entirely new concepts of what a psyche is—along with an entirely new view of what psychology is. However, as the work of B. F. Skinner has shown, such a psychology would merely accept conditions as they are, having lost its critical perspective. But then, did not Freud and the individualists lack such a critical point? How many laudable human characteristics constituting the group psyche of the age of community were swept under the scientific rug in the triumph of individualism? The entire question of whether there is an absolute once or future human nature has not been answered. And yet, if human experience is not to be totally ignored, we owe it to those suffering the transition from the individualist age to the bureaucratic age to record their agonies from their perspective.

Bureaucratic Personalities

The time is past when one could say with Freud that "all our social institutions are framed for people with a united and normal ego, which one can classify as good or bad, which either fulfills its function or is altogether eliminated by an overpowering influence."[39] The institutions that dominate the bureaucratic world promote no "united and normal ego." The choice between ego function in the sense of an autonomous, self-directing individual and the elimination of ego by an overpowering influence has long been made. Organizational forms shape skills and behaviors—ultimately personality types—that "directly reflect the demands of the organizational society."[40] What type or types of personality can or do the institutions of the bureaucratic world promote?

Given recent developments in the new science of psychoanalytically informed organization analysis, this question can be answered in three ways: sociologically, psychoanalytically/situationally, and existentially. In summary:

---

*Except that the subordinate is in no condition to make that judgment.

1. Sociological analysis can pinpoint those basic forces in organization structure that directly attack the basic structures of the psyche. When the impact of the structural forces of the organization upon the structure of the psyche is logically reasoned out, we arrive at a number of "ideal types" of personalities as they can be shaped by bureaucracy according to *logical* analysis.
2. Beginning at the opposite end of the puzzle, not with social structures but with psychic structures, we can also logically predict which types of psychological structure (personality) will blossom and bloom in certain types of bureaucratic situations.
3. Beginning with a normative or philosophical base of what constitutes the lasting essences of human beings, we can look at both organizational structures and psychological structures of modernity and logically arrive at an answer to the question: What is it, in the essence of humanity or the human soul, that is fundamentally put at risk in modernity?

Bureaucratic Personalities: Socio-Psychic Analysis

The many structural faces of bureaucracy produce a variety of psyches, all variants of the bureaucratic personality. Take Max Weber's six structural characteristics (discussed in Chapter 2); now ask what impact on personality each of these is likely to have.

Depending on their ability to adapt themselves to the pressures of hierarchy, division of labor, and the rest of the structural characteristics of bureaucracy, a variety of personalities or role identities can be expected to develop among successful functionaries and managers.

BEINGS WITHOUT CONSCIENCE, BEINGS OF DEPENDENCE

The individual entering bureaucracy from society who adapts most easily to the pressure of hierarchy will find himself or herself asked to leave personal norms at home, submit to superiors in matters of conscience, and assume a position of dependence in moral judgment. Not to reason why, but to do. In those organizations that rely heavily on hierarchy and its prerogatives, conscienceless dependency-oriented beings, incapable of making moral judgments of right or wrong on their own, can be expected to proliferate as the superego is systematically externalized. At the same time, externalization of ego mastery produces a third characteristic: inability to make sound judgments on how to get a piece of work done combined with dependency on being told how to work by superiors. Since hierarchy is a key structure in all modern organizations, this is probably the most general type of bureaucrat—dependency oriented in matters of moral judgment and mastery over work. It was of this type that Max Weber wrote: "Specialists without spirit, hedonists without heart; this nullity imagines that it has reached a level of civilization never before achieved.[41]

Beings Without Mastery

Where the division of labor is emphasized, there may be limited mastery over a small piece of work but functionaries lose the sense of how a task is integrated into the larger environment. They are denied, at least officially, the knowledge of how their piece fits together with the pieces worked on by their neighbors. Such knowledge is arrogated to their superiors. The entire power of hierarchy comes out of the ignorance and ego diminution that division of labor produces. Beings without mastery are also beings of great dependence: accustomed to being told what to do, they are unable to respond to the challenge from the environment that a normally developed personal ego would handle.

Beings Without Experience

In organizations or in specific places of work where the job involves heavy reliance on written documents, records, and communications—for example, information storage and retrieval sections but also in staff versus line jobs or in street-level functionary roles relying heavily on written instructions—the function of memory fades away. Personal memory is supplanted by organizational memory. Access to the organizational memory would seem to give great power, but it also tempts one into no longer relying on personal memory. The modern computerized campaign manager or the high-ranking staff analyst of a multinational corporation is far more dependent on organizational structure than was the political boss of *The Last Hurrah* who relied on personal knowledge of his work and workers or an organization creator like Henry Ford. A bureaucracy does not rely on personal memory. In this lies its great strength: the impersonal files don't lie, don't forget, and are difficult to "bribe"—their "interests" are not human interests; the biases of a machine storing data are not human biases.*

But what is human memory but the filing away in the subconscious of data that would encumber the conscious mind? And how are data from the unconscious retrieved normally? The ego must have learned tricks that will trigger access to the data bank of the unconscious. With the substitution of written records, the need for such tricks disappears. The entire art of memory (mnemonics) is lost, and with it easy access of the ego and the conscious mind to the unconscious. The distance between conscious and unconscious widens.

The being without experience stands outside both the context of his or her own past, for memory keeps us in touch with our past whether in

---

*So only experts can corrupt them, which opens interesting scenarios for those fascinated by the potential of modern organizations themselves to become victims of a knowledge elite. In passing, the entire question of the psychological impact on personality of specific organizational structures, such as information systems, has hardly been explored.

society or at work, and the context of the depths of human experience in general.[42] Beings without experience are thus peculiarly flat, without depth, or, more accurately, out of touch with the depths of the human species. A depth psychologist would have a hard time reconnecting such a being to any depths, and even if reconnection was achieved, the depths might be empty of meaning for such a being[43]

ASOCIAL BEINGS

In modern organizations hiring and promotion are based on trained expertise. What is trained expertise? It is learned and developed skills for a particular kind of work and not another. Further, expertise is free of social constraints. Competency, which used to be a concept understood in both the social and the work-oriented sense—i.e., does an action get the work done and is that action and its work result socially useful?—now becomes task-oriented competency. To the extent that holding a job and being rewarded in it are determined by the organization purely on the basis of getting work done, the sense of social responsibility to people outside the plant gates is weakened, as is the sense of solidarity with coworkers. Expertise is an attack on the superego, removing from it social standards for judgment and behavior though not work standards. The personality type who best succeeds in organizations where expertise is a dominant theme climbs coldly and without concern over the bodies of coworkers to greater and greater job success. The relevant role type is that of the professional who knows only professional standards.

WORLD-CLOSED BEINGS

Full-time devotion to one's work, structured into the concepts of career and job, focuses emotions and attachments very narrowly. The potentially diffuse attachments to the real world, which the psyche arranges to satisfy needs originating in the id, become highly channeled and specific. Whereas biologists and psychologists in general agree that, in contrast to more instinctually determined animals, human beings are only to a limited degree predetermined in their responses to the world, we must pay attention to the fact that only organizationally predetermined responses will bring job success in the bureaucratic world. From a world-open being, the individual becomes essentially a world-closed being. Objects of satisfaction to which attachment is allowed are strictly defined for the functionary through management's or the profession's definition of problems previously left wide open to ego mastery. Ego no longer selects on a daily basis the objects that best satisfy demands of the id—demands for love or satisfaction of aggression. To the extent that love (eros) is repressed in organizations, aggression (thanatos) is let loose and given satisfying objects—subordinates or clients—by the organization.

Table 3.1
ORGANIZATION STRUCTURES' IMPACTS ON THE PSYCHE

Characteristics of Modern Organizations	Area of Impact on Psyche	Functional Effect	Ideal-Typical Examples	Real World Examples	Personality Type
Hierarchy	superego	Superego function externalized.	Functionary suppresses personal values when faced with organization's.	Anti-pollution citizen accepts working at GM.	Dependent being without conscience
Division of labor (jurisdiction; specialization)	ego	Ego range narrowed; ego externalized.	Functionary accepts organization's definition of mastery range.	Craftsman over entire work accepts specialization on part.	Being without mastery
Written records (recorded and retrievable information base)	ego access to unconscious	Obsolescence of memory; functionally inadequate access to unconscious.	Reliance on personal memory superseded by impersonal memory: records.	"Let's look it up."	Being without experience
Task-oriented competency (hiring and promotion based on trained expertise)	ego/superego split	Work separated from social approval; competency is context-free.	Functionary now capable of applying expertise apart from conscience and morality; survival capacity in doubt.	Chemical engineer ignores effects of organization's pollution on own family living nearby. Extreme: Eichman excuse.	Asocial being

Fulltime devotion to job/career	ego-superego id	Mastery function technically defined within limits of career; id repressed.	Potentially diffuse attachments and activities are now focused; sources of diffuseness repressed.	Career priorities or superior's demands are accepted over needs of self or kin.	World-closed being
Rules	superego, ego, id internally uninte-grated	Organizational rules serve as external reference points for personal conscience and social morality; continued externalization of superego and narrowing of ego range.	Experimental function of ego reduced; recipe action; irrelevance of personal sense of right and wrong; evocative function of unconscious reduced.	"Never mind that following the rules leads to disaster; as long as you follow the rules, you're safe." Loss of feel for reality: space shuttle mentality.	Rule-bound being

Source: Derived from R. P. Hummel, "Are There Groups in Organizations?," paper presented to the fifth scientific meeting of the A. K. Rice Institute, Washington, D. C., April 2–4, 1981.

Repression of love turns institutions into implements of death-dealing (thanatoic) tendencies. The perfect bureaucrat shapes others and is in this sense destructive of the capacity of others to shape themselves. Further, the bureaucrat becomes incapable of judging when these activities become destructive of himself or herself.

Organizations that emphasize the functioning of the employee within strictly predetermined channels, thereby controlling the distribution of affect, not only change individuals from world-open into world-closed beings but convert them into world-closed beings of a limited sort. In such organizations the successful are those who seek rewards in aggressive behavior, for aggression is the only channel left open for the exercise of affect where love is forbidden. The individual who is aggressive both to others and to oneself, responding to a strictly limited set of cues in the organizational environment, is a personality ideal.

RULE-BOUND BEINGS

No one has yet investigated the effect on the psyche of being governed by rules rather than by human superiors. The presence in modern organization of universal rules to which employees attach themselves suggests the development of a personality type different from the type of followers who attach themselves to a personal leader or even functionaries who orient themselves to a manager. Rules, at the least, are much more abstract than a human superior. A rule has less of a reality base than the objective presence of a human superior. A rule by itself can be interpreted and distorted endlessly; a human superior will come down on a subordinate like a ton of bricks—physically, if need be—when he or she is thwarted.

Rule-bound beings live in an abstract world that is mistaken for reality. Reality has a basis both inside the individual who experiences it and in itself: a rock does not go away no matter how hard I imagine it away. Rules, however, do go away under interpretation unless they are objectively sustained by other human beings or organizational structures. Yet, increasingly, many functionaries—especially those in specialized jobs and those at the top—work in a rules context whose only reality is a set of figures on a cathode ray tube or on a piece of paper. Everyone "knows" these figures are not reality; yet everyone treats them as if they were. The rule-bound being has the peculiar knack of letting physical or social reality get out of hand, clinging to his or her faith in written reports, figures, and the rule book. As science itself becomes increasingly mathematized, the ideal type becomes the being capable of working easily in a world of abstractions, who may never see a stroke of real work being done and wouldn't know what to do with such reality contact if it occurred. The rule-bound being is an abstracting personality detached from physical and social realities.

In summary, of the six personality types above, no single one is independent from the influences of the other types. No pure type *ever* appears. The influences of bureaucratic structures like hierarchy and division of labor are not capable of being separated from one another. Yet, to the extent that any given organization emphasizes one of the six major structural characteristics of bureaucracy, the part of the psyche most directly affected by the environmental structure will produce a dominant personality characteristic in the bureaucrat. The logical relationships between organizational structures, psychic structures upon which these impact, and personality types are summarized in Table 3.1 on pp. 156–57.

Bureaucratic Personalities: Psycho-Social Analysis

If we want to know what kind of personalities to expect in bureaucracy, we can also begin with personalities shaped in early childhood and ask which of these are going to be recruited and supported by bureaucratic social structures.

MICHAEL A. DIAMOND AND SETH ALLCORN: PERSONNEL SELECTION BY DEFENSIVE TYPE

Psychoanalytical organization theorist Michael Diamond and collaborator Seth Allcorn suggest that the bureaucratic machine is a particular kind of stressor that exacerbates human anxiety. Such anxiety is built into us all in childhood because we at one point had to deal with the loss of the mother and the resulting loss of interpersonal security. Since such bureaucratic structures as hierarchy and division of labor strictly control relations, which in turn produces regression among personnel, experience in such structures is likely to reawaken childhood defenses against anxiety. Bureaucracy selects certain defensive personality types—and it selects them for either management or the rank and file. There prevails an unconscious selection process in bureaucracy that reinforces and reproduces the bureaucratic structural and normative status quo.

Managers: Because of its power, hierarchy attracts as managers those people who already have an extraordinary desire to control events and contain feelings of anxiety. Among these types are: the *perfectionist*, the *arrogant-vindictive*, and the *narcissist*.[44] Their behavior is structurally supported or tolerated by their position. Perfectionists are allowed to carry out rigid and self-righteous attitudes. The arrogant-vindictives are allowed to carry out an "I win, you lose" attitude. And the narcissists are allowed to express the kind of convulsive self-importance of which Max Weber already spoke in characterizing bureaucrats.* It may be guessed

*For details, see the last section of this chapter, "The Psychological Dilemma of Bureaucratic

that, from the viewpoint of the average employee, these are wonderful people to work for, but the reality—both from the human and the organizational point of view—is worse than that; for the bureaucratic structure also selects in for survival specific defensive types among employees—easy sheep for the slaughter.

Employees: Because of the lack of autonomy and power built into subordinate positions, organizations will be bottom-heavy with people who tend to rely on *self-effacing* and *resigned* tendencies in dealing with security from anxiety.[45] *Self-effacing* employees tend to look to others to take the lead in meeting their security and safety needs. They minimize their own sense of having been effective in an accomplishment. And they find sustenance in the belief that they are sensitive, lovable, and deserving of being loved. Naturally such an individual is extremely vulnerable to manipulation by perfectionist, arrogant-vindictive, or narcissistic superiors. *Resigned* employees bring to work past experience in dealing with anxiety through suppressing all awareness of internal conflict and even of anxiety itself. They simply withdraw from events and from people. They want to be left alone. Since bureaucracy is not designed to leave anyone alone, this type eventually comes into conflict not only with others but with the organization itself unless sustained by the jurisdictional autonomy.

Diamond and Allcorn's model of personnel selection in bureaucracy hinges on Diamond's discovery of a fundamental irony. Bureaucracy, he argues, is the modern human being's most perfect instrument for dealing with the kind of anxiety[46] that comes to all human beings when they face loss of a beloved other: this could be the mother in childhood or other loved figures in adulthood. Bureaucracy stabilizes all personal relationships. However, bureaucracy does this at a cost. Stability of fixed roles is offered as a substitute for real people-to-people relations that human beings construct on their own.[47] The impersonality of role relationships also takes all emotion out of human relationships. In short, bureaucracy deals with everyone's craving to love and be loved, but it does this by successfully suppressing into the unconsciousness of its members that there even is such a craving. As long as this cold machine faces stable conditions—of environment, of personal relations, or of work—all may be well. However, when any kind of stress enters the machine—as it will, for example, in firings or budget cutbacks—the human element is ready to explode. Then, all the defensive tendencies, learned early on to guard against the anxiety of loss of interpersonal security, collide with one another. Manager psychologically beats up on employee and employees

---

Self-Integrity." See also the behaviors described and advocated in the last section of Chapter 5, "Surviving Political Attack in Modern Organizations."

Figure 3.3: Distribution of Defense Types in Hierarchy

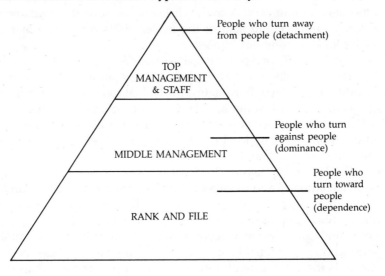

try to defend themselves, or managers find employees unable to deliver what is needed.[48] Such stressful events need not be an organization-wide crisis; *any* manager-employee encounter is potentially loaded with the collision of incompatible defenses to anxiety. Whenever the thin layer of organizational protection of security is scratched, an explosion is possible. In short, the Diamondian irony of modern organizations is this: designed to reduce interpersonal insecurity in work operations, bureaucratic structure tends so much to suppress basic human needs for self-constructed interpersonal security and love that bureaucracy actually heats and stirs a hidden cauldron of insecurity always ready to erupt.

KAREN HORNEY'S NEUROTIC TYPES AND BUREAUCRACY

Bureaucracy, because it takes over basic functions of the self-reliant and loving individual, tends to attract what in society would be called individuals who have neurotic responses to challenges to self-reliance and love. Psychoanalyst Karen Horney suggests that there are three types of such neurotic responses: turning toward people (dependency); turning against people (dominance); and turning away from people (detachment).[49] I would like to suggest that bureaucratic structures tend to attract different types of neurotics into different levels of the hierarchy, as illustrated in Figure 3.3.

People Who Turn Away From People—Top Administrators: There simply is no time for the top administrator to deal with real people. This is the fate of his or her role. Organization of reality here must be in terms of concepts and numbers. A cold, self-loving personality would be ideal for this role. What Freud said of the leader holds of the top manager: the leader loves no one but himself.

People Who Turn Against People—Middle Managers: While many middle managers actually succeed in their role by informally nurturing, even "mothering," their subordinates, the formal role requires attitudes, skills, and behaviors of turning against the needs of subordinates when these conflict with the needs of the organization. People attracted are types who can play roles of dominance. They need other people, but they need them to dominate them.

People Turning Toward People—Employees: Structures requiring obedience to command and to impersonal rules select from society and nurture within the organization those people who have a need to depend on others. Such employees need to be led through guidance in getting work done, initiating the construction of work relationships, and initiating the satisfaction of personal love needs: sense of belongingness, being appreciated, being taken care of. Others (for example, professionals deriving a great deal of a sense of autonomy from their professional status and values) have a difficult time. At the least, they live in constant conflict between their need for professional autonomy and the required dependency. But any worker who retains any sense that he or she is best able to judge, from personal and intimate experience, the work at hand has the same problem. The danger is that the organization designed to take personal relations out of work tends ultimately to remove all work out of its organized (emotionally repressed) impersonal relationships.

Douglas LaBier: Power Positions and Technical Positions

What kind of people are attracted to wield the power in government bureaucracy and what kind of people are attracted to do the work?

Psychoanalyst Douglas LaBier found that "The answer lies in the observation that different roles call for more or fewer irrational attitudes.[50] For example, people handling power relations between individuals tend to manifest more irrational attitudes. Those involved in getting work done, such as auditors, tend to come from a more normal range. LaBier's suggested distribution of different types attracted to different levels of the hierarchy are illustrated in Figure 3.4.

LaBier says that power roles attract a different kind of person than work roles: "Certain roles are more likely to select and support the development of irrational attitudes. These include various 'power positions' found throughout government, such as policy formulation, high administration, or positions of assistant to presidentially appointed

Figure 3.4: Distribution of Passions at Work

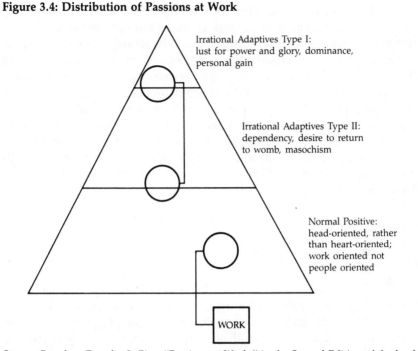

Irrational Adaptives Type I:
lust for power and glory, dominance,
personal gain

Irrational Adaptives Type II:
dependency, desire to return
to womb, masochism

Normal Positive:
head-oriented, rather
than heart-oriented;
work oriented not
people oriented

WORK

Source: Based on Douglas LaBier, "Passions at Work," in the Second Edition of the book.

administrators."[51] While LaBier suggests that a power-hungry type is usually found at the very top, for example, among presidential appointees picked to push programs through very quickly, and a masochistic type among the middle levels of the bureaucracy, we can probably generalize that dominance/submission relations occur generally wherever the maintenance of power and not getting work done is the prime object of a pairing of roles.

Irrational Adaptive Type I: These persons show a lust for power and glory, desire to subjugate and/or destroy others, and greed for personal gain; all of which have come to dominate the person to a pathological degree. That is, the behavior is really beyond their control.

Irrational Adaptive Type II: These persons show passive dependency, a desire to return to the womb, and submission to masochistic humiliation. This dependence and submissiveness is also pathologically ingrained.

Normal Positive Type: These individuals are, by traditional psychiatric criteria, normal. However, they are not fully healthy, having failed to develop "such qualities as love of life, concern for others, affirmation of truth"[52] (characteristics of the heart) while having overdeveloped particular concrete technical skills—such as those of accountants—favoring accomplishment of work. Their character fits the bureaucratic setting where the rationalism of head work is prized but not the vagaries of the judgmental heart. These people tend not to be found in power positions.

Finally *irrational nonadaptive* and *normal negative* types simply do not fit well into bureaucracy. The first type because its members either show emotional disturbances (rather than keep pathology under wraps). Unlike the irrational adaptives, their pathology simply does not fit into the role requirements assigned to them, which gives rise to conflicts and observable symptoms. The second type because the work environment also stimulates the "negative or unproductive sides of their character; traits like loyalty, fairness, authority, and assertiveness turn into submission, dominance, withdrawal, and destructiveness."[53]

Existential Analysis

THE ANXIOUS PERSONALITY AND THE BUREAUCRATIC DRIVE

The psychological analysis of bureaucratic personality rises and falls on the validity of the individualist perspective. That perspective sees the bureaucrat's psyche as sick or distorted; yet from the technological and organizational perspective, the bureaucrat is functional. Similarly, while some inmates of bureaucracy find the bureaucratic experience psychologically devastating, an administrator might argue that many seem to find in bureaucracy the satisfactions of their life's work. A value relativism pervades both viewpoints. Unless the critical perspective, and its experiential and empirical results, can be based on something more solid than what could be attacked as arbitrarily chosen values, a valid psychology of bureaucracy can ultimately *not* stand. Because of this problem, raising to the forefront the concept of anxiety as the prime motivator in bureaucracy takes on crucial importance.

Many industrial and organizational psychologists have pointed out that modern organizations must satisfy primarily the physical and psychological needs of inmates for survival and existence. Here the names of the organizational humanists come to mind: Maslow, Herzberg, McGregor, Argyris, and others. Why the need for survival and existence is basic—and the experiential testimony of people in bureaucracy also bears out that it is—does not become evident, however, until we take a critical perspective. What this perspective allows us to see is that bureaucracy creates the bureaucratic personality by attacking existence. It begins by disintegrating, if not forever destroying, the social personality. This explains the sense of loss experienced by those who are recruited from society into bureaucracy, the feeling of emptiness at work, and the inability of retired bureaucrats to get along outside the institutional context.

Bureaucracy gets its power exactly because it creates for us an existential dilemma by promising to solve our existential crisis. The individual is deprived of the feelings of human solidarity that a healthy superego provides and denied the sense of individual self-being that the independent exercise of mastery over a piece of work brings about. He or she does not merely become dependent on organizational structures for a sense of "ersatz" interpersonal inclusion—the sense of society—and for a sense of having a self provided by the replacement identity of the role. The individual is also continuously at the mercy of the institution to fulfill these needs. Yet anxiety is pervasive and profound. It is based on the knowledge that, in any matter of crisis, the organization will put its own survival before the existence of the employee. The arrangements for getting work done provide in subtle ways daily experience of the essentially dispensable, interchangeable, and replaceable roles that employees play in the larger picture. Employees are not simply afraid of losing their jobs, a real fear that managers exploit; they are pervaded on a minute-to-minute and day-to-day basis by a vague feeling of dread—nothing you can put your finger on, a dread that must in fact appear irrational but which is always there. Employees of modern organizations are in fact afraid not of anything specific but of the general and ever-present possibility of having the essential nullity of their importance in the values hierarchy of the organization exposed to themselves and to others. Anxiety as the dread of nothingness keeps me with my nose to the grindstone. The grindstone reassures me that I have a nose and that there is a "me."

Support for the anxiety concept comes also from a quite different source, the philosophical work of the phenomenologist and existentialist Martin Heidegger. Heidegger characterizes the condition of human beings in modern society as an escape into institutions and anonymity away from the one fact of life that no human being can look straight in the eye: that on the other side of or below the foundations of institutions there is nothingness.[54] The social world is made by humans. The psyche is a social product. The psyche, in our context, is an institutional product.

Modern organization constantly places us in contact with nothingness in two ways. First, at the point of transition between society and bureaucracy, we suddenly sense that the ground for our lives has been torn out from under us. It is an experience no one is likely to forget, even if we do not understand it. Secondly, the day-to-day management of modern organizations continually brings us into contact with nothingness: it is a managerial technique to deprive us of the grounds for assuring ourselves of existence (self-assurance) in order to continually recreate the need for the assurance that managers and the institution can provide.

Bureaucratic Ontology: Psyche versus Being

Psychological approaches to bureaucratic personality tend to focus on the problems of organizational attack on the self, raising problems of insecurity. At bottom is a focus on anxiety. Bureaucracy is seen as the modern person's way to create stabilized conditions in the world and at work. These promise to get the person away from the anxieties of interpersonal insecurity that Thomas Hobbes's state of the war of all against all represented. At the same time, it is the contribution of psychoanalysis to have shown that new insecurities are created by bureaucracy, turning people back to anxiety. The psychoanalytical, like the general psychological solution, however is to heal either the assaulted psyche or fix the offending bureaucratic structures or both. Anxiety is seen as an illness of the psyche that can be cured—either by healing the psyche or by improving environmental conditions. This assumes that the bureaucratic assault is an assault on the integrity of our *psychic structure*. Such an assault questions whether we "have it all together." But the assault may be more basic. It may be an assault against our being. This puts in question whether modern institutions allow us to have any existence at all. It is the final question of whether we are "out of touch with ourselves." The second possibility is *not* a psychological problem. It is an ontological problem. Psychology studies what makes us tick. Ontology studies who or what we are (from the Greek *ontos* + *logos* = the logic of our being). This distinction forces us to ask whether we are dealing, inside modern organizations, with neurotic anxiety or existential anxiety.[55]

The ontological approach argues that anxiety is not a disease but *the* most fundamental human condition.[56] Psychological descriptions of anxiety are quite accurate: we sense ourselves as filled with a nameless dread of *nothing* in particular; unlike fear, anxiety has *no* object; *nothing* in particular seems to trigger it.[57] This is exactly the existential ontologist's point: human beings normally must confront the fact that beyond their own existence there is nothingness. We live our lives as beings confronted by the abyss of nonbeing. Throughout history, humankind has tried to find refuge from the threat of nonbeing—but in no culture or civilization, the ontologist argues, have human beings ever *denied* their existential suspension between being and nonbeing. Modernity is the first culture to deny there is a problem. Bureaucracy is the most advanced institutional attempt to hide the problem. Bureaucracy—as organization theorist Robert Denhardt has pointed out in regard to one problem of being/nonbeing, namely mortality—promises immortality.[58] Individual members may come and go but in the programs and structures of the bureaucracy they will live on forever: "Contemporary organizational thought provides a comprehensive, although often disguised, scheme of moral behavior to which the member's actions can be related; by following this code, we presume our soul will be granted continuity."[59]

MARTIN HEIDEGGER: COGNITION WITHOUT THINKING

As an ontologist, Martin Heidegger looks at this personal problem on a larger scale. He is critical of modern science, modern technology, and modern organizations exactly because they pose one central danger: they enable Man to lose touch with his own being. What is wrong with bureaucracy is exactly that it attempts to reduce anxiety. Reducing anxiety absolutely is the absolute denial of the prime human condition. The member of the human community that denies his or her anxiety in the face of the daily confrontation with nothingness is also out of touch with the one great human power: the ability to leap ahead of ourselves into the dark, to leap from moment to moment into a future that can never be known fully ahead of time, to leap into our own potential—the ability of Man to create himself.[60] Instead we proceed by taming nature through science, manufacturing a world of our own design through technology, and controlling everything including human beings by an administration that treats everything as things. Thus we foreclose our own possibilities. We tend to think that nuclear extinction is our greatest danger today—and we look to technological solutions like Star Wars (the Strategic Defense Initiative). Yet Heidegger argues that we are in the greatest danger exactly when the nuclear bombs do not explode:

We do not stop to consider that an attack with technological means is being prepared upon the life and nature of man compared with which the explosion of the hydrogen bomb means little. For precisely if the hydrogen bombs do *not* explode and human life on earth is preserved, a change toward feeling homeless in the world moves upon us.[61]

What is the basis for this change? ". . . our inability to confront meditatively what is really dawning in this age."[62] We have not merely stopped emoting, we have stopped thinking. In a world in which everything is provided for, there is no more room for Man to think about providing anything for himself. In this age, science, technology, and organization still claim to be able to provide total security—despite all indications to the contrary: nuclear war, runaway technologies no longer under control, rampant insecurity in organizations. All that is demanded is enough time and money. All things can be fixed, and Man becomes a thing among things. We may conclude that the paradox Man confronts is this: in the bureaucratic world we have created a barrier against the anxiety of having to confront nothingness. Yet, nothingness—Cindy Confer, among others, called it being a "nonentity—intrudes into our daily lives as the condition of our modern being.

Is the experience of anxiety over being treated like a nonentity a *disease?* We sense it is not. It shows itself not as a disease but as a condition we find ourselves in. Anxiety—as silent suffering or in full cry—is the human condition in the bureaucratic world. But who suffers? We suffer, not bureaucracy. Anxiety is ours, yours and mine. It belongs to us. It is one of the very few things we can call our own in this world. But that makes it something to be treasured. We can treasure it as a sign. Signs point from where we are to where we might be able to go. As a sign, anxiety shows us our present condition: that of false security within the bureaucratic order. As a sign, too, it points beyond that order: to a place where anxiety is once more in our hands rather than we in the hands of anxiety disguised as security.

In sum: those who see anxiety in these terms will care for and take care of others. But they will not be satisfied merely with easing pain psychologically, nor will they obscure its origins organizationally. Neither as a healer nor as an architect, but with the word will they proceed. This means thinking—even before assuaging pain. In fact, it is thinking that builds on the pain. It also means thinking before rebuilding. The ontological position is that the "psychological" problem of bureaucracy is not one of emotions or irrationality, nor even of rationality. Neither the emotional nor the cognitive psychology of the modern individual is at stake. What is called for is a new kind of thinking, deeper than emotion and harder than rationality, that cuts like the sword through the false peace of bureaucracy.

WHAT PEOPLE CAN DO:

The Psychological Dilemma of Bureaucratic Self-Integrity

*Michael A. Diamond**

Those of us who appreciate the social and political "good" served by public bureaucracy know psychic trauma may arise from the interaction of human personality and bureaucratic structure. What do bureaucrats need to know in order to do something about the bureaucratic psychological predicament? How can we counter the psychic assault on self-integrity?

*Professor Michael A. Diamond teaches in the Department of Public Administration, College of Business and Public Administration, University of Missouri—Columbia. A

The bureaucrat needs a theory to identify and interpret psychological responses to organizational traumata. Organizational traumata (stressors) are triggers most readily, but not exclusively, observable when organizations change. Examples are leadership transitions, cutbacks, administrative audits, departures, transfers, changes in policy commitment and direction, and rapidly increasing or decreasing demands for services. Critical events in the life of a public agency impose an alteration in the status quo unleashing actions rooted in the unconscious. The experience is often one of anxiety. This produces unconscious adaptive and defensive psychological responses.

Unconsciously motivated defensive actions are the intersubjective data of bureaucratic experience. When we reflect upon and analyze these data within the situational context of roles in hierarchical positions, we often uncover invariant characteristics of the bureaucratic personality. More significantly, we see rigid and compulsive patterns of response to stressful circumstances and critical institutional events. Psychologically, defensive adaptations to anxiety over loss and insecurity associated with change and instability represent "a wished for return to the status quo," which unconsciously signifies "a wish for retrieval of the lost (maternal) object." Defensive and adaptive responses to loss due to change recall the infant's behavioral patterns clinging to and following the mother-caretaker; they signify adults' regressive responses to loss and uncertainty (the experienced anxiety), responses that are more characteristic of infancy and childhood.

To understand and appreciate the impact of these regressive responses to anxiety, organizational members need a psychologically based theory for practice. This knowledge should enable organizational participants to explain nonrational behavior and interpret outcome and, more importantly, enable them to claim responsibility for the outcome of their own actions. A psychologically informed organization theory must assist intentional self-organization of experience under stressful circumstances. It must enable us to convert otherwise unintelligible and incoherent patterns of behavior into intelligible and coherent patterns of human response to change that are more than merely a defensive response to the loss of the status quo. It must take into account the developmental psychodyamics of total dependency, separation, and individuation renewed in the adult personality under conditions of organizational distress. And it must give us alternative responses to recurrent problems and offer a remedy for psychic assault in bureaucratic hierarchy.

In this essay, I offer a model for achieving self-integrity in the

consultant to federal and state governments, he is co-founder of the International Society for the Psychoanalytic Study of Organizations.

Figure 3.5.

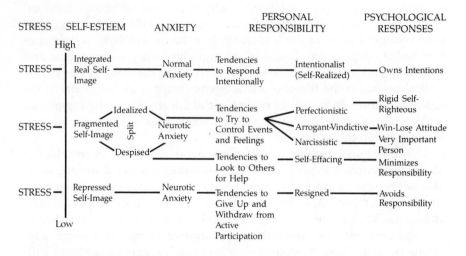

bureaucratic environment. The model describes the psychodynamic impact of stress on self-image and personal responsibility and provides a conceptual framework for assessing the psychological costs to bureaucratic members of functioning at the interface of social structure and self. Self-integrity rests on the coherent organization of self-experience. This is achievable only if we minimize defensiveness and anxiety. Instead, we must maximize self-esteem, intentionality, and opportunities to assume personal responsibility for our actions. A conscious "working through" process is required if we are to identify psychological defensive actions and to change them for individual and organization. The model is designed to assist the bureaucratic administrator in the maintenance of self-integrity and intentionality. It is constructed to facilitate "reflection-in-action" by cognitively mapping the variety of human responses to organizational stress. The bureaucratic practitioner is encouraged to recognize defensive and adaptive behavioral patterns to critical events. He or she is further encouraged to identify the effect of certain types of response on the ability or inability to assume personal responsibility for the outcome of one's official actions. The model is an interpretive framework for participant-observation, enhanced self-consciousness, and the promotion of greater intentionality among members of bureaucratic organizations.

A Conceptual Model for Bureaucratic Self-Integrity

Three general defensive responses are available to counter stress in bureaucracy. These responses involve diminished self-integrity and low self-esteem. Organizational participants must pay greater attention to these responses because they distort relations with others and produce dysfunctional consequences. The first two responses involve the defensive maneuver of "splitting" in which a whole self structure is cognitively and affectively split into two or more part structures. Usually one part structure is perceived as all "good" (accepting) and the other part structure is perceived as all "bad" (rejecting). The all-good response is represented by an "idealized" self-image made up of three distinctive tendencies: perfectionistic, narcissistic, and arrogant-vindictive. The all-bad response is represented by a "despised" self-image consisting of a self-effacing tendency. The third defensive response to stress involved the common avoidance strategy "repression" in which the stressful event and one's accompanying feelings of anxiety are denied by shutting the event out of consciousness. This defensive response is illustrated by the "repressed" self-image consisting of a resigned tendency.

There is also a healthy response. If the bureaucratic member does not perceive the situation as stressful and does not experience disorienting and fragmenting anxiety (alienation of self and others) as a consequence, then he or she may respond in a nondefensive fashion. This nondefensive, noncompulsive, unexaggerated response to change in the bureaucratic environment can be called the "intentional" response: self-integrity and personal responsibility are characteristic features. Intentionality assumes the individual is able to maintain and institutions reinforce an integrated self-image. This stands in contrast to the fragmented experience of the idealized and despised self-image and in contrast to the repressed self-image. Under stressful circumstances where anxiety is experienced, intentionality emerges only after the bureaucrat acknowledges his or her initial defensive response to the situational event.

An individual's response to stress has deep roots. It grows out of personality, out of a self-structure that represents individual characteristic (invariant) defensive and compensatory solutions to anxiety and conflict. These solutions originate in the bureaucrat's organization of experience with attachment, separation, and individuation during infancy and early childhood. The manner of adult psychological responses to stressful situations is often determined by how one unconsciously perceives an event and the personal meaning that situation carries subjectively. In bureaucracy this understanding must take into account the hierarchical position and role of superordinacy and subordinacy that influence the bureaucrat's interaction with others, and the nature of his or her intersubjective response to events. For example, a perfectionistic superordinate may appear self-effacing when functioning from a subordinate position in bureaucratic hierarchy. We turn now to a description and typology of psychological responses to stress.

INTENTIONALIST

The intentionalist response to organizational stress, as mentioned, is hard to achieve in bureaucracy for it assumes the person either does not experience alienation or disorientation or recovers intentionally after an initially defensive reaction. The intentionalist style of work is often contradictory to bureaucratic job norms described by Hummel (1977; 1982; 1987). Intentionalist organizational members are not dependent on bureaucratic structure for personal security and avoidance of anxiety. Rigid and routine structure is not relied on for unilateral protection and defense against anxiety. There is, therefore, no "need" to perpetuate control in the form of organization (Diamond and Allcorn, 1985).

In contrast to psychological responses drawn from the idealized, despised, and repressed self-images, intentionalists confront rather than avoid conflict and anxiety arising from change. This enables them to solve problems by "reflexive inquiry" (Argyris and Schön, 1978). In positions of leadership, intentionalists can facilitate learning under stress and anxiety by encouraging self-reflection, a balance between feeling and thinking and the claiming of responsibility for actions and outcomes. The intentionalist represents an ideal type of organizational member who is capable of maintaining both individuality and affiliation—a psychic equilibrium at the heart of healthy alignments between individual and organization.

THE IDEALIZED AND DESPISED IMAGES

Psychological responses to critical events may result in the "splitting" of self-image into two or more part structures. These include expansive tendencies of the idealized variety: perfectionistic, arrogant-vindictive, and narcissistic; and self-effacing tendencies of the despised variety. Perfectionistic bureaucrats harbor feelings of superiority over others. They set unusually high standards of performance (moral and intellectual) that justify "looking down" on others (Diamond and Allcorn, 1985). In addition, "bad" feelings of self-condemnation for not living up to their own standards are displaced onto others; thereby they come to denigrate others for not living up to their standards (Diamond and Allcorn, 1985). On the positive side, they are capable of attending to great detail in their work overlooking little in detection of organizational and programmatic errors.

Arrogant-vindictive bureaucrats appear emotionally cold and prefer to produce prodigious amounts of work. They are highly competitive and perceive interactions at work as win-lose encounters where triumph and success are of greatest value. They show arrogant contempt for others and believe that only they can do the work properly. They tend to intimidate and exploit others. Work is not intrinsically valued nor viewed as a collaborative effort. Rather, work becomes a game of calculated strategy to ensure triumph over defeat. In extreme circumstances, these bureaucrats' behavior may be self-destructive and destructive to others. On the positive side, they are resourceful, efficient workers and rather good planners and organizers (Diamond and Allcorn, 1985).

Narcissistic bureaucrats express unusual self-pride and view themselves as having boundless energy in solving problems. Their grandiose and omnipotent self-image tends to contribute to an overvaluation of their work and, particularly, an overemphasis of the importance of their role in the production of services. They use most of their energy on conceiving grand schemes and developing new opportunities but often lose interest in carrying them out (Horney, 1950). They require admiration and loyalty from others, in order to reinforce their idealized self-image. On the positive side, narcissistic administrators are productive in inventing original ideas and may remain productive so long as they are not placed in charge of carrying out the details of their grand designs.

Self-effacing bureaucrats identify with a despised self-image that perpetuates a dependency-oriented response to stressful circumstances. They often seek to minimize their self-accomplishment by measuring their performance against perfectionistic standards of excellence that inevitably result in finding fault with themselves (Diamond and Allcorn, 1985). This results in significant inhibitions at work. Adequate productivity can be maintained where authority directs and imposes deadlines along with constant recognition for any work performed. Self-effacing bureaucrats prefer not to do for themselves. Conformity, compliance, and overdependency serve security needs by finding others, often those in superordinate authority positions, to idealize. Authoritarian tendencies, and the combined self and other (often client) destructive potential of self-effacing functionaries, cancel out most positive attributes of this role response in bureaucracy. However, self-effacing characteristics are to some degree necessary for learning and correcting errors, which require humility and a willingness to question one's self competence.

THE REPRESSED SELF-IMAGE

Finally, resigned bureaucrats repress feelings associated with stressful events by withdrawing from active participation in organizational life. This functionary expresses a strong preference to be left alone and views as coercive others' efforts to interact or request his or her participation. Working with others and having to follow rules and procedures is disliked as they tend to limit personal freedom. In contrast to the self-effacing response, this response is for the most part inconsistent with bureaucratic organization norms (Presthus, 1978; Diamond and Allcorn, 1985). Freedom is sought above all else by avoiding feelings of coercive pressure and by restricting or repressing desires to accomplish anything (Diamond and Allcorn, 1985). The resigned functionary assumes the status of an onlooker in organizational life (Diamond and Allcorn, 1985). On the positive side, organizational outputs are possible when subordinates assume unofficial authority and authentic leadership (without any resistance from the resigned bureaucrat) to direct staff operations (Diamond and Allcorn, 1986).

CONCLUSION

In this essay, I have suggested what the bureaucrat must know about human responses to stress in large organizations. Change means loss; and loss often triggers in us "a wished-for return to the status quo" and an underlying desire for "retrieval of the lost (maternal) object." Here, momentary psychological regression among adult organizational members ignites infantile psychological defenses and security-oriented behavior. Becoming aware of one's own and others' typical ways of dealing with stress is a first step in learning what to do to keep or construct self-integrity. In part, the model explains perpetuation and reinforcement of the bureaucratic status quo. A psychological theory of human response to organizational traumata has been proposed to conceptualize and predict individual, interpersonal, and organizational consequences of stressful events. The theory for practice is offered to enable organizational participants to claim personal responsibility for their actions which permits intentional, constructive change in the status quo.

NOTES

1. Max Weber, *Economy and Society: An Outline of Interpretive Sociology*, 3 vols. Guenther Roth and Claus Wittich, eds., E. Fischoff et al., trans. (New York: Bedminster Press, 1968), p. 998.

2. Interview with the author, May 1975. Anonymity requested.

3. Interview with the author, May 1975. Anonymity requested.

4. John J. Sirica, *To Set the Record Straight* (New York: New American Library, Signet, 1980), p. 180.

5. Weber, *Economy and Society*, p. 968.

6. Quoted in Philip M. Boffey, "F.D.A. Sets Rules on Artificial Heart Implants," *New York Times*, Jan. 9, 1986, p. A15.

7. My thanks to Cheryl Smith, then medical records administrator of Penobscot Bay Medical Center, Rockport, Maine, for permitting me to contribute to a seminar on DRGs and ethics, 1984, Penobscot Bay Medical Center.

8. See Marcia Chambers, "Criminal Lawyers in Study Say New Laws Inhibit Case Choices," *New York Times*, Nov. 21, 1985, p. A20.

9. In Freud's own words, the ego is "an intellective activity which, after considering the present state of things and weighing earlier experiences, endeavors by means of experimental actions to calculate the consequences of the proposed line of conduct . . ." (Sigmund Freud, *An Outline of Psychoanalysis* [New York: Norton, 1936]).

10. Personal conversation with psychoanalyst Douglas LaBier, November 1985.

11. The discussion of the growth of self-love here is taken from Howard S. Schwartz, "Immoral Actions of Organizationally Committed Individuals: An Existential Psychoanalytic Perspective," Draft 1.1, circulation draft of paper delivered at the annual meeting of the American Society for Public Administration, April 13–16, 1986, Anaheim, California.

12. Schwartz, op. cit., p. 7.

13. See the sections on charisma in Max Weber, *Ancient Judaism*, Hans H. Gerth and Don Martindale, trs. and eds. (New York: Free Press, 1952); *Economy and Society* (New York: Free Press, 1964); *The Religion of China*, Hans H. Gerth, tr. and ed.; and *The Religion of India*, Hans H. Gerth and Don Martindale, trs. and eds. (New York: Free Press, 1958). See also R. P. Hummel, "Charisma in Politics: Psycho-Social Causes of Revolution as the Preconditions of Charismatic Outbreaks within the Framework of Weber's Epistemology," Unpublished Ph.D. dissertation, New York University, 1972.

14. My thanks to Professor Charles Hayes for this case.

15. Paul Roazen, *Freud: Political and Social Thought* (New York: Knopf, 1968), p. 247.

16. For an understanding of what communal life is like psychologically, see the example Bruno Bettelheim draws from contemporary *kibbutzim* in *Children of the Dream: Communal Child-Rearing and American Education* (New York: Avon Books, 1970). See especially his concept of the "collective superego" in contrast to the individual superego of the individual in society, pp. 142–43.

17. Roazen, *Freud*, p. 234.

18. Ibid., p. 233 ff.

19. Freud, Sigmund, *The Standard Edition of the Complete Works*, James Strachey, ed. (London: Hogarth, 1955), vol. 9, p. 237.

20. Roazen, *Freud*, p. 248.

21. For the definitive work on the meaning of modern liberalism since Hobbes, and on the elective affinity of Hobbesian-Lockean politics and Lutheran-Calvinist theology, see H. Mark Roelofs, *Ideology and Myth in American Politics: A Critique of a National Political Mind* (Boston: Little, Brown, 1976).

22. See B. F. Skinner, *Science and Human Behavior* (New York: Free Press, 1965), and Edgar H. Schein, *Organizational Psychology* (Englewood Cliffs, N.J.: Prentice-Hall, 1965). Thus, for example, psychiatrist Gregory Zilboorg, in commenting on "this sacrifice of the individual," speaks of a "disindividualized concept of the human personality" and the "rather sickening phenomenon of the disindividualization of man in favor of his serving the social, or mass machine." (Gregory Zilboorg, "The Changing Concept of Man in Present-Day Psychiatry," in Benjamin Nelson, ed., *Freud and the 20th Century* [Gloucester, Mass.: Peter Smith, 1974], pp. 31–38.)

23. Freud, *Group Psychology and the Analysis of the Ego* (New York: Boni and Liveright, undated), p. 1.

24. Thigpen, Corbett H. and Cleckley, Hervey M., *The Three Faces of Eve* (New York: Popular Library, 1957).

25. On the object-relations relations approach, see for example the *SASP Newsletter* issued by the Society for the Advancement of Self-Psychology, New York City, and Jay R. Greenberg and Stephen A. Mitchell, *Object Relations in Psychoanalytic Theory* (Cambridge, Mass.: Harvard University Press, 1983).

26. On social psychiatry, see the work of Harry Stack Sullivan and Erich Fromm; see also the work applied to private bureaucracies by Michael Maccoby and the work applied to public bureaucracies by Douglas LaBier. See also the article by Michael A. Diamond, "Organization Psychiatry," *The Bureaucratic Experience*, 2nd. ed. (New York: St. Martin's Press, 1982), pp. 134–137.

27. See Michael A. Diamond, "Bureaucracy as Externalized Self-System: A View From the Psychological Interior," *Administration and Society*, vol. 16, no. 2 (August 1984), pp. 195–214.

28. Interview with Cynthia Confer, Jan. 13, 1986, and completed Feb. 23, 1986, for the following quotations.

29. I would like to thank Professor Michael A. Diamond of the University of Missouri-Columbia for raising, in reviewing parts of the introduction to this edition, the issue that the

fundamental problem of the psychology of organizational life is not simply the pain of inmates but is a question of "basic humanity."

30. I am taking this phrase from the title of Ernest Keen's summary of existential psychology, *Three Faces of Being: Toward an Existential Clinical Psychology* (New York: Appleton-Century-Crofts, 1970).

31. Ibid., p. 59.

32. Ibid., p. 59.

33. Ibid., p. 46. Keen continues: "This is a highly subtle and yet very important phenomenon. When the child presents himself to his parents as 'good' and knows he is 'bad,' that is not a lie-for-oneself. But when a child invests so much in the being-good-for-his parents that it becomes an overwhelming concern, then his honesty in confronting himself is likely to suffer. Extremely punitive parents, therefore, undermine the child's honesty with himself. The experience of guilt can be so threatening that one effectively loses control with what one really feels or desires. In the place of this honest reckoning of oneself emerges an 'idealized self,' as Horney (1950) has called it, which may come to dominate one's entire being." Keen here refers to Karen Horney, *Neurosis and Human Growth* (New York: Norton, 1950). An interesting application of this theory of child development would be an investigation of the childhood of former President Richard M. Nixon, with whom the press experienced the great difficulty of finding the "real" Nixon.

34. Ibid., pp. 330–31.

35. Max Weber, *The Protestant Ethic and the Spirit of Capitalism*, trans. Talcott Parsons (New York: Scribners, 1958), p. 181. Weber is equating the entire modern economic order with his "iron cage."

36. Robert F. Pearse, "Manager to Manager II—What Managers Think of Their Managerial Careers—an AMA Survey Report" (New York—AMACOM, A Division of the American Management Association, 1977), p. 3.

37. I derive this thought from the first edition of this book. It is developed in R. P. Hummel, "The Work Bond," paper delivered at the first annual scientific meeting of the International Society for Political Psychology, New York City, Sept. 1–4, 1978.

38. See, for example, R. P. Hummel, "Freud's Totem Theory as Complement to Max Weber's Theory of Charisma," *Psychological Reports*, 35 (1974), 683–86, and "Psychology of Charismatic Followers," *Psychological Reports*, 37 (1975), 759–70.

39. Sigmund Freud, *The Standard Edition of the Complete Psychological Works of Sigmund Freud*, J. Strachey, ed. (London: Hogarth and Institute of Psycho-analysis, 1961), vol. 20, p. 221.

40. Robert Presthus, *The Organizational Society* (New York: St. Martin's Press, 1978), cited in Diamond, "Bureaucracy as Externalized Self-System: A View From the Psychological Interior," cited.

41. Weber, *The Protestant Ethic and the Spirit of Capitalism*, p. 182.

42. This discussion of memory benefited from the suggestions of my students in the seminar "Organization Psychology," Brooklyn College, Spring 1981, and from an exchange with Dr. Roger S. Mazze at the Institute for Applied Phenomenology, Summer 1981. I am aware of only one other source for a discussion of memory in this context, David S. Schuman's brilliant *Bureaucracies, Organizations, and Administration—A Political Primer* (New York: Macmillan, 1976), which touches on practically all important issues of bureaucracy today.

43. This is said in the sense of the depth psychology of Carl Gustav Jung. For some recent works in public administration utilizing Jung, see Orion F. White, Jr., *Psychic Energy and Organizational Change* (Beverly Hills, Calif.: Sage Publications, 1973), and "The Concept of Administrative Praxis," *Journal of Comparative Administration* (May 1973), pp. 55–86; Robert B. Denhardt, *In the Shadow of Organization* (Lawrence: The Regents Press of Kansas, 1981), especially Chapter 3, "Science, Organization, and Psyche." Cynthia McSwain, "Beyond the Instrumental Model of Leadership," *Dialogue—The Public Administration Theory Network*, vol. 7, no. 2 (Winter 1985), pp. 13–24; and Richard B. Polley, "Organization and Myth: The Consultant as Shaper," paper and presentation prepared for the First Cornell Symposium on the Psycho-Dynamics of Organizational Behavior and Experience, New York City Industrial and Labor Relations Conference Center, Oct. 1–2, 1983.

44. Michael A. Diamond and Seth Allcorn, "Psychological Responses to Stress in Complex Organizations," *Administration & Society*, vol. 17, no. 2 (August 1985), pp. 217–39.

45. Loc. cit.

46. Michael A. Diamond, "The Social Character of Bureaucracy: Anxiety and Ritualistic Defense," *Political Psychology*, vol. 6, no. 4 (December 1985), pp. 663–79.

47. Michael A. Diamond and Seth Allcorn, "Role Formation as Defensive Activity in Bureaucratic Organizations," *Political Psychology*, forthcoming.

48. Michael A. Diamond and Seth Allcorn, "The Role of Unconscious Actions in Work Relations," paper presented to the 1984 annual meeting of the American Political Science Association, Aug. 29–Sept. 3, 1985, New Orleans: specifically, see Table 2 outlining types of work relations.

49. Karen Horney, *Our Inner Conflicts* (New York: Norton, 1945), pp. 48–51, 53–55, 63–67, 73–77, and 79–81.

50. Douglas LaBier, "Passions at Work," in R. P. Hummel, *The Bureaucratic Experience*, 2nd ed. (New York: St. Martin's Press, 1982), pp. 141–47; citation from p. 142. See also LaBier, "Emotional Disturbances in the Federal Government," *Administration & Society*, vol. 14, no. 4 (February 1983), pp. 403–48; and LaBier, *Modern Madness: The Emotional Fallout of Success* (Reading, Mass.: Addison-Wesley, 1986).

51. LaBier, "Passions at Work," p. 143.

52. Ibid., p. 145.

53. Ibid., p. 146.

54. Martin Heidegger, *Sein und Zeit* [*Being and Time*] (Tübingen: Max Niemeyer Verlag, 1976 [originally published 1927]). See also *Heidegger and Psychology*, special issue, *Review of Existential Psychology and Psychiatry*, vol. 16, nos. 1, 2, and 3 (1978–1979).

55. Neurotic anxiety is merely an overdetermination of the ego from the outside, opening the ego up to the flood of forces emanating from the id. Existential anxiety is seen as the human condition. Freud: "In view of the dangers of [external] reality, the ego is obliged to guard against certain instinctual impulses in the id and to treat them as dangers" [pp. 81–82]. Ego fends off this danger by mobilizing a limited amount of anxiety [p. 71], which mobilizes unpleasure [p. 70] as a signal that something must be done to control "the unpleasure which the instinctual process was threatening to produce" [p. 71]. Sigmund Freud, *Inhibitions, Symptoms and Anxiety*, Alix Strachey, tr. (New York: Norton, 1959 [originally published 1926]), pages cited. Heidegger: "Warum sich die Angst ängstet, ist das In-der-Welt-sein selbst." Heidegger, *Sein und Zeit* [*Being and Time*], cited, p. 287, paragraph 40.

56. R. P. Hummel, "Heidegger, Freud and Anxiety in Organizations: Consultants and the Crisis in American Psychoanalysis," paper presented to the annual scientific meeting of the International Society for Political Psychology, June 1983, Toronto.

57. Sigmund Freud, *A General Introduction to Psychoanalysis*, Joan Riviere, tr. (New York: Pocket Books, 1969 [originally published 1920]), pp. 402 and 404; and Freud, *Inhibitions, Symptoms and Anxiety*, p. 91.

58. Robert B. Denhardt, *In the Shadow of Organization* (Lawrence: Regents Press of Kansas, 1981), Chapter 5, "Organization and Immortality."

59. Ibid., p. 83.

60. Martin Heidegger, "The Origin of the Work of Art," in *Poetry, Language and Thought*, Albert Hofstadter, tr. (New York: Harper & Row, Colophon, 1971), pp. 15–87; reference to p. 71; see also Heidegger, *Sein und Zeit* [*Being and Time*] on the concept of "thrownness" [*Geworfenheit*].

61. Martin Heidegger, *Discourse on Thinking*, John M. Anderson and E. Hans Freund, trs. (New York: Harper Torchbooks, 1969), p. 52. I have taken the liberty of retranslating the last clause, originally rendered as: ". . . an uncanny change in the world moves upon us." The original German word for "uncanny" is *unheimlich* [unhomely], which Heidegger uses to refer to Man's sense of not feeling at home in the world.

62. Loc. cit. Heidegger distinguishes meditative thinking from calculative thinking.

Bibliography: Michael A. Diamond

Argyris, Chris, and Schön, Donald. (1978). *Organizational Learning: A Theory of Action Perspective*. Reading, Mass.: Addison-Wesley.

Baum, Howell. (1986). *The Invisible Bureaucracy: Problem-Solving in Bureaucratic Organizations*. Oxford, England: Oxford University Press.

Diamond, Michael A. (1984). "Bureaucracy as Externalized Self-System: A View from the Psychological Interior." *Administration and Society* (vol. 16, no. 2, August), pp. 195–214.

Diamond, Michael A. (1986). "Resistance to Change: A Psychoanalytic Critique of Argyris and Schön's Contributions to Organization Theory and Intervention." *Journal of Management Studies* (vol. 23, no. 5, September).

Diamond, Michael A., and Allcorn, Seth. (1985). "Psychological Responses to Stress in Complex Organizations." *Administration and Society* (vol. 17, no. 2, August), pp. 217–39.

Diamond, Michael A., and Allcorn, Seth. (1986). "Role Formation As Defensive Activity in Bureaucratic Organizations." *Political Psychology*, vol. 7.

Horney, Karen. (1950). *Neurosis and Human Growth*. New York: Norton.

Hummel, Ralph P. (1977; 1982; 1987). *The Bureaucratic Experience*. eds., I, II, III. New York: St. Martin's Press.

Kets de Vries, Manfred F. R., and Miller, Danny. (1984). *The Neurotic Organization: Diagnosing and Changing Counterproductive Styles of Management*. San Francisco: Jossey Bass Publishers.

Kets de Vries, Manfred F. R. (1980). *Organizational Paradoxes*. London: Tavistock Publications.

Kohut, Heinz. (1977). *The Restoration of the Self*. New York: International Universities Press.

Levinson, Harry. (1981). *Executive*. Cambridge, Mass.: Harvard University Press.

May, Rollo. (1977). *The Meaning of Anxiety*. New York: Norton.

May, Rollo. (1969). *Love and Will*. New York: Dell.

Presthus, Robert. (1978). *The Organizational Society*. New York: St. Martin's Press.

Sullivan, Harry Stack. (1953). *The Interpersonal Theory of Psychiatry*. New York: Norton.

Van Den Daele, L. (1981). "The Self-Psychologies of Heinz Kohut and Karen Horney: A Comparative Examination." *American Journal of Psychoanalysis* (vol. 39, no. 1).

Zaleznik, Abraham, and Kets de Vries, Manfred F. R. (1975). *Power and the Corporate Mind*. Boston: Houghton-Mifflin.

4

The Language and Thought of Bureaucracy

Bureaucratic administration always tends to exclude the public, to hide its knowledge. . . . The treasury officials of the Persian Shah have made a secret science of their budgetary art and even use a secret script.

—Max Weber[1]

Language used to separate countries. Today it separates bureaucracy from its clients in society, functionaries from one another, and even managers from employees.

HOW PEOPLE TALK

One-Directional and Acausal Language

The language of society was causal ("Would you start the fire? I'm cold.") and two-directional ("But there's no wood."). The language of bureaucracy is one-directional (Manager: "Turn up the thermostat!") and acausal (Manager again: "So what if it's 90° outside! Do what you're told!"). Try to find the reason why. Try to talk back. Try to find somebody to talk back to.

Clients and customers feel this one-directionality most acutely when they try to talk back to a computer. They don't know computer language, and even if they did, the program would not allow them to be heard. The complainant who asks after the identity and purpose of the miscreant who set up the program is effectively blocked by that very program from pursuing the question. The computer, through its requirement for specialized language knowledge to operate it, protects its operators from attempts by lay people to find the cause of their discomfort and power-lessness. Once programmed, the computer talks only one way, from the top down. Its language is one-directional. The fact that the language itself contains no clues as to why the program was set up in one way and not another means it is also acausal. Acausal language hides the power interests of those who control it.

One-directionality and acausality are the two major characteristics not only of computer language but of bureaucratic language in general, of which computer language is an advanced case. Bureaucratic thinking also—the processes of cognition, analysis, and synthesis—is handi-capped by such language.

CLIENTS: A MAN ON SOCIAL SECURITY

The client is the first victim of the language barrier that bureaucracy erects—and not necessarily an unconscious one. In the client all the conflicts between bureaucracy and society come to rest. Listen to Pasquale Plescia, who went by bus from California to Washington, D.C., to find out about delays in his Social Security checks:

Well, I'll tell you something about this town. They got a secret language here. You know that? Bureaucratese. Same thing we used to call double-talk. These government people, they don't hear you. They don't listen. You start to say something and they shut you out mentally, figuring they know right away what you're going to say before you say it.

I knocked on doors here for two weeks but everyone's so busy with paperwork, they got no time for nothing else. I go to see one Congressman—a priest, so I figure he's got humanitarian interests—and his aide says I got to write him a letter first. Another one won't let me in cause I'm not in his constituency. Another gives me a press release and says, "This is the Congressman's position on Social Security." No kidding, that happened. So I go down to HEW. They've got 180,000 people working for HEW, and you know what? They've got nobody to make a complaint to.[2]

The client's misunderstanding of bureaucracy is classic. He assumes bureaucrats are people, but finds they can treat him only as a "case." He assumes a priest-congressman's values might include humanitarian ones, but the priest in congressional "office"—the priest as bureaucrat—must carefully apportion his time, and efficiency demands a written letter first. He assumes that bureaucrats are people like himself—personalities with a head on their shoulders, able to respond to human complaints, able to make decisions—but he finds no one in Washington corresponding to that personality type. The bureaucrat's psyche has been lobotomized.

And finally, although he recognizes that bureaucrats speak a dif-ferent language, he commits the error of interpreting the language they use as double-talk, a deliberate attempt to mislead him.

Indeed the systemic function of bureaucratese is fundamentally to make outsiders powerless. But that is a secondary function. The fact is that the people who speak bureaucratese do not design what they say and how they say it with Pasquale Plescia in mind at all. As he correctly perceives: "These government people, they don't hear you. They don't listen." Bureaucratic specialized language is specifically designed to insulate functionaries from clients, to empower them not to have to listen, unless the client first learns the language. For a client who has learned the language is a client who has accepted the bureaucrat's values. Language defines both what problems we can conceive of and what solutions we can think of. Once a client uses the bureaucracy's language, the bureaucrat may be assured that no solutions contrary to his interests and power will emerge.

Just follow all the changes your mind has to go through before you can understand—much less use—this example of language from the Federal Register:

The determination in these decisions of such prevailing rates and fringe benefits have been made by authority of the Secretary of Labor pursuant to the provisions of the Davis-Bacon Act of March 3, 1931, as amended (46 Stat. 1494, as amended 40 U.S.C. 276a) and of other Federal statutes referred to in 29 CFR 5.1 (including the statutes listed at 36 FR 306 (1970) following Secretary of Labor's Order No. 24-70) containing provisions for the payment of wages which are dependent upon determination by the Secretary of Labor under the Davis-Bacon Act; and provisions of part 1 of subtitle A of Title 29 of Code of Federal Regulations Procedure for Predetermination of Wage Rates, 48 FR 19533 (1983) and of Secretary of Labor's Orders 9-83, 48 FR 35736 (1983) and 6-84, 49 FR 32473 (1984) . . .[3]

In case you are wondering, the excerpt deals with how much people should get paid when they work on construction projects that get federal aid.

Once we recognize the mind-changing function of language, it is only one further step toward recognizing the ultimate function of bureaucratic language: a bureaucracy's language is usually so constructed as to prevent both bureaucrats and outsiders from ever formulating questions that might attack the underlying assumptions of the bureaucracy itself.

A bureaucracy's language hides the questionability of that bureaucracy's own existence. Jargon is a mystery even to those who daily use it.

In summary, everyday experience raises in us the sense that, just as bureaucracy differs from society in all other ways, it differs from society in the use of language. This difference presents itself in two aspects:

1. Based on our use of language in social life, we often would like to talk back to bureaucracy, but we can't. This is the phenomenon of one-directionality. Bureaucracy speaks; we listen.
2. Because we learn to do so in society, in our attempts to talk back to bureaucracy, we naturally look for a person to talk back to. In finding the person who utters a word, we get *behind* the word and hope to discover the

person's meaning. People have intentions; they can be asked, "What did you mean when you said that?" In bureaucracy, utterances are impersonal, not personal. That means if there is anything to talk back to, it is a *structure*, not a person. But we all know that structures, like offices, are things; and things, unlike people, appear not to have intentions. So we don't ask structures what they mean by a word. It seems an absurd thing to do. Structures just are; they give no clue as to their origins. Neither do their utterances.

Pasquale Plescia finally found the office of the secretary of HEW and in it a responsive administrator over the entire bureaucracy. But normally bureaucracy is so designed as to make unavailable or invisible from below the person who is the cause of a citizen's discomfort. In the succeeding sections of this chapter, I shall argue that not only is bureaucracy structurally designed not to reveal its causes of action, but the language it uses is itself couched in terms that dissolve the concept of responsibility. The result is a language that is acausal because it is impersonal.*

Clients as a Source of Insight

People are not stupid. A man having trouble getting his Social Security checks goes to Washington to ask why and immediately puts his finger on two central qualities that distinguish bureaucrats from regular people:

1. "They got a secret language here. . . . Bureaucratese."
2. "These government people, they don't hear you. They don't listen. You start to say something and they shut you out mentally. . . ."

Without being a specialist in linguistics, our man, Pasquale Plescia, has clearly identified two distinctions between social and bureaucratic language. One concerns the quality of bureaucratic language: it is strange; it has its own words; it is a foreign language popularly known as bureaucratese. The other distinction concerns how language is used, how persons relate to one another in acts of speech. Here he finds that, in dealing with bureaucracy, he is expected to listen while bureaucrats talk, and when he speaks, bureaucrats don't listen.

Should such insight surprise us? No. Anyone using a social language is an authority in it. Social languages are participatively constructed. Everyone who has grown up with such a language has taken part in determining what words mean and has experience in the oral exchanges through which meanings are worked out:

---

* The experience of acausality in bureaucratic language is fostered by the structure of that language itself. Bureaucratic language is functionalist; that is, it is so constructed as to make easy and clear to read what functions or activities have to be going on together at any given time. It is not constructed to reveal which activity *causes* the next activity. More of this later in this chapter. For now it may be sufficient to refer you to your own inability to gain access to the cause of your financial embarrassment when Macy's sends a computer-printed statement canceling your credit.

MAN IN A MUSEUM: Isn't this what they call a unicorn?

WOMAN: Looks like a horse with a horn to me.

MAN: But it's a white horse with a horn. Don't most people call that a unicorn?

WOMAN: Looks like a palomino to me.

MAN: Well, a palomino unicorn?

WOMAN: Seems like most people would call only a white horse with a horn a unicorn, but if you want to call it a palomino unicorn, I'll go along with you.

MAN: Okay. A palomino unicorn.

In social speech there is a kind of democracy in language construction. Sure, some people's words count more heavily than others'. But everyone takes part in defining words, if only by accepting a particular definition. A word doesn't mean anything after I utter it until you actively accept my meaning. That's minimal. But in most cases the meaning of a word is constructed by all who use it and who redefine and refine the meaning as it fits into a specific context. "Fire!" yelled by a person in a crowded theater means something different from "Fire!" gleefully shouted by that same person laboring at length to ignite some sticks in our fireplace. It is the variability of what words mean, according to context, that gives a social language like English its liveliness. That liveliness shows that living people constantly construct and take apart and rebuild again the meaning of words according to their shared needs. It is exactly this kind of language construction that bureaucracy must at all costs prevent if the meaning of what a bureaucracy is ordered to do is to remain the same when bureaucrats carry out those orders. The bureaucratic construction of language must always be from the top down, as in this entertaining but nevertheless essential example taken from *The New Yorker*:

THE BUREAUCRATIC MIND
AT WORK
[Notice distributed at the United States
Environmental Protection Agency]

OFFICE OF
THE ADMINISTRATOR

MEMORANDUM FOR
    Associate Administrators
    Assistant Administrators
    Office Directors
    Regional Administrators
We have had some confusion as to the designations A/O and O/A. To avoid further conflicts, A/O will mean the Office of the Administrator and O/A will be Office of Administration.

JOHN E. DANIEL
Chief of Staff[4]

What top bureaucrats say is so. At least, those below are officially obligated to pretend it is.

The Newly Hired: Ambivalence and Ambiguity

Top-down language in modern organization can also be ambivalent and ambiguous. A typical example of ambivalent language that misleads newcomers to organizations is the manager's "suggestion." When managers say, "Please try to get to that as soon as you have a chance," managers tend to mean: "Do it now, or you're in trouble." Managers may be trying to contain contradictory values in one statement: their need to have the results of your work now and their understanding that you can't drop everything. Only experience will show you what a particular manager really means in such statements. Similarly, "Don't worry!" is an ambiguous statement coming from a manager or supervisor when your question was, "Is this really what you want?" Newcomers to organizations, basing themselves on their previous experience in the reciprocal construction of social language, often expect and demand clarity by asking questions and believing the answers. In the words of one career counselor speaking of recent MBAs: "Kids out of school are apt to take things literally."[5]

To expect superordinates to clarify their instructions, however, is to overlook that their power is enhanced exactly to the extent that they can keep you guessing by *how* they say *what* they say. Exactly to the extent that a manager's words are vague, an employee must orient himself or herself more and more acutely and desperately toward discovering what it is the manager meant. (See also Chapter 5, "Bureaucracy as Polity.") This is such a generally valid rule that organizational communications expert James R. Killingsworth warns that, "Organizational talk is not made to be taken at face value by hearers. . . .As a text, it means what it says. As a pretext, administrative talk is a clue to still other, potential meanings."[6]

When a manager tells you, "You're being certified for our outplacement program," he or she is not simply using an apparently neutral or even upbeat expression for "You're fired." The manager is conveying information he or she is required to pass on but is doing so in words that evade personal responsibility for the act.

Killingsworth has produced a chart that shows both the utility and the absurdity of vague, ambivalent, and ambiguous speech: almost any phrase can be combined with any other, thus achieving nearly total meaninglessness. The chart's utility comes from two facts. It must be taken seriously both by employees or clients. If they don't, they are not

Table 4.1
EMPTY TALK IN ORGANIZATIONS

Column I	Column II	Column III	Column IV
Gentlemen,	the realization of the program's goals	leads us to reexamine	existing fiscal and administrative conditions.
Equally important,	the complexity and diversity of the committee's areas of concentration	has played a vital role in determining	areas of future development.
At the same time,	the constant growth in the quality and scope of our activity	directly affects the development and advancement of	the attitudes of key members regarding their own work.
Still, let us not forget that	the infrastructure of the organization	requires the clarification and determination of	a participatory system.
Thus,	the new shape of organizational activity	insures the participation of key members in	new proposals.

Source: James R. Killingsworth, "Idle Talk in Modern Organizations," *Administration and Society*, vol. 16, no. 3 (November 1984), pp. 346–384; chart from p. 352, originally produced as a satire by Polish students.

likely to survive in or with the organization. And it does not need to be taken seriously by managers. There's always a way of interpreting the meaning in many ways, and the person who has the power to interpret is in charge. The very fact that, in the chart, any combination of apparently differentially meaningful terms can be applied to almost any situation indicates how far detached organizational speech has come from referring to reality. Such speech can be used only in an organization in which internal performance standards outweigh any contact with reality: that is, where job performance is more important than getting work done. All bureaucratic organizations—public or private—tend, because of their inner logic, to become detached from the boundary with outer reality, where work is done. In short, the detachment of modern organizational language from real referents indicates the general detachment of modern organizations from human social and physical reality.

The Uses of Jargon

People complain about bureaucratese, secret professional languages, and jargon because their use by members of a bureaucracy or profession keeps other people outside. Jargon prevents us from knowing what the jargon users are talking about. But one would assume that as soon as an outsider learns the insiders' language, the outsider will be one of them and know what the words mean and what is being talked about. That is true to an extent, but somehow a mystery remains.

All words more or less hide their origins. This is due in part to the fact that we simply *use* words in daily life for practical and present purposes. We ask such questions as, "Where's the Empire State Building?" or "Where's the bathroom?" We give such practical answers as, "Turn left at the next corner," or "There isn't one." We don't inquire about the origins of such a word as "bathroom." In fact, a stranger would probably think that the term referred to a room that had a tub.

But if ordinary words hide their origins and meanings to some little extent, jargon words hide their foundations almost totally. This is especially true of abbreviations. Such a hiding of origins is of great power advantage to those who have an interest in the use of "inside" words, jargon, or abbreviations: what is hidden are the values of those who standardized the vocabulary. For instance, what were the values of those who standardized the American practice of calling a toilet a bathroom? A simple-minded example? Words were also able in the late 1970s and early 1980s to hide the fact that investment bankers were running New York City and that neither the inhabitants of the city nor of the state nor of the United States were ever consulted about *how* the bankers were to run the city—quite aside from the fact that words that ask no questions make it easier for professionals serving the bankers to think they are engaged in neutral acts. Take the case of "GAAPS":

An interesting case is a term relatively new to municipal finance. When New York City almost went bankrupt, the state legislature mandated that budget audits be done according to "generally accepted accounting practices." This long term soon became shortened to GAAP. Auditors and the press started talking about GAAPs as if they were things. To an accountant a GAAP means certain procedures that he will follow. But what an abbreviation like GAAP hides are questions like: What are accepted accounting practices? Who accepts them? What are the interests of those who accept them that must be reflected in such practices? How did they come to be generally accepted? Such questions might raise the issue of whom GAAPs are designed to serve: investment bankers or people who ride the city's disintegrating subway system? Or the issue of how an accounting practice becomes a political value might arise: who was or should be involved in legitimating "*generally* accepted accounting practices"? Accountants, the bankers, the public? Behind the thing GAAP, which simply *is* and which at best evokes procedures that *must* be carried out, hide questions of causality—who started it?— and legitimacy—who properly decides what a GAAP should be?[7]

FUNCTIONARIES: POLICE, FIREFIGHTERS

Functionaries themselves often don't understand the need for one-directional speech that forbids backtalk and for hiding the origin of a word or a policy when knowing it would cause orders to make much more sense.

Employees experience bureaucratic language always in the imperative voice and bureaucratic utterances as always coming from the top, that is, as one-directional: "When the orders come down, you can't talk back." Or in terms of the favorite gripe of the policemen I used to teach: "We're the guys who know what's going on in the street better than anybody. You'd think they'd want to know about that upstairs. But the hardest thing for us is to try and get to talk to them." Employees often tend to attribute causality to the commands they receive; that is, they assume there is both a reason and a person behind them. This assumption is erroneous to the extent that the officer in charge does not officially act on behalf of the office and the organization at large in personal terms. Nevertheless, the favorite line in a large East Coast fire department undergoing painful management changes was: "If it weren't for ⸺ [the fire commissioner] all these changes wouldn't be happening to us."[8]

The fact is, of course, that bureaucracies are designed to carry out orders, but the orders have their meaning defined in a context higher up and far removed from the work situation. "Retreat!" in the specific context of soldiers engaged in hand-to-hand combat with the enemy and knowing themselves to be winning is likely to mean to them, at the most, a call to disengage and fall back to established positions. That is the kind of sense the word makes in the context of their "work." But consider the general back at staff headquarters who issued the order after being informed of a massive enemy advance rolling up his army's left flank. To him, "Retreat!" meant something much more absolute and final, such as "Run like hell and don't stop until you get back home."

The overview that high position in hierarchy provides administrators must give them a different sense of what their commands are intended to convey than that allowed by the parochial view of an employee locked into his or her job by the division of labor and layers of superiors. The entire strength of bureaucracy as *the* form of modern organization superior in power to any other type of organization—one, for example, in which kinspeople pause in the midst of battle to dispute what their tribal chief meant—lies in the fact that language and speech acts are so structured as to forbid employees' asking "the reason why." Theirs but to do or die. Individuals are responsive to a narrow work context; the bureaucracy is responsive to a vast organizational context.

The experience with social speech was that people became personally attached to what they said. They made judgments, dependent on work and social contexts, as to whether one should be committed to carrying into action the implications in one's words. This caused all kinds of trouble: a soldier might not obey a general when ordered to shoot a member of his own family, a necessity perhaps in a civil war; a tax officer might not collect taxes from relatives; a road worker might not paint the yellow stripe down the center of a road during a rainstorm even though the performance of the road department was judged by how much paint was used up. When language was made impersonal (one function of jargon, which covers up any human values involved) and speech one-directional, a major problem of gaining obedience was solved. Impersonal language takes the burden of guilt off the executioner or the tax collector and the responsibility of making sense off the road worker. The inability to talk back, which can be a frustration, is also a relief: "There's nothing I could do even if I wanted, so I'll keep painting in the rain."

Administrators and Managers: A Secretary of State

Words make power. This can be understood when we ask ourselves how we react to the words of the powerful. These individuals, especially if they run a bureaucracy, have us in their power to begin with: if I want to keep working for, say, the State Department, I will obey. But their control over the language used adds to their power—and in a way that the rest of us do not normally perceive as an exercise of power. That, of course, is the beauty of it: to be exercising power without seeming to.

Take the specialized words used by an American secretary of state and future presidential aspirant, a lifelong bureaucrat who, though a general, had never exercised a combat command. Some of the words and phrases used by this top administrator, along with some *Time* magazine comments, can be found in the box that follows.

Observe your reaction to this idiosyncratic use of what are mostly common words with a long and meaningful history in the social language in which we were raised: English. Amusement? Disgust? Confusion? Disdain? Perhaps all of these went through your mind. But now imagine you are somehow obliged to deal with the man who uses words in such a strange way. If you are a Russian diplomat, or a subordinate in the State Department, you *must* deal with the secretary of state. But the only way of dealing with him, especially if you are a subordinate, is by trying to understand what he means. You must try to understand him because you are in an inferior power position to begin with; if you don't try or if your attempt fails, you may act in the wrong way and you risk disfavor. So you turn your entire attention to the speaker and become a total listener.

Like most subordinates, you do not have a chance to ask the speaker, "What is it you meant?" Much less can you challenge him by saying,

Haigledygook and Secretaryspeak

Alexander Haig is conducting a terrorist campaign of his own—against the English language. His war of words with the Kremlin has turned into a war on words, presumably much to the consternation of Russian translators. Herewith a lexicon of Haigisms:

Careful caution. A repetitious redundancy but preferable to careless caution. Similar to his "longstanding in time."

Caveat. An Al-verb, a victim of the general's verbification program, to which resistance is *verboten* for even the most insolent little noun. As in: "I'll have to caveat my response, Senator."

Contexted. The past tense of Haig's verbicose veins. As in telling Senator John Glenn that his question cannot be answered "in the way you contexted it."

Epistemologicallywise. The only thing less clear than the meaning of this word is how many hyphens it should have.

Exacerbating restraint. A Pushmi-Pullyu, as in expressing the hope that the Soviets would do nothing "to exacerbate the kind of mutual restraint that both sides should pursue."

Menu. Used with careful caution as in: "In each instance

Source: *Time*, February 23, 1981, p. 19.

the menu—and I use that term guardedly—of assets available to the West will vary."

Nuanced and nuance-al. As when the secretary of solecism talks of "nuanced and fundamentally sharp departures" and "nuance-al differences."

Posthostage-return attitude. An imploded word cluster that may be the result of reading too many NATO command manuals in German.

Saddle myself with a statistical fence. A techno-cowboy's metaphor that borders on the kinky.

The very act of definitizing an answer. A punishable act in most English-speaking countries.

This is not an experience I haven't been through before. Definitely not a non-Haigism.

Out of context these phrases make no sense; in context they make even less sense. Maybe, just maybe, the Haigledygook is deliberate. As the Secretary said at his press conference when asked to clarify a statement: "That was consciously ambiguous in the sense that any terrorist government that is contemplating such actions I think knows clearly what we are speaking of." Well, perhaps *they* do.

"What you have just said doesn't make any sense." What the powerful say makes sense because, like a character in *Alice in Wonderland*, they command it to make sense. I mean exactly what I mean, neither more nor less—and it is for you to find out what that is. So you look at the speaker's language use and at the contexts within which he speaks. You see what actions his words refer to, and what things. And after a while you think you have an idea of what he means by "careful caution," "definitizing," and "menus." Then you act on your understanding of his orders containing such usage, and, if nothing adverse happens, you assume you have understood him.

Note the strange and twisted attitude you must take toward a powerful speaker: you engage in a turning toward the other, but the other makes not the slightest effort to turn toward you.

The mandated turning toward the other in language use, in which the other merely speaks over the shoulder *at* us, deprives us not only of participation in the construction of language but also of the ability to think independently and, ultimately, of the ability to take part in the construction of reality.

This is, of course, exactly what the specialized language of bureaucracy, extending far beyond a secretary of state's idiosyncracies, is intended to accomplish. From the viewpoint of citizens, legislators, and administrators—if we may change roles for a minute—we do not want bureaucrats who redefine the meaning of a law or a policy or a memo. We do not want independent thinkers to reshape what the polity has decided. And we do not want the illegitimate reconstruction of our social world by bureaucrats who are intended to be our servants, not our partners.

WHAT THE EXPERTS SAY

Wittgenstein: The Abolition of Language

In bureaucracy, we may be moving in a direction where language is not language at all. One of the strongest arguments on behalf of the death of language can be drawn from the philosopher Ludwig Wittgenstein. Language is communication, this argument runs; what goes on in bureaucracy is not communication but information. Communication is a two-way construction of meaning between at least two human beings; information is literally the molding and shaping of one human being by another. In fact, information does not necessarily involve human beings: machines can "inform" one another.

COMMUNICATION AND INFORMATION

Language originates in the common life that human beings share as members of a community, Wittgenstein seems to argue.[9] Within this communal context, we engage in "language games."[10] That is, we engage in mutual interaction through language that is based on taken-for-granted rules silently agreed upon among ourselves. The fundamental agreement of the game is agreement in "what we do."[11] We might think of such agreement as a result of convention: "Okay, Joe, let's agree on not killing each other in this game by calling this a head and we all know heads are easily injured." But before I can even begin to agree with you on such definitions, I must already have an understanding of what a head is and what it means to be injured. That is, I must share with you my humanity. "If language is to be a means of communication there must be agreement, not only in definitions, but (queer as this may sound) in judgments."[12] As one Wittgensteinian commentator said, "Unless people agree in their reactions to colours they will not have the concept of colour they need to have to see certain behavior as 'agreement in reaction to colours'. Unless they agree in their expressions of, and reactions to, pain, they will not have the concept of pain they need to see behavior as 'pain behavior'."[13]

In summary, what makes language as a means of communication possible is the shared experience of being human. This shared experience Wittgenstein called "forms of life" [*Lebensformen*]. Forms of life are specific expressions of behavior among human beings that rest on the organic peculiarities of the species. In the words of another Wittgensteinian commentator:

Language, and therefore the higher forms of consciousness, depend, logically, for their existence on the possibility of common "forms of life." Hence, also, they depend, as an empirical matter of fact, on the existence of human beings regarded as members of a (fairly gregarious) species. To assert the existence of *such* forms of consciousness is in part to assert the existence, not of a single person, nor even of several separate persons, but rather, of people, that is to say of groups of individuals having not only common characteristics but also common (mutual responses), interactions, etc.[14]

The relevant question to be asked about life in bureaucracy is whether such life still maintains the characteristics of human "forms of life" based on our biological characteristics as a species.

Specifically we can address this question to two kinds of "communication" within bureaucracy: (1) "communication" between bureaucratic structures and individual functionaries; and (2) "communication" between computers and individual functionaries or clients.

One of the leaders in modern organization theory, Herbert Simon, considers bureaucratic structures to be frozen decisions.[15] In other words, the office of the sales manager in a vacuum cleaner company is set up to perpetuate the decision that whenever a customer comes in to buy a vacuum cleaner there will be adequate sales staff to effect the sale. Setting up this structure once—the structure of the sales manager's office—for all time hence, or until another decision is made, obviates the need to have unqualified and ill-informed personnel run around, when a customer comes, searching desperately for vacuum cleaners, price lists, and the proper procedures for recording the sale so that inventory can be brought up to date, new machines ordered, and so on. In this sense, the office structure is not simply one frozen decision—the decision to sell—but many frozen decisions: on how to sell, what price to ask, how and when to reorder.

Nonhuman "Language"

The question that arises here is: Are the instructions contained in the frozen decision—i.e., the sales manager's office—really communication? That is, are they language? Or are they something else?

Let me tentatively suggest that the instructions so frozen are neither communication nor language in the traditional sense, but information. That is, for the very good reason of achieving predictability of behavior by the sales staff, the instructions encoded in the sales office are not subject to mutual agreement from below. They are one-directional. They shape behavior from the top down. As soon as, and because, it becomes detached from the original decision-makers, who then become inaccessible to communication from below, information of this technical sort loses an essential characteristic of human language. The office in question is not a living thing, although it might be argued that it is usually inhabited by a living thing, the sales manager. But what characterizes the bureaucratic office is that its frozen decisions exist no matter whether there is a sales manager or not and no matter who he or she is. Even when the office is temporarily empty because the manager has been fired, the office "exists" and even "talks." It "talks" because many of its frozen decisions are encoded in price lists and work rules, which serve me as external guides to my behavior as sales clerk.

But does the office talk and exist the way human beings do? As a sales clerk, I am quite aware I can never talk back to it to inquire after the original decisions under which it was structured. One of these decisions was to have an office that would talk to me without having back talk. But, more importantly, in bureaucracy the office is specifically not the human being who fills it. Rule is impersonal. This means that even if I were to try to engage in back talk, I would be addressing a "partner" of intended communication that very specifically, and by design, lacks experience in the human condition. The office, after all, is the attempt to mechanize and automate both perceptions of what goes on in the sales process and instructions based on such inputs. Lacking human experience, the office as such can never become, under Wittgensteinian concepts of language, a partner for mutual agreement about a language game called "sales."

Because the office is inhuman, it can only treat me as a thing like itself. I, who think of myself as a human being, am "thought of" and treated as an analogue to the machine—another machine. I can understand it only to the degree that I accept the rules it imposes on me, that is, to the extent that I become mechanical not only in my behavior but also in my conception of what language is. At this point whatever "talk" goes on between me and the office is no longer "language" in the Wittgensteinian sense. As Vesey notes, with tongue-in-cheek, about similar situations: "Arguments from analogy haven't a leg, even *one* leg, to stand on."[16] This is, of course, because offices, unlike humans, do not have legs. Given such a handicap we might, under Wittgenstein's premises, have assumed from the beginning that neither communication nor language is possible between human beings and the structures of bureaucracy.

But something does go on between the two, and if it is not language in the traditional sense, what is it? Here we may look to what Herbert Simon considers the ideal structure of modern organization, the computer, for an answer.[17] Don't computers speak to us? Don't programmers "program"—that is, "speak" to—computers?

Before proceeding to an answer, let us emphasize that the above argument on the linguistic relation between office structure and functionaries already demonstrates our main point: language in bureaucracy is radically different from language in society. Wittgenstein's argument in fact suggests that language is not only different in bureaucracy, it is abolished.*

Nowhere does this become more clear than when people freeze business or public-service decisions into a computer and then make other people subject to the computer's instructions. Like the relationship between organizational structure and functionary, and for exactly the same reasons, the one between computer and functionary is not one of communication. The computer provides us with an especially clear–cut example of the difference between communication and information precisely because the last human element has been squeezed out of the computer, seen as an organizational structure into which decisions are frozen. An office, on the other hand, still seems to be occupied by a human manager, giving the impression of a human-machine symbiosis. In general, computer-human exchanges can no longer be understood in terms of how language used to link humans because a computer is not part of the human species.

A computer is as different from humans as humans are from dogs or

---

* Similarly, Jenny Teichman on the concept of "inaudible" language: "He [Wittgenstein] seems to be saying . . . that a language which cannot be used in communications is not a language at all (any more than infinity is a number)." (Teichman, "Wittgenstein on Persons and Human Beings," in Royal Institute of Philosophy, *Understanding Wittgenstein* [New York: St. Martin's, 1974], p. 145).

stones. As one Wittgensteinian put it: "Why can we not intelligibly say of a dog or an infant that it is hopeful? Or of a stone that it is in pain? Why can we not say that a computer calculates?"[18] Pointing out that Wittgenstein himself asked this last question,* the same author summarizes Wittgenstein's reply:

A computer can reel out unimpeachable answers to the questions we feed into it. It may be tempting to think that here is exemplified the kind of competence that makes us speak of thought and intelligence in a mathematician. If the mathematician differs from the computer in *other* respects why should that undermine the similarity in their mathematical performance? Certainly if a man or a child writes down the answer to a mathematical problem this, in *itself*, does not prove that he has intelligence. To think of him as having mathematical ability we want him to be able to solve *other* mathematical problems. Whether or not his present performance exhibits ability and intelligence depends on what he does on *other* occasions. But when we call a man who solves a wide range of difficult mathematical problems intelligent, we take it for granted that the symbols, formulae and simple operations he uses have meaning for him, that he understands them. We cannot take this for granted in the case of the computer. Merely responding to the problems fed into it with the correct answer does not show that the computer understands what it prints. . . .

In short, if the computer is to calculate it would have to have something like the human body, with arms, face, eyes, and enter into various activities in which the symbols and formulae it prints play a role. It is their role in these many activities, in shopping, measuring, accounting, engineering, that gives them the sense they have.[19]

In other words, without participation in the human experience, the computer is not capable of something like understanding. For the same reason, we can argue that the interaction between people and computers can never fully partake of the characteristics of communication, because one of the basic requirements for communication, the capacity for understanding on the ultimate grounds of sharing the human condition, is not available to the computer.

Similarly, the more human beings, who are dependent on modern organization for employment, adjust to the machine, the less likely they will remain capable of communication. As Wittgenstein points out, if a human responded to mathematical questions with the quickness of a computer and always came up with the correct answer, could carry out complicated formal transitions, and could work out involved mathematical proofs, but was "otherwise perfectly imbecile," then he or she would be "a human calculating machine."[20] In yet other words:

A person who produces such answers, whether in words, writing or print, is performing an activity in which thought and intelligence are displayed *only* if he

---

* In *Remarks on the Foundations of Mathematics* (Oxford, England: Basil Blackwell, 1956), Part IV, Section 2.

lives a life in which this activity has a point and a bearing on other things he does, *only* if he has other interests—interests independent of producing these answers. In the absence of such a life even a being who is alive is not a human being.[21]

As we move from the society of human beings to the bureaucracy mix of functionaries and machines, we thus experience a sense of strangeness in the kind of language spoken there. According to the Wittgensteinian explanation, this is because structures of the bureaucratic type are incapable of producing human language, human communication, and human understanding.

Searle: The Separation of Language from Meaning

There is a very basic experience in bureaucracy in which we sense that speech there is radically different from speech in society. We reflect this when we call an institution's press spokesperson a "mouthpiece." We encounter a similarly strange experience when we see computer specialists "talk" to their machines. In both cases we sense that something strange is going on, but we don't understand why. In both cases we are right.

DETACHING MEANING FROM MESSAGE

What we are observing when bureaucrats or bureaucratic structures (including computers) speak, or are spoken to, is often something unparalleled in human history—the separation of meaning from the message. It was of such language that bureaucratic practitioner and critic C. P. Snow wrote, "It was a curious abstract language, of which the main feature was the taking of meaning out of words."[22] Marshall McLuhan may glibly tell us that the "medium *is* the message," that the form of a message is its meaning; and he may be right: all communications media shape what they are capable of saying. But what is happening in bureaucracy is very specifically the separation of the message from both its content and its context.

Press secretaries of government institutions are very specifically understood by reporters *not* to be involved in what they are saying. They do lend, as the derogatory but very descriptive appellation of "mouthpiece" suggests, the mouth to the conveying of the institution's message; but his or her personal meaning is detached from what is said—the impersonal message. This is the function of the "good" bureaucrat's detachment from his or her acts. It is a sign of insufficient bureaucratization that news reporters held President Nixon's press secretary, Ronald Ziegler, personally responsible for the misinformation he distributed. On the other hand, Ziegler showed he understood the function of his office in purely bureaucratic terms when he chose to characterize previous statements exposed by the press as falsehoods as "inoperative" instead of as "lies." A lie is a concept that belongs to the world of social language in which individuals are held responsible for what they say, and their intentions are expected to be congruent with their words. Within the world of bureaucratic language, "inoperative" is a perfect term for a statement that no longer functions in the bureaucracy's overall attempt to remain adaptive to its environment—that is, in a world where means and meanings no longer matter but results do.

Nevertheless, those of us coming to bureaucracy from society are right in feeling there is something very strange going on in the way bureaucrats use language, though perhaps our sense of strangeness should be resolved through understanding rather than outrage. What can explain our sense of strangeness when confronted with bureaucratic language? For something to be strange, it must differ from what we are used to. How does bureaucratic language differ? If we could answer this last question, we could also understand our sense of being strangers in a strange land.

But first another example. Our sense of strangeness reaches a peak when we are spoken to by computers. Computers interest us here because they have replaced large segments of bureaucratic structures, are in fact often used *as* bureaucratic structures. A computer can, for example, replace a large section of a business's or civil-service institution's accounting or payroll office. To a large degree it is, in effect, the accounting or payroll office, and it is more bureaucratic in Max Weber's sense than any structure that preceded it. Precomputer structures are mixtures of people and machines in which people still visibly dominate even if, for the sake of bureaucratic control and stability, they are supposed to act like machines. For the segments that the computer takes over, this duality is resolved: the structure in which formerly twenty accountants performed calculating operations on a payroll is now a computer. The computer *is* the ideal bureaucracy.

When such a structure speaks, as we have said, the speech seems very strange to us—because all human components have been removed from the speaker. What is left is myself and the IBM terminal, myself and the printout.

Here, because the computer presents us with an extreme or "pure" example, we begin to see clearly the nature of bureaucratic talk—machine language—as opposed to people talk—human language.

The difference, as we have already indicated, is that in bureaucratic talk the message has to be so encapsuled and protected against the personal interests of its human carriers that it can stand by itself—apart from, and even despite, these human carriers. With the machine language of the computer, the designers of bureaucracy have finally reached that goal. There now is an impersonal language. And it is free from human interference. It is this fact that is unique in human history. No wonder we feel strange!

At this stage we may call upon the services of an expert linguist, John R. Searle, to deepen our understanding of just how serious this difference is.

A Retreat from Language

In ordinary human discourse, Searle argues, what is said (language) is never separate from the intentions of the person who says it (the speaker). The purpose of language, in fact, is to have the listener recognize the intention or meaning of the speaker.

Now, one of the strangest things about observing people who program computers—that is, who work with what computer specialists call "machine language"—is that they "utter speech," or construct speech, which the machine will then be able to use, without having in mind anything specific that they want to communicate. They are simply laying down the *means* of communication without reference to any specific *meaning*. Someone who wants to use the computer to communicate will come along later and use the means laid down—I hesitate to call it language for it is nothing of the sort in traditional terms—by attaching a meaning to it. This process of attaching meaning to the means of a language is one of the strangest experiences in which humans have ever engaged. Not that definitions have not been imposed from above for millennia. But the permanent, and very visible, separation of what is said, the signs and symbols, from what is meant has been experienced only for short spans at most, as when a child or a newcomer to a country uses a new word before learning the meaning attached to it. In the past such separation was always a handicap, a barrier to communication, but now the computer promises that separating means from meaning will encourage communication and make it more certain.

Some further exploration of Searle may deepen our understanding of this difference between what is said and what is meant. He writes:

Human communications has some extraordinary properties, not shared by most other kinds of human behavior. One of the most extraordinary is this: If I am trying to tell someone something, then (assuming certain conditions are satisfied) as soon as he recognizes that I am trying to tell him something and exactly what it is I am trying to tell him, I have succeeded in telling it to him. Furthermore, unless he recognizes that I am trying to tell him something and what I am trying to tell him, I do not fully succeed in telling it to him.[23]

That is, in ordinary human life the act of telling and the meaning attached to what is told are usually inseparable.* In contrast, the computer, and to

* In social life having meaning attached to what is told us is best achieved by having the

a lesser degree the thoroughly bureaucratized bureaucrat, separates the two. Computer "language," as a pure example of an ideal bureaucratic "language," is not fully language until it is applied *by someone* to a *particular case.** That is, it requires someone to come along and put what is a highly abstract and detached system of signs into a human context.

Such "language" is strange to us because most language we are acquainted with ordinarily appears in some sort of context related to a problem, interest, or activity in which we are engaged. Computer language, and to a large degree bureaucratic language in general, is in this sense "context-free." It lacks a context in the same way that a tongue would lack a context if I saw it going for a walk unattached to a head. And bureaucratic language thus unattached appears strange to us users of attached language in much the same way.

Linguists, who take language apart in their day-to-day work, have of course encountered language in this amputated form before. But, as Searle says, in real life, "speaking a language is everywhere permeated with the facts of commitments undertaken, obligations assumed, cogent arguments presented, and so on."[24] Those of us toying playfully and naively with computer "language," and the "language" of bureaucracy in general, might well be forewarned by the caution Searle addresses to his fellow linguists:

The retreat from the committed use of words ultimately must involve a retreat from language itself, for speaking a language. . . . consists of performing speech acts according to rules, and there is no separating those speech acts from the commitments which form essential aspects of them.[25]

While Searle does not address himself to what we have observed—that people in ordinary bureaucratic life are now playing games with a language that involves the separation he fears—it is perhaps not too impertinent for us to read into his specific caution a general warning for ourselves as speakers, as listeners, and, above all, as human beings. The fact is that in everyday life we have begun to use "language" in a way that heretofore only linguistic analysts have encountered in their scholarly

---

speaker remain personally attached to his or her words. For example, juries apparently tend to lend more credence to narrative testimony offered by a witness than to the same information presented in a non-narrative manner (for example, signed depositions), according to a research group headed by anthropologist William O'Barr of Duke University. (As reported in "Verdicts Linked to Speech Style: Anthropologists Say Subtle Patterns Influence Juries," *The New York Times*, Dec. 14, 1975, p. 88). Contrasting mock juries' reaction to narrative versus non-narrative information, the report concluded: "The result: The juries considered the narrative form of testimony to be more authoritative and stronger, even though the substance presented in the two varieties was indistinguishable." The narrative style, of course, is *social* speech. In contrast to bureaucratic speech, it allows speakers to become directly involved in what they say.
* I am putting the word "language" in quotation marks here to indicate that these are not language in the traditional sense.

studies. And I am certain we are dealing with such "language" without being aware of its truncated nature and without a single thought of its consequences—except the vague sensation that something strange is going on.

THE NATURE OF BUREAUCRATIC LANGUAGE

Bureaucracy separates people from their language. This is the major conclusion to be drawn from the Wittgensteinian and Searlean analyses of the nature of bureaucratic language and computer language as its logical extension

A Language of Functions

Both experts specify that language is not language unless what is spoken is attached to the intentions of the speaker and addressed to the understanding of the hearer. In Wittgenstein's judgment, a person who speaks outside this human context "is not a human being." Searle similarly comments that human language is never separated from the meaning of the speaker and that "the retreat from the committed use of words ultimately must involve a retreat from language itself. . . . But it is the pride of designers of bureaucratic systems that the individual functionaries are in the anomalous position of not being personally committed to their words.*

The bureaucratic language—always unique in its systemic definition of terms and its structural echoing of the bureaucratic processes it enshrines—is designed before the first functionary ever arrives at the place of work. It is protected by underlying cultural imperative against the process of ordinary dialogue that changes and amends meanings. It also exists apart from the speaker and will continue to exist long after the speaker is gone. It is in this sense a dead language. If it were a living language, it would be subject to modification by every user. But the terms that define what operations a bureaucracy may and may not engage in must not be so amendable, otherwise the certainty of having the lowest functionary do what the highest echelons command is gone and with it the raison d'être of bureaucracy. It is for these reasons that the problems with language that we cited at the beginning of this chapter exist.

At the boundary between the two linguistic communities, functionaries must not be allowed to change the meaning of an official term one iota from its legal and administrative predefinition. For example, the term

---

* In contrast to society, where a man's or a woman's word is his or her bond, in bureaucracy it is exactly the *lack* of personal attachment to one's words that guarantees the reliability of the functionary—especially in cases in which there is a danger of conflict between personal values and the values contained in the words he or she must officially use.

"welfare mother" can only mean an unemployed, husbandless female of a certain age, with a certain number of children. Similarly, an official term must be encapsuled through administrative and legal sanctions against attempts by a potential, but not quite qualified, client to engage in the normal dialogue usual in human relations and persuade the functionary to amend what he or she "means" when using the term (e.g., "welfare mother") in the officially defined way.

The functionary's only survival strategy is to teach a potential client the meaning of official language—its categories and procedures—as he or she has learned them. And the central tactic of that strategy, especially if the functionary has personal sympathies with the client, is to separate what he or she says officially, including the choice of terms and grammar, from any private intentions. Only if the functionary and the client both understand that in bureaucracy it is never a human being speaking—to whom intentions, empathy, or responsibility of a human sort might, after all, be prescribed—will bureaucracy work.

The client who blames functionaries personally for what they officially utter commits the serious misunderstanding of associating speech with the speaker. Such an expectation is reasonable only in social life. How else are people ever to trust one another? Why else, except that you mean what you say, should I pay attention to you? How else, but with mutual willingness to listen and talk back, can we ever hope to communicate and act together on a problem? But in bureaucracy such two-directionality of speech is forbidden for the simple reason that whatever the problem with which we approach a bureaucracy, the solution has already been predesigned for us.

The "language" through which bureaucracy speaks to us is not designed for problem solving; it is designed for passing on solutions in as precise and efficient a manner as possible. As such it is a language of functionality: in content as well as in form, bureaucratic language consists of fragments of information. These fragments each describe actions that the client must carry out if he or she is to become a part of the system of administration which the bureaucracy represents—that is, if he or she is to become "functional." The language bits passed on by functionaries to clients are descriptions of functions the client has to perform, in exactly the same way that the functionary's work sheet or code book is nothing but a listing of functions he or she has to perform.

It is for this reason that clients, much to their surprise and often to their irritation, hear themselves spoken to predominantly in the imperative. At the New York State Motor Vehicle Department:

1. CHECK if you have your Registration, your Insurance Form (F-1), and your Completed Application for Renewal!
2. Go to Line 1. Get your Application Form checked, stamped, and fees calculated.
3. Go to Cashier's Line. Pay fees.

These instructions are designed not only to reinforce the division of clerical labor but also to shorten lines to a physical length the building can handle, to separate evaluation and money-handling functions to ensure honesty—or at least make collusion between evaluator, cashier, and client difficult—and so on.

What is most striking about this language of functionality is that its content and structure coincide: it is a series of imperatives stated in the imperative.

"If . . . then" Language of Computers

The parallel with computer language can hardly be overlooked. A simple program to average a large number of figures might read:

CALL PROGRAM*
PROGRAM: AVERAGE

This section of the program tells the computer in imperative terms what functions it will be asked to perform, in this case averaging. The term "AVERAGE" here is predefined by the computer engineers to describe a number of mechanical functions that the machine will perform when that cue is given. It is predefined and immutable in its meaning in exactly the same way that the terms "Registration," "Insurance Form (F-1)," and "Application" are in the case of the car registration bureaucracy. Misinterpretation of the term "AVERAGE" by the computer user will have exactly the same results as misinterpretation of the term "F-1" by the client: the machine—mechanical/electronic or human—will not work for either of them unless they understand its terms *in* its terms.

The program continues, probably with some further definitions that translate social language into machine language. For engineering and programming reasons, some computer languages limit the use of certain letters to certain functions. Therefore certain social terms have to be translated into computer language, as follows:

CARD = KARD

COUNT = KOUNT

This is likely to be followed by instructions to perform the first function in averaging a number of data; that is, to count the number of data:

KOUNT DATA

Without previous translation—or from another point of view, adaptation—of social language to computer language, this simple instruction could not be "processed" by the machine.

---

* I am here using the now virtually obsolete Fortran IV, which makes the assumptions of all computer language clear.

More instructions would then follow, narrowing or further specifying the functioning of the machine. For example, if the user wants the machine to skip numbers smaller than 1.01, he or she would write into the program:

IF NUMBER .LT. 1.01 GO TO 100

I have purposely introduced this complication into the averaging operation to bring out the importance of a standard form taken by both computer language and bureaucratic language. This is the "if . . . then" form.

In exactly the same way that the computer is instructed to go on to the next item if an item has a number smaller than 1.01, the welfare case evaluator is told by rules and regulations to go on to the next case if a "welfare mother" candidate has fewer than the requisite number of children or more than the requisite maximum number of dollars. In fact, as the rationalization process of the world proceeds, computer thinking is increasingly being imposed on the judgment of bureaucrats through the processes they are obliged to adopt to get their work done.

Thought: An End To Causality, An End To Possibility

Thinking by analogy marks the computer era and computerized bureaucracies. The danger is that analogous thinking ends an era and forecloses another one. The era that computer technology ends is the scientific era. Scientific thinking, and language, was originally causal: the warmth of this rock is caused by the sun. Causal thinking always leads back, to original causes, and ahead, to ultimate consequences: light speeds up the molecules in the rock, thus causing warmth, *and* if we artificially speed up the molecules too much, we will have an explosion. Such causal thinking is now replaced by analogous thinking: high intensity of sunlight correlates with high rock warmth. Falling by the wayside are both the need and the possibility of explaining. The computer era is the end of the scientific era exactly because it makes scientific calculations possible, because of computer speed and scope, that were never possible before. All such calculations now must be conducted within the framework of analogizing computer language. Science has been framed.

The computer mind—whether encased in a machine or machined into handling of a case—also forecloses possibility. This is the greater danger. Foreclosure means that only those parts of reality already framed into the questions are suitable for the computer or the computer-minded; nothing else can find a home in the computer or bureaucratic reality.

Table 4.2

CONDITIONS	RULES 1 2 3 4 5 6 7 8 Else
1. Does the applicant have (a) minor(s) whom he/she is living with <u>UNDER THE AGE OF 18 OR BE-TWEEN 18 AND 21</u> who is/are regularly attending high school, college or undertaking an approved course of vocational or technical training, or is the applicant pregnant? DSS 1994, Section A, E. (See Notes 1, 2 and 3)	Y Y N
2. Is the minor deprived of parental support or care because of parent death and/or continued absence from home of a parent and/or mental or physical incapacity, or pregnancy, or unemployment of father? DSS 1994, Sections F, G, H, I, J, K, L. (See Note 4)	Y N N

ACTIONS	RULES 1 2 3 4 5 6 7 8 Else
1. This is not an ADC case, <u>these tables are not to be used.</u> Explore HR category for possible assistance.	X X
2. This is a possible ADC case. Go To Next Table.	X
3. Ask Supervisor for assistance.	X

Source: Welfare Research, Inc., *Decision Logic Table Handbook* (Prepared for the State of New York, undated), p. DLT 2.

WELFARE CLIENTS AND DECISION LOGIC

Take the use of decision logic in the processing of welfare clients in New York State. In a pilot project in Albany and New York City, a team of management consultants reduced the thousand-page set of New York State welfare regulations to 140 pages of decision-logic charts. Instead of using their own judgment as to how to proceed in client intake from regulation to regulation, intake workers were now guided through the regulations by following the set of charts, each of which told them: If you get results A, B, C, from your interview of the client, then go to appropriate next chart A, B, or C, respectively. For example, Table 4.2 illustrates what might be a decision-logic chart to screen applicants for Aid to Dependent Children.

The intake worker simply looks at the two questions provided, registers the answers (three possibilities are open: Yes, Yes; Yes, No; and

No, Yes), and then checks under the "Rules" heading what the next step is.

Using charts such as this one, the offices increased the accuracy rate for processing welfare clients by more than 40 percent—from 51.5 percent to 94.6 percent.

If citizens believe that what happens in the world—including its future and its alternate possibilities—can be captured in a few questions, then they would be well advised to take to computer logic processes such as decision-logic tables that enhance bureaucrats' accountability and responsibility. However, if the world is still an open thing—to be continuously constructed from the inside out by those dwelling in it, then the use of such closed systems as these is inappropriate.

Why Computers—and Bureaucrats—Don't Think

The most immediate danger in the increased use of computers in the public service, as elsewhere, is that we begin to assume that computers think. But the fact is: computers are logic processors; they are not able to think themselves into situations. So it is exactly in those circumstances in which human beings have always had the most difficulty—in the making of judgments (Does *this* act fit into *this* situation?)—that computers let us down.

A patient waits for a diagnosis in the emergency room of a hospital. Excruciating pain indicates a kidney stone, but the intern reads off a long list of possible diseases including an East African one. An East African one? This is Brooklyn, New York. East Africa? After the pain subsides, the patient walks out. He passes a computer. He looks at the printout. It is printing out lists of diagnoses. Aha! That's where the East African disease came from. The intern simply had failed to use good judgment, judgment that fitted the situation, and had unnecessarily troubled a patient with a low probability diagnosis that was *implausible* under the circumstances.[26]

Computers don't think exactly because they are unaware of the situations to which their logic applies. People who follow computers in their thinking don't think for the same reason: they believe reality is in the computer display or printout, not on the spot. To the extent that bureaucrats follow the grammar of institutional rules that demand action without thinking ourselves *into* the situation of clients, bureaucrats don't think.

Why People Who Imitate Computers Don't Think

If we follow the way computers operate in our own thinking, it is likely that we will stop thinking altogether. How can such an assertion be demonstrated?

The logic structure of the computer—its imperative to pair terms—is the beginning of the end of thinking for those who follow this practice. For example,[27] the computer can, once people make the initial judgment and set standards, distinguish between writing that is "poetic" and writing that is "nonpoetic"; it can in fact judge a literary contest. However, there is no way of instructing the computer to recognize the "unpoetic," an expression that is not yet poetic but that has poetic possibilities locked within it. Such an expression would have to be categorized by the computer in the same category as "nonpoetic." In short the computer does not recognize possibility or potential.

A totally different type of thinking, however, prevails in entrepreneurial efforts and even some established large corporations. When conditions are recognized that fall short of sales goals and production standards, the entrepreneur or the corporate officer cannot be satisfied with a success/failure judgment. A consultant is called in exactly to get those in the organization out of established modes of thinking. The first thing the consultant does is to sit down with the client in order to mutually define the problem. The aim is not to show that failure has occurred, which is already known, but *to bring out of the situation* those potential ideas or acts that can free managers and employees from their circumstances in order to succeed.

But this entrepreneurial or consultative thinking implies that there is something already in the situation that thinking can *bring out*. Widespread success with this kind of approach seems to prove that human situations are not end games in which there is an ultimate stopping point where a definite determination of "success" or "failure" can be pronounced.

Thinking

Martin Heidegger, one of the critics most concerned with developing a way of thinking our way out of modernity without returning to times past, has warned that the technological revolution could so captivate, bewitch, dazzle, and beguile people that calculative thinking might someday come to be accepted and practiced *as the only* way of thinking.

If calculative thinking imprisons us within the logic of things as they are—and no logic can ever provide an escape from itself—then what is the role of any alternative mode of thinking? Obviously it is to get us out of the logic that imprisons us, as exemplified in the logic systems embedded in institutions.

How does thinking get us out of the reality that is? Thinking can disclose hidden opportunities for escape. But if such opportunities are hidden in our bureaucratic and technological actuality, then that also means that they are stored away in that actuality. Hidden opportunities are waiting to be discovered.

One place in bureaucratic and technological reality where a basis for thinking other than the calculative mode has recently enjoyed a resurgence has been in industrial production management. Hit by Japanese competition combining premodern and modern ways of thinking and managing, American industry has recently rediscovered the value of bottom-up knowledge. Bottom-up knowledge comes from the particular, often unique, hands-on experience of workers dealing with particular physical objects: for example, the worker fitting a fender to a car. The physical fit of parts assembled into a product can be calculated up to a point, but in final assembly points the actual fitting ultimately must be designed not according to the universal rules of quantitative scientific design or scientific management, but "by the feel of things" in the workplace.

Another place for an alternative to calculative thinking has already been mentioned. One of the most widespread consulting practices is that of Organization Development (OD). Here outsiders—a third force—are brought into on-the-job relationships. Their aim is to free up job relations bogged down in their own logic. Through group sessions, OD attempts to reestablish enough of what used to be called social relations to free individuals for working out problems together. Admittedly these groups are usually run without getting rid of bureaucratic structure, specifically the division of labor. The fact that outsiders are needed to bring about original thinking reflects how serious is the frozen state of mere calculative thinking in most organizations.

SUMMARY

We can reiterate the key distinctions between bureaucratic language and social language and between bureaucratic thinking and human thinking. These distinctions explain much of the language relations and thinking barriers between bureaucracy and society that have hitherto been left incomprehensible or explained only in a fragmentary fashion. The language distinctions are as follows:

Social Language	Bureaucratic Language
1. causal	1. analogous (acausal)
2. two-directional	2. one-directional

The analogous, or acausal, nature of bureaucratic language is mainly responsible for bureaucracy's resistance to penetration by outsiders. A language that lacks causal paths and consists merely of lists of conditions against which reality must be tested by the user (i.e., the functionary) is not a language that lends itself to the question "why?"

Second, a language that does not allow mutual definition and redefinition by speaker and hearer is admirably designed to maintain a one-way power relationship from the top down, especially in situations in which people are dependent on bureaucracy for their survival. The client's only choice is to learn the language of the agency from which he or she seeks service and accept the kind of help that is codified into its vocabulary, whether it fits a need exactly or not. Functionaries bow the more easily to the absurdities and inhumanities of such language for the simple reason that bureaucratic language is so designed as to separate surgically the speaker from involvement with, and often understanding of, what he or she must say.

Finally, a seemingly terminal problem arises with thinking. It is no longer certain that any of us think as long as we follow pure rational rules. Especially those of us involved in computerized bureaucracy, and all preprogrammed bureaucracy in general, tend to do the kind of thinking that gets us out of touch with reality.

For this thinking that loses reality there are two reasons:

1. In attempting to imitate life, programmed thinking is able to reflect only one quality emanating from reality at a time. As in science, this quality can either be affirmed or negated. In real life, however, the negation of a quality does not exhaust its alternatives. We can still dig for the possibilities inherent in it. For example, a welfare program designed to negate poverty does not necessarily achieve the social goal of citizens who want the poor restored to full participation in the economy as productive fellow citizens.
2. Programmed thinking as an imitation of life requires categorical statements, the perfect expression of which is numbers. Numbers, however, are *quanta* (measurements), which can describe the extent of a quality in real life but which cannot, by their nature, express the quality itself. The hardness or softness of an object, the dependence or independence of a client, are not themselves present in a preprogrammed formula for providing service; what is present consists only of *measures* of softness or hardness, independence or dependence.*

In sum, bureaucracy endangers both language and thought.

WHAT PEOPLE CAN DO:

Nurturing Straight Talk in Modern Organizations
Sandra Fish[†]

People encountering bureaucracy ask, "How can a person be really human at work? Can I talk in a human way? Isn't it too great a risk?" The questions reveal an implicit understanding of the personal threat that bureaucracy poses, primarily separation from other people.

* See also the discussion in Chapter 2, on the charring of O rings in the section on the space shuttle disaster of January 1986.
† Professor Sandra Fish is chairperson of the Corporate/Organizational Media Department, School of Communications, Ithaca College. She is also a consultant with Training for Change, Inc., Ithaca, N.Y.

The hierarchical structure of bureaucracy fosters an attitude of monologue, an orientation to communication that is manipulative, coercive, exploitative, defensive, and untrusting.[1] In contrast is an attitude of dialogue that, unlike monologue, is an orientation to communication characterized as genuine, supportive, empathic, and cooperative.[2] The purpose of this essay is to demonstrate how the communication process of listening promotes dialogue and counteracts the dehumanizing effects of bureaucracy.

LISTENING

Listening can be defined as actively attending to the verbal and nonverbal messages of another person with the intention of understanding what the person *means* and simultaneously communicating an appropriate response. Genuine listening goes far beyond merely receiving the verbal transmission of another. First, words themselves require deciphering. Of less interest is the objective meaning of what someone says, and of greater interest is what he or she *means* by the words chosen. Second, genuine listening includes attending to nonverbal messages that accompany the words and that affect our interpretation of their meaning. *People* mean, and our goal as listener is less to analyze and more to synthesize what their meaning really is.

Probably the single most significant feature of listening is empathy, which consists of imagining how we would feel if we were in the other's place, requiring a shift of perspective, a genuine attempt to see the world from the view of the other.[3] Shifting perspective reduces the distance created by one-directional communication and, in fact, increases efficiency because it allows us to understand a problem or concern from the view of the person experiencing it.

Effective listening requires that we *stop* what we are doing, temporarily set aside our own thoughts and feelings, and devote attention to another person. Such an act of care for the other may produce surprise or incredulity; but if the listener is genuine, the other person experiences a "letting go," a reduction of defenses or anxiety, and consequently feels gratitude.

Not only does listening require energy focused on the other's message, but it also requires communicating a response. At the very least, our response tells the speaker that we are present and attending to the message. Further, by responding, we offer our own perspective, share ourselves, and give the other person an opportunity to respond to us. The process of communication is not complete without reciprocity which, of course, makes us vulnerable—which may explain our reluctance to listen. Reducing acausality—the detachment of meaning from persons—requires the reattachment of meaning to individuals. Thus, the apparently

simple act of genuine listening becomes a radical tool to subvert bureaucratic impersonality.

How can we increase listening effectiveness? Two techniques can be
useful: paraphrasing content and reflecting feeling.[4] The manager who
restates and confirms what a subordinate says and accurately reflects the
feelings expressed not only is likely to win the trust and support of the
subordinate but also gains access to information that can be helpful in
problem-solving. For example, if an employee says in response to a new
deadline, "Gee, I'm not sure I can do that,"[5] a typical bureaucratic
response is, "Sure you can." However, if the manager asks, "What
concerns you about the deadline?", he or she has acknowledged the
employee's hesitation and has asked for information which could forestall
a delayed report. While reassurance may ultimately be an appropriate
response, the manager cannot know that without the intervening act of
listening.

A situation which puts our listening skills to the test is receiving
criticism. No one likes to be criticized and the usual response is to defend
ourselves or turn a deaf ear. There are again, however, two techniques
which can help us *listen* effectively to criticism. If, for example, my
employer tells me that my budget presentation was inadequate and
ill-prepared, I need to stop my usual pattern of protection and, *first*,
gather data: That is, *ask* for more information. Rather than an exercise in
masochism, this technique allows me simultaneously to obtain necessary
facts and perceptions and also to have time to slow my defenses. After
listening carefully to the additional information, the *second* technique is to
agree with the critic where possible.[6] For example, I might be able to say
honestly, "I can see how you must have felt," or "I can see how it must
have seemed to you." It is worth noting that good listening cannot be
faked; anything less than a genuine response is likely to be met with
increased defensiveness. Often even managers need training in effective
listening.

COMMUNICATING FOR ACHIEVEMENT

The seemingly simple act of listening by a person in a position of
authority can create a climate that supports the *human* function of the
organization in which people are encouraged to develop their potential
and reach satisfactory levels of achievement.[7] Managers often wonder
what motivates people to achieve and how they can improve communication in the existing hierarchical structure. One straightforward method
is to ask people—and to listen to their reply. I recently attempted such a
task with a group of graduate students in my organizational communication class. I asked the group of 12 to recommend changes in organizational policy and improvements in the motivational climate.[8] They were

instructed first to list current policies (in the graduate program, in this case) that had an effect on their motivation, and second to identify specific actions their immediate superiors (the graduate faculty) could take to develop a more supportive climate. Predictably, the answers to the first question were issues of structure or regulation such as stipends, space, and scheduling; and the answers to the second focused on desired communication practices of the faculty such as increased interaction with students and a more thorough orientation to the program. While the concerns expressed were not new, they gave sharper focus and greater urgency to what needed to be done to improve the program. Asking people directly what they need or want, in order to improve their motivation, will frequently elicit a useful response.

Bureaucracy fosters a kind of "quiet violence."[9] By rendering personal relationships subordinate to institutional needs and goals, bureaucracy encourages manipulation of the individual and systematic denial of options. The individual is subject to manipulation most obviously by those in authority who systematically "violate" the individual by failing to listen and respond to the person as a whole human being. Indeed, bureaucracy is arranged precisely to compartmentalize everything—people, tasks, responsibility—in order to gain efficiency and control.

Bureaucracy sends contradictory messages to its managers. Many bureaucratic institutions ostensibly promote a human resources development model which, if actually enacted, would stand in opposition to the underlying assumptions on which bureaucracy rests. Managers are thus faced with a unique opportunity to select an interpretation of guidelines consistent with their own value system. Much has been written about methods of human resource development—such as participative decision-making, training and coaching, developing teamwork, and so on.[10] Ironically, bureaucracy may offer its members a method by which to use the system against itself. People respond positively to being involved and being listened to, and ultimately a system rises or falls on the collective action or nonaction of its members. Human resources development, by synthesizing task, maintenance, and human functions, promotes a balance which legitimizes and rewards behaviors antithetical to bureaucracy.

The immediate goal, however, is survival. Even if unified collective action were directed at the transformation of bureaucracy into a humane workplace, it would be a long time coming. In the interim, practices such as effective listening can retard and resist further encroachment of bureaucratic norms. As Robert Bellah says:

Communication and sympathy cannot fully humanize the world of bureaucratic work, but they can make it more comfortable and cooperative. They can smooth conflict between people and help them through the regulated channels they must negotiate to get the job done while looking out for themselves.[11]

NOTES

1. Max Weber, *Economy and Society: An Outline of Interpretive Sociology*, 3 vols., Guenther Roth and Claus Wittich, eds. E. Fischoff et al., trans. (New York: Bedminster Press, 1968), p. 992.

2. Reported in the *Los Angeles Times*, reprinted as "He Forces Bureaucrats to Hew to the Line," *New York Post*, July 29, 1975, p. 62.

3. *Federal Register* cited in Marjorie Hunter, "In Plain English, Gibberish," *The New York Times*, June 4, 1985, p. A22.

4. "The Bureaucratic Mind at Work," *New Yorker*, Dec. 21, 1981, p. 120.

5. Career counselor Betty Harragan quoted in Mary Bralove, "Taking the Boss at His Word May Turn Out to Be a Big Mistake at a Lot of Companies," *Wall Street Journal*, June 4, 1982, p. 3.

6. James R. Killingsworth, "Idle Talk in Modern Organizations," unpublished paper, p. 21.

7. Based on Paula Gelbard, Robert Greenblatt, Jay Hershenson, Ralph Hummel, and Edward Rogowsky, "The New Governance of New York City: Financiers, Administrators, Politicians, Labor Unions, Neighborhoods, Minorities," paper delivered at the annual meeting of the American Political Science Association, Washington, D.C., September 1979.

8. For the same reason that the police officers behind the composite quotation here must remain anonymous, I am extending the same courtesy to the fire commissioner in question.

9. The representation of Wittgenstein attempted here follows closely the work of Jenny Teichman, "Wittgenstein on Persons and Human Beings," in Royal Institute of Philosophy, *Understanding Wittgenstein* (New York: St. Martin's, 1974), pp. 133–48. The other major source is Ludwig Wittgenstein, *Philosophical Investigations* (Oxford, England: Basil Blackwell, 1953).

10. Wittgenstein, *Philosophical Investigations*, Part I, paragraph 241.

11. Godfrey Vesey, Foreword to *Understanding Wittgenstein*, p. ix.

12. Wittgenstein, *Philosophical Investigations*, Part I, paragraph 207. In this case judgment as to what a head is when I see it on someone else's shoulders. Such judgments can, according to Wittgenstein, only be based on shared concepts. And shared concepts, according to him, can emerge only out of a shared human nature and the behaviors that nature leads people to share. See also R. M. White: "The fact that human beings do in general react in the same way . . . is a contingent anthropological fact, but one without which language could never get off the ground . . ." (White, "Can Whether One Proposition Makes Sense Depend on the Truth of Another? [*Tractatus* 2.0211-2]," in *Understanding Wittgenstein*, p. 26.)

13. Vesey, p. x.

14. Teichman, *Wittgenstein on Persons*, p. 145.

15. See, for example, Herbert Simon's widely read article "Decision-Making and Organizational Design: Man-Machine Systems for Decision-Making," in D. S. Pugh, ed., *Organization Theory: Selected Readings* (Baltimore: Penguin, 1971), pp. 189–212.

16. Vesey, p. x.

17. Simon, especially p. 194.

18. Ilham Dilman, "Wittgenstein on the Soul," in Royal Institute, *Understanding Wittgenstein*, p. 165.

19. Ibid., p. 166. Dilham's italics.

20. Wittgenstein, *Remarks on the Foundations of Mathematics* (Oxford, England: Basil Blackwell, 1956), Part IV, Section 3.

21. Dilman, pp. 166–67. Human beings who behave like machines have been analyzed in modern psychology as early as Freud. Machinelike functionaries are no strangers to anyone who has visited a bureaucracy.

22. C. P. Snow, *Corridors of Power* (New York: Scribners, 1964), p. 371.

23. John R. Searle, *Speech Acts: An Essay in the Philosophy of Language* (London: Cambridge University Press, 1969), p. 47.

24. Ibid., p. 197.

25. Ibid., p. 198.

26. Personal experience of the author.

27. This example is based on the historical dispute in logic on whether it is adequate to be content with the simple negation of a term ("A") or whether something that is "not A" should be defined in terms of privation—the lack of something that would make it "A" and that would imply even and especially by its absence that "not A" has the potential of becoming "A." Both the example and the reference to the history of logic are from Martin Heidegger, "Das Wohnen des Menschens" (The Dwelling of Man), in Heidegger, *Denkerfahrungen* [Thinking Experiences], (Frankfurt am Main: Vittorio Klosterman, 1983), pp. 153–160.

Sandra Fish: Nurturing Straight Talk in Modern Organizations

1. Richard L. Johannesen, "The Emerging Concept of Communication as Dialogue," *The Quarterly Journal of Speech*, 57 (1971), pp. 376–77.

2. Ibid, pp. 374–76.

3. Jack R. Gibb, "Defensive Communication," in John Stewart, ed., *Bridges, Not Walls*, 3rd ed. (Reading, Mass.: Addison-Wesley, 1982), p. 239.

4. Robert Bolton, *People Skills* (Englewood Cliffs, N.J.: Prentice Hall, 1979).

5. See *Session Builders, Series 100, No. 145*, Harrisburg, Pa. Training Resource Associates, 1982.

6. Ronald B. Adler, *Confidence in Communication: A Guide to Assertive and Social Skills* (New York: Holt, Rinehart and Winston, 1977).

7. W. Charles Redding, *The Corporate Manager's Guide to Better Communication* (Glenview, Ill.: Scott, Foresman, 1984), pp. 54–56.

8. See *Session Builders*, cited fn. 5, no. 158.

9. Newton Garver, "What Violence Is," in A. K. Bierman and James A. Gould, eds., *Philosophy for a New Generation*, 2nd ed. (New York: Macmillan, 1973), pp. 260–65.

10. See Paul W. Cummings, *Open Management: Guides to Successful Practice* (New York: AMACOM, 1980): Jack R. Gibb, *A New View of Personal and Organizational Development* (Los Angeles: The Guild of Tutors Press, 1978); William Howell, *The Empathic Communicator* (Belmont, Calif.: Wadsworth, 1982); and Sandra E. O'Connell, *The Manager as Communicator* (New York: Harper and Row, 1979).

11. Robert N. Bellah et al., *Habits of the Heart* (Berkeley: University of California Press, 1985), p. 125.

5

Bureaucracy
as
Polity

In a modern state the actual ruler is necessarily and unavoidably the bureaucracy. . . .

—Max Weber[1]

In a world of bureaucracy, administration replaces politics. As citizens accept bureaucratic values, they begin to judge the performance of politicians according to bureaucratic standards. Bureaucracies move into this field of opportunity. They begin successfully competing with political institutions. These now must measure up to rationalized standards in the shaping of issues and the making of policy. Inside bureaucracy itself, subordinates are told that politics has no place there; and everywhere they are discouraged from taking politics into the workplace. Yet they find politics whenever and wherever their managers make decisions. Politics seems to continue to exist within bureaucracy—except now citizens and the ordinary rank-and-file bureaucrat feel excluded from it. Bureaucratization conceals and denies the political experience.

At the same time, especially private bureaucracies are beginning to recognize the fact that their participation in a bureaucratic politics alone cannot solve problems of survival. Such problems emanate from those sources of "irrationality" that continue to exist in the increasingly rationalized world. Unrationalized international money markets and free trade cause troubles for American industry, accidentally giving a head start to the Japanese competition. Unrationalized citizens increasingly make new political demands on a system in which the bureaucrats thought they had figured out all the problems and were controlling all the answers. Here technology—rationalized science—seems to play a role:

leading humanity into situations—such as the artificial prolongation of life or its artificial termination—for which there has been no previous human experience. As the fundamental questions of human life—What is it all about? What is the good life?—keep being reasserted, bureaucracies themselves initiate a third form of politics, neither traditionally political nor purely bureaucratic. (See section below, "Post-Bureaucratic Politics.") How can we make sense of these developments in the confrontation between politics and the bureaucratic experience?

In this chapter, we address this question in three ways:

1. We describe the bureaucratization of the wider political arena.
2. We describe the birth of a truncated bureaucratic politics within bureaucracy, a living paradox arising out of bureaucracy's own rationalizing tendencies.
3. After consulting two experts, Jürgen Habermas and Martin Heidegger, we try to describe the subtle and yet vague third-force political experience that crystallizes out of a reaction against both traditional interest politics and bureaucratic politics.

HOW PEOPLE POLITICK

The Bureaucratization of Politics

How do people experience the bureaucratization of politics?

TWO PRESIDENTS

Even top politicians, the leaders of America, seem to notice that before they can get to an issue bureaucracy has already been there.

> John F. Kennedy:

Sooner or later it seems that every problem mankind is faced with gets dumped into the lap of the president right here in the center of it all. But by the time it reaches here, the problem has been dissected, sanitized, and cast into a series of options—almost as though they were engraved in stone. What is missing is the heart behind them, what they mean in human terms.[2]

President John F. Kennedy's complaints—that problems have been "dissected, sanitized, and cast into a series of options" long before reaching the White House—do not stand alone. If agencies and staff purportedly under the command of the chief executive are capable of pre-decision-making because of their superior knowledge and information about problems, they are also entirely capable of independent decision-making and of entering the political arena to get their own way. Listen to what another president, Franklin D. Roosevelt, is reported to have said in conversation with one of his top administrators:

When I woke up this morning, the first thing I saw was a headline in *The New York Times* to the effect that our Navy was going to spend two billion dollars on a

shipbuilding program. Here I am, the Commander in Chief of the Navy, having to read about that for the first time in the press. Do you know what I said to that? No, Mr. President.
I said, "Jesus *Chr*-rist!"[3]

Roosevelt is reported to have continued:

The Treasury . . . is so large and far-flung and ingrained in its practices that I find it is almost impossible to get the action and results I want—even with Henry [Morgenthau] there. But the Treasury is not to be compared with the State Department. You should go through the experience of trying to get any changes in the thinking, policy, and action of the career diplomats and then you'd know what a real problem was. But the Treasury and the State Department put together are nothing as compared with the Na-a-vy.[4]

Thus a president of fifty years ago experienced in a very practical sense the error of Woodrow Wilson's statements of 1887:

Administration lies outside the proper sphere of politics. Administrative questions are not political questions. Although politics sets the task for administration, it should not be suffered to manipulate its offices. The field of administration is a field of business. It is removed from the hurry and strife of politics.[5]

Literary reports from practitioners—see, as a classic, C. P. Snow's *Corridors of Power*—established long ago that the permanent bureaucracy channels the currents that temporary political masters buck at their peril. Only recently has the dominance of bureaucracy over politics been recognized by American academic specialists. The bureaucratic experience of presidents is not unique. This is verified in a recent comparative study of bureaucracies here and elsewhere by B. Guy Peters. According to Peters, not only are agencies marked by "the ability of the permanent staff essentially to determine the agenda for their presumed political masters," but also:

Through the ability to control information, proposals for policy, and the knowledge concerning feasibility, the bureaucracy is certainly capable of influencing agency policy, if not determining it. It requires an unusual politician to be able to overcome this type of control within an agency.[6]

More sweepingly, Peter Woll comments in his study of the political role of bureaucracy in America:

The bureaucracy continues to run the government and often formulates its major policies, while the President and Congress play out the power game between them, and the courts stay in the background.[7]

While recent presidents (Jimmy Carter and Ronald Reagan) have attacked bureaucracy, through reorganization and budget cuts, their control seems not to have improved much. Whether from the liberal or the conservative perspective, there is every reason to believe that fiascoes such as Kennedy's Bay of Pigs decision and similar problems during the

Iranian hostage crisis can be laid at the foot of the lopsided relations of power and influence between bureaucracy and the purported decision makers in the political realm.

In analyzing the disastrous invasion of Cuba at the Bay of Pigs, Arthur Schlesinger, Jr., a Kennedy adviser, pointed his finger at bureaucracy. As political scientist James David Barber reports, "The Bay of Pigs muckup, he [Schlesinger] suggested, had stemmed in large part from 'excessive concentration' on military and operational problems and wholly inadequate consideration of political issues."[8] If by this Schlesinger meant an overemphasis on means and a neglect of considering ends and overall purpose, we are on familiar ground. It is the typical problem that arises in any attempt to solve human problems when bureaucracy gets involved.

At one point during the Iranian hostage crisis, President Carter found that, to deal with "the apparent reluctance in the State Department to carry out my directives fully and with enthusiasm," he had to ask the Iranian desk officers and a few others to come to the White House:

I laid down the law to them as strongly as I knew how. I pointed out how difficult the Iranian question had become, and described my procedure for making decisions. [Ambassador to Iran William] Sullivan had not been the only one who had caused trouble. . . . I told them that if they could not support what I decided, their only alternative was to resign—and that if there was another outbreak of misinformation, distortions, or self-serving news leaks, I would direct the Secretary of State to discharge the officials responsible for that particular desk, even if some innocent people might be punished.[9]

While some might consider such an event a temporary breakdown in command control, there is every historical reason to believe that bureaucracies in America—especially the State Department—behave in political ways repeatedly and permanently. They base themselves on their own constituencies providing a power base separate from their political masters.

When there is an intellectually weak president, such as Ronald Reagan, the country can expect muffled wars between departments competing in a policy area, such as the State Department and the Defense Department. Such wars can usually be understood as contests over turf and power—each department head following the imperative of maximizing survival for his agency through constantly expanding its imperium—and the public be damned.[10]

The experience of chief politicians seems to be that they feel surrounded by bureaucracy.

1. Presidents seem to sense that bureaucracy gets to problems before they do, *pre-deciding* decisions by *defining* the problem.
2. Presidents seem to feel that bureaucracy unduly *controls solutions*, manipulat-

ing them according to its own interests, which may not be the President's intent or the public interest.

LEGISLATORS

Lawmakers sense a loss of integrity of the legitimate lawmaking bodies of the country, the legislatures, in the face of the private and public institutions the lawmakers are intended to control.

A speaker of the U.S. House of Representatives, Thomas (Tip) O'Neill (D-Mass.):

The House has always been a difficult body to lead; I do not believe, though, that even Henry Clay, despite the many problems he had with John Randolph of Roanoke who brought his hunting dogs on the floor of the House, ever had to deal with as many independent members as are found in the modern House of Representatives. The result has been a breakdown of party discipline and a refusal to follow party leadership, which leads in turn to congressional paralysis and an inability to act coherently as a legislative body.[11]

While the perception of a threat to the integrity of Congress is clear, the reference to members' growing "independence" needs explanation. This is forthcoming from another Congressman, Rep. Barber Conable (R-N.Y.), who put the apparent independence of Congressmen into context:

I'm scared. I'm scared. [So said Conable, the House expert on tax reform who later decided not to run again.] These new PACs [political action committees] not only buy incumbents, but affect legislation. It's the same crummy business as judges putting the arm on lawyers who appear before them to finance their next campaign.

Conable was referring to growing control by modern institutions in the private sphere, especially corporations, over individual members of Congress through the use of political action committees (PACs).

Personal experiences are supported by measurement of their distribution. According to measurements of the percentage change in Congressional campaign contributions between 1974 and 1982, Congressmen's experience of the growing impact of PACs was backed by an actual 235 percent increase of PAC contributions compared with a 47 percent increase in contributions from individuals and candidates and a 176 percent increase from political parties. Senators were impacted by a 220 percent increase in PAC contributions versus a 68 percent *decrease* in party contributions and a 109 percent increase in contributions from individuals and candidates themselves.[13]

PRESIDENTIAL AIDES

So deeply accepted is the influence of private organizations on lawmaking that White House aides speak easily of teaming up with it. A White

House Aide, 1982, speaking of coordinating spending by PACs and the Republican Party's national committee for twenty vulnerable Republicans:

If we can't buy half these races, we don't know our business.[14]

A former White House aide, in 1973, speaking of his experience under President Richard M. Nixon:

We don't have a democracy of the people now. We have a special-interest democracy. We have the auto lobby, the oil lobby. The individual has no way of appealing to the government.

The true democracy is where the individual is able to affect his own situation. That is not true in this country anymore. The big lobbies can do it, but the individual can't.[15]

So much for the influence of private bureaucracies. What about public ones?

POLITICAL SCIENTISTS

How do private organizations like corporations, public organizations like government bureaucracies, and politics fit together?

Economist and political scientist Charles Lindblom:

The large private organization fits oddly into democratic theory and vision. Indeed, it does not fit.[16]

Yet somehow private organizations and politics are made to fit. How?

Political scientist Theodore J. Lowi explains that lawmaking is achieved through what he calls a "triangular trade in politics" among private groups, public bureaucracies, and congressional committees. But to make political deals, each participant has to have a power base. It is easy to see where the power base of private groups, especially corporations, is: in money. But only Congress can make laws; it divides up this legitimate authority among its committees. The money groups can do nothing politically legitimate without the authoritative lawmakers; the lawmakers will not get reelected without support from the money groups. Each needs the other. Where does bureaucracy come in?

Political scientist Peter Woll suggests two reasons for bureaucratic power: First, Congress has delegated authority to government bureaucracies. It is hard to take this power back. Second, those who run congressional committees, where the deals are made, have a harder time lining up constituencies for each of the many policy problems that pass through the committees. In contrast, each specific bureaucracy already has a supporting group or several lined up to back its demands. That is how the iron triangle comes together. Woll:

Administrative policies often have virtually automatic political support which will in turn have significant impact upon Congress, for the groups that support the bureaucracy are more frequently than not very powerful economically and politically.[17]

We may conclude that modern organizations—bureaucracies, both public and private—are the leading forces in contemporary politics because:

1. Bureaucracies with their centralized command structure are *structurally superior* to fragmented political institutions and the entities that make a democracy: individuals. Democratic institutions are simply more *dis*organized, and cannot get their act together; so are lone individuals.
2. Bureaucracies have their *own competitive cultural base* in citizens' belief in modern values. Rationalism, efficiency, and formal equality are seen as producing a life of seeming stability, a refuge against the life of politics with its emotionally upsetting human passions and basic "irrationalism." Given the choice, citizens will often, in their attitudes and behavior, prefer stability to politics.

The result is that we often accept bureaucratic criticisms of politics such as the following.

BUREAUCRATS

Playing on modern human beings' search for stability and security, bureaucrats tend to attack politics.
A federal bureaucrat:

We draw up good legislation in the national interest with all the parts fitting into the whole properly, and what happens to it when it hits the [Capitol] Hill is like a Christian among the heathen. . . . So we spend lots of time figuring out how we can do something we want to do and think we should do, without taking a new piece of legislation over to Congress. . . .[18]

Apart from the use of engineering models in which all the parts neatly fit the whole, bureaucrats also tend to treat political issues as technical issues: matters for scientific research that will uncover the "facts" just waiting out there to be discovered.
Another federal bureaucrat:

The bureaucrat has a program to carry out that he believes in. The question of whether or not Congress has authorized it is not so important to him. He figures that if Congress really had the facts and knew what was right, it would agree with him.

There is a tendency among bureaucrats to denigrate the official political process. Yet in it politicians get a sense for the needs and wants of their constituents by discussing such often barely formed needs and wants in public and shaping them into a problem. Used to dealing with the administration of preformed policies and programs, bureaucrats themselves become easy victims to those who are aware that the party who defines a problem also wins the power to shape the range and the quality of solutions. At other times, bureaucrats believe they can play this political game of shaping problems without reference to the public at all—a kind of nonpublic or apolitical politics.

Lawmakers themselves are seduced into accepting the bureaucratic approach viewing politics as technical issues to be decided according to technical (problem-solving) rather than political (problem-shaping) standards. For example, one political scientist studying the increased use of staff and reliance on experts by members of Congress observed:

Overburdened and somewhat intimidated by the material the "experts" throw at them, they [Congressmen] are delighted when issues can be resolved in apparently noncontroversial, technocratic terms.[19]

In trying to compete with the organizational superiority of public and private bureaucracies, some state legislatures have tried to rationalize their politics by bringing in the foremost tool of bureaucratic rationality: the computer. However, early studies have shown that an increase in legislative technology simply centralizes the power of decision-making at the top and center. Legislative leaders or the governors gain. But there is no evidence of any improvement in the *political* process of shaping reality-based problems founded on a sensitivity to the experiences of citizens.

As one political scientist, and former staff member of the Massachusetts legislature, observed:

A legislature can be entirely functional without being either efficient or productive.[20]

Finally we get to citizens' experience of bureaucratized politics. Not surprisingly their experience is as split as the two sets of values on which they operate: political values and bureaucratic ones.

CITIZENS

Citizens at large agreed by a majority of 65 percent with the statement offered by a congressional survey in 1973 that "The trouble with government is that elected officials have lost control over the bureaucrats, who really run the country." Agreement among elected officials registered at 57 percent.[21]

When the question was put slightly differently, 73 percent of citizens and 80 percent of elected officials agreed with the statement that "Federal Government has become too bureaucratic."[22]

At the same time, citizens were carried along in a continuing decline of participation in official politics. In contrast to the era of the *political* "machine"—in which voter participation in presidential elections, for whatever reasons, reached nearly 80 percent (1880–1896)—in the era of the *bureaucratic* machine such participation has hovered barely over the 50 percent mark (1952–1984).[23]

The correlation between the rise of perceptions of domination by bureaucratic power and the decrease in participation in official politics can hardly be overlooked. Learning how to work the bureaucracies pays; politics doesn't.

In summary, just about everyone—presidents, aides, legislators, political scientists, and citizens—faces up to the growing experience that:

1. Bureaucracies are increasingly *politically active*.
2. Bureaucracies are more than simple conduits for the flow of authority originating in the political sphere and serving to implement legal policies and programs; they *generate their own power*.

Something paradoxical, unintended, and dangerous happens when bureaucracies use this self-generated power politically: the tool of politics tends to become the master of politics in the polity at large. Internal politization ultimately would seem to threaten to undermine even bureaucracy's own power base if bureaucrats lose faith in their bureaucratic values and adopt political ones. We next turn to this second danger and what it means to the institution and society at large.

The Politization of Bureaucracy

One of the worst-kept secrets is the politization of bureaucracy internally. Unlike constituency-based political power, the control power of bureaucracy is entirely self-generated. This means that, unlike political power, control power does not arise from the consent of external constituencies allowing themselves to be led, but from internal structures of the organization. When Max Weber concluded from his comparative study of traditional and modern organizations that modern bureaucracy is a control instrument without compare, he pointed to specific sources of power within: hierarchy and division of labor.

Divided Labor as a Source of Control

Assume you go to work for a modern organization. You are given a job description and you are assigned to a desk or a production line position. Next to you are other employees with their own duty assignment. You don't do what the person next to you does, and he or she doesn't do what you do. This is division of labor or rule of jurisdiction. The overall work is a task broken down into individual tasks. But these somehow must be reassembled. The problem arises of how your work and everyone else's work is to be fitted together. In premodern organizations, you would simply turn to your neighbor and talk about it. In "working things out," you would not only share your knowledge and product but the two of you would, by working together, "gain the power" to get something accomplished. This is exactly what bureaucracy, by dividing labor, seeks to avoid. Control *over* any individual's task performance can only be exercised to the extent that that individual's tasks are radically distinguishable from the neighboring individual's. In short, organizational designers and managers can be in control over the exact task to be performed by defining it as purely as it can be defined and then manipulating the conditions that affect accomplishment of that individual task. Frederick Taylor, the father of scientific management, experimented with varying the length of shovel handles of coal shovelers; the experiment would have been disrupted if, unbeknownst to him, several shovelers had collaborated and helped each other shovel the coal.

In short, division of labor makes possible the *technical* definition of work, its *technical* (that is, scientific/experimental) manipulation to find ways of accomplishing it that take less input and produce more output, and therefore its *technical* control from above. The result is hierarchy. Hierarchy responds to the need of subordinates at one level to turn to someone immediately above them who has an overview (supervision) over their divided work. Supervisors must be able to oversee a large enough segment of the work process to be able to judge whether a change in the efficiency of one worker's work actually leads to a fitting of that worker's work into another worker's work.

HIERARCHY AS A SOURCE OF POWER

Hierarchy in the *technical* sense originates from *the* one great, single invention of the modern organization of work: the rationalized division of labor. Once tasks are scientifically divided, two kinds of knowledge are possessed only by management:

1. Precise knowledge of the *standards* according to which tasks are divided and jobs designed.
2. Precise knowledge of how each divided task *fits* with every other divided task.

It is no longer either the responsibility of workers to work together nor is it possible. The knowledge for working together has been scientifically, almost surgically, removed from them. It has been placed into the next higher level of supervision. The division of labor is therefore the source of *control* power for hierarchy. While the division of labor runs contrary to human instincts (I naturally turn my head to see what the person working next to me is doing), it *is* the basis for modern organization of work. In fact, to the extent that I am not divided from what the coworker next to me is doing to that extent I am also not required, in a technical sense, to lift my head upward with the spoken or unspoken query: "Boss, what do I do now?"

But that turning of the head upward also makes me dependent not only on the superior knowledge of technical task division and coordination possessed by my superior—*it also makes me dependent on that superior in a personal political way.* If that superior chooses to tell me to do things that express his or her personal self-interest rather than the requirements for scientific task design or technical task coordination, *I am no longer in a position to know or judge whether such demands are technical or political.*

The breaking apart of technical working together on a job also means the breaking apart of politically working together. Technically divided labor also surrenders political judgment. At the most basic level—two people working in a situation of divided labor—you and I are no longer able to judge whether what we are told to do by our superiors accords with the self-interest of the two of us—to say nothing of the public interest!

The potential for political misuse of technical control power is unlimited. This may explain why, next to bureaucratic structures and overlaying them (encapsulating their potential political power), we find civil service systems to control the narrowly political, self-serving misuse of technical power for personal political purposes of managers.

We are all acquainted with typical examples of the political misuse of technical control power by managers.* As bureaucrats we are subject not only to the bureaucratic experience but to the political experience within bureaucracy.

POLITICAL MANAGERS

In personality, the politician is an individual who displaces his or her private motives upon public objects. So Harold Lasswell, the late dean of American political science, told us.[24] Often childhood scripts of family passions are acted out again and again in adulthood as Erik H. Erikson has pointed out in regard to Martin Luther and Mohandas Gandhi.[25] On the more narrow stage of bureaucracy, balancing precariously on a platform provided by hierarchy and division of labor and hemmed in by civil service regulations, political managers often act out their psychological predispositions—their traumas, agonies, and pleasures—in more narrow ways. Their office politics gains in pettiness, intensity, and viciousness what it lacks in the broad, creative stroke. Nevertheless, with the bureaucratization of the world, the impact of the office politician can be worldwide and the sword just as cutting. We all recognize the type of political manager. Whether the politicized manager's impact is personal

---

* Technical control aims to get work done; political power in the American mold aims to satisfy individuals' personal interests and passions.

or national or worldwide in scope, the political attack is always experienced with considerable surprise by those who trust in the ideology that bureaucracy is nonpolitical. To the victim the political managers' actions are never trivial. History has shown us:

1. The manager with a dislike for sweaty or moist palms—whose employees are driven to seek medical or psychiatric advice before facing an occasion on which they were expected to shake hands with him.
2. The manager who transfers an employee to Butte, Montana, on discovering the employee has uttered a critical comment.
3. The manager who forbids coffee drinking on the job, checks up on unmarried employees' sex life, and dismisses anyone knowing of illicit relations but failing to report them.
4. The manager who distrusts anyone who hasn't gone to the type of school he has gone to, especially those from higher status schools, and gets others to ghost write academic articles for him.
5. The manager who, coming in on a cold winter's day that is blowing snow, will comment on the nice weather we're having—expecting and getting employees to agree with him.
6. The manager who projects a childhood need to protect the mother into an adulthood obsession to protect the country—and uses his office to engage in national witchhunts that reenact the childhood script against contamination from without.

All of the above were attributed to the late FBI Director J. Edgar Hoover.[26]

Manager-Employee Relationships

Why do bureaucratic employees put up with politicized managers?

A disturbing possibility is raised by the research of public administration theorist and planner Howell Baum about the institutionally created gap in knowledge between superior and subordinate in hierarchy. It is possible that this gap, so essential to generating the technical control power of the superior, also sets the superior up so that political manipulation is expected of her or him. When this manipulation, however, is actually applied to a subordinate, the subordinate goes into a syndrome of shame and doubt about his or her own autonomy. There is a shift from an emphasis on getting work done to pleasing the boss. The Baumian paradox is this: apolitical bureaucracy itself creates superior/subordinate relationships that are technically necessary but which the human beings engaged in them translate into dominance/submission relationships. Bureaucracy creates both itself and its antithesis—politics.

Baum presents what he calls a "puzzling relationship":

The superordinate is significant, as an authority, and yet this person reveals virtually nothing personal about him- or herself. In order to make sense out of this relationship, in the absence of clues from the person in authority, a subordinate is compelled to turn to imagination to fill in personal characteristics of the authority and to define the relationship with the authority. Subordinates are likely to reflect on earlier experiences with authority figures. . . . One is likely to transfer much of the childhood feeling [for such a figure]. Because bureaucratic power is elusively difficult to understand, members find it hard to identify the ways in which the feelings may be inappropriate to the actual bureaucratic [technical] situation and to develop a realistic perception of the authority relationship.[27]

While this explanation of how politics arises in the technical work structure draws on psychoanalysis, it is not itself psychoanalytic. Rather, Baum, in his study of planners, recognizes the *knowledge gap* that division of labor and hierarchy structurally produces on behalf of the control imperative. The Baumian paradox is an explanation of political power in bureaucracy based on a structural epistemology. It is a theory of how knowledge is distributed through structure.

Managers, of course, are quick to pick up on the potential for power presented them by the knowledge gap. Managers may not care whether they are exercising legitimate technical control based on the rational division of labor or illegitimate political power based on a psychological deficit in mutual understanding (also produced by the division of labor and hierarchy). Confronted with the task of control, the individual manager may carelessly seize on any tool that comes to hand. If this tool happens to be based on a subordinate's transfer of feelings onto the superordinate and if manipulating such feelings "works" for the manager, all the better. Now the manager finds he or she has both technical control power and psychological political power. Add to that the fact that the manager may also have his or her psychological needs unsatisfied by a pure rational relationship and you have a recipe of a living hell in which the subordinate is trapped by acceptance of rational bureaucratic rules that produce psychological dependency.

As psychoanalytic organization theorist Michael Diamond has pointed out, this type of situation is an opportunity without parallel for the self-absorbed, narcissistic manager.

SUSTAINING THE KNOWLEDGE GAP

How can employees, especially professionals, live with themselves once they recognize they have surrendered not only professional but personal power to their managers?

The answer is that they don't. Employees develop a broad shield of unconsciousness to protect themselves against having to recognize that their integrity, their work, their professional values are undermined by submission to the political power of their manager.

Objectively, also, two cultures are promoted, and reinforced through disciplinary action, one for managers and a different one for employees. Employees are structurally encouraged to accept the existence of these

Table 5.1

False self	True self
Cannot take personal responsibility	Can take personal responsibility
Lacks intentionality, 'I can't' attitude	Intentionality, 'I can' attitude
Disconnectedness from actions	Connectedness to actions
Maximum defensiveness	Minimum defensiveness
Engages in projections and distortions	Counter-projective remarks
Security oriented	Competence oriented
Compulsion to repeat mistakes	Reflective, learns by experience
Passive and submissive	Collaborative and consensually-vali-
Adaptive to bureaucratic demands	dating
Narrow-minded	Nonadaptive to bureaucratic demands
Closed to criticism	Open-minded
Blind loyalty and conformity	Open to criticism
Dependency-oriented	Questions authority
Responds to external authority	Relatively independent
Form-oriented, stresses formal organi-	Responds to internal authority
zational attributes	Substance-oriented, stresses informal
	and interpersonal attributes

cultures as "normal"—one set of values for their manager, another for themselves.

In the first type of response (the psychological response) knowledge of wanting (professionally) to do one thing but having to (politically) do another is repressed. It is pushed into the unconscious. When this fails, pathologies result.

In the second type of response (the structural/cultural response) knowledge of wanting to do one thing and being forced to do another is externalized. That is, it is explained in terms of an external reality that, though contradictory in demands, must be obeyed.

In personal practice, this may mean that an individual employee simply alternates between two stances toward the world. In a truncated political stance he or she attempts to adjust himself or herself to political demands. In a second, professional stance he or she attempts to act out professional and social reality-oriented obligations. Michael Diamond has distinguished between the roles of a "false self" and a "true self"; clearly the first role is narrowly political and refers to constellations of self-interest; the second is professional and even open to recognition of public interest.[28]

Objectively, modern management systems simply enforce a dual system of discipline. For example, a study of arbitrators' awards in private management showed that, while a general bureaucratic culture was upheld in terms of values expected to be adhered to by both management and labor, arbitrators expected different types of behavior from managers and rank and file.[29]

In general, arbitration awards from 1953 through 1972 tended to reward managers for being just and fair, generous, *dominant*, decisive and firm, intelligent, careful and self-controlled, obedient to rules; trustworthy, reliable, truthful; and friendly and cooperative toward workers. At the same time workers were commended in arbitration awards if they were *at work* and *working well*, *obedient*; trustworthy, reliable and truthful; careful and self-controlled, intelligent; friendly and cooperative with management, and tolerant.*

In short, employees, reminded in disciplinary actions that theirs is to work and the managers' is to command, may simply accept illegitimate dominance/submission relationships as part of legitimate hierarchical separation in the broader context of a rule-bound organization. That is when they choose to face up to the political implications of work in organizations at all. Most of the time, one study found,[30] employees, especially those with claimed professional status, simply prefer to know nothing and admit nothing about the political realities of their organization—at great psychic cost to themselves.

Most important, the dynamic model here pursued—that bureaucracy both creates stability and predictability of behavior (through the division of labor) and opportunities for arbitrary political evaluation (through the personal psychological contract with superordinates that division of labor makes possible)—should get us away from simple assertions that bureaucratic structures either make people happy or unhappy. The model suggests that the rules of bureaucracy are appreciated by workers when they protect *work* autonomy as against the arbitrary evaluation by superiors.[31] Rules and the other characteristics of bureaucracy are likely to be appreciated when, and to the extent that, they are congruent with the worker's hands-on experience of reality (see Chapter 2). However, bureaucratic job definition itself is likely to run up against the worker's experience of what he or she needs to do to get work done. The cutting apart of work into jobs is generally undertaken from the top down and by individuals with scientific, engineering, or management background. In such cases, those designing the division of labor fail to appreciate what the quantitative division of labor according to mathematical principles does to actual work experience.

In summary, two dangers emanate when bureaucracy confronts politics:

1. Bureaucracy creates the illusion that all problems, including political ones, can be translated into administrative and technical ones.
2. Even when bureaucracy becomes sensitive to politics or generates its own politics, it produces a truncated politics that itself rests on bureaucratic assumptions, thereby obscuring the possibility of a full, human politics.

* Here the *differing* categories for proper management and worker behavior are italicized.

Against the first possibility, there are and have been recurrent "political" revolutions in America, including the cultural revolution of the 1960s and the cutback revolution of the 1980s. Can the world be rescued from the bureaucratization of politics? Can it be rescued from the narrowness of office politics? Can a fully human politics emerge out of and against bureaucracy, yet without a loss of the benefits of bureaucracy? The thinking of two experts orients our thinking on these questions.

WHAT THE EXPERTS SAY

Two futures arise out of the confrontation between bureaucracy and politics. One future sees more rationalization, more bureaucratization of politics. This view is represented here by the analysis of sociologist and philospher Jürgen Habermas. The other future is more hopeful and calls our attention to the seeds of a fully human politics inherent even in bureaucracy. This second future is represented here by the thinking of the philosopher Martin Heidegger and by the doings of a number of analysts, consultants, and citizens.

Jürgen Habermas: Technical Power and the Decline of Politics

Jürgen Habermas distinguishes between the nature of power in society and in bureaucracy. These are contrasting life worlds: a world of "symbolic interaction" and "work." In the world of symbolic interaction, we orient all our activities, including our work, toward approval by other human beings. In the world of work, including bureaucracy, we orient all our activities toward work, making human relations secondary. In the first, work is a means; in the second, work becomes an end. How does this transition come about? How does work change power?

In the world of work, violation of a rule, that is, opposition to the exercise of power, has a totally different consequence from such violation in society; it is punished differently. "*Incompetent* behavior," Habermas states, "which violates valid technical rules or strategies, is condemned per se to failure through lack of success. . . . The punishment is built, so to speak, into its rebuff by reality."[32] It is this rule of nature on which the power of managers and technocrats is built. Science has created a world in which human beings manipulate nature (technology) and, in order to do so, manipulate other human beings (bureaucracy). In contrast to the worlds of community and society, what matters in the new world is whether such manipulation *works*, not whether it is approved by others. In such a world, managers have power as long as they succeed in manipulating functionaries.

In short, what is right and wrong in a technically work-oriented world is evident in the success or failure of any given piece of work as technically conceived.

In contrast, what is incompetent behavior in bureaucracy was deviant behavior in society. Not that work done in society did not have its own internal indicators of success or failure, of competence. But there also was a higher standard than competence in a given task. That standard was whether the task itself was considered by society at large as a desirable task, as a means toward an overall end that helped society to survive or achieve whatever cultural goals it might set for itself. In Habermas's words: "*Deviant* behavior, which violates consensual norms, provokes sanctions that are connected with the rules only externally, that is, by convention."[33]

In the world of society, we develop social competence, which resides in our personality. In the modern world of work, bureaucracy, we develop technical competence, skills: "Learned rules of purposive-rational action supply us with *skills*, internalized norms with *personality structures*. Skills put us in a position to solve problems; motivations allow us to follow norms."[34] Habermas offers an explanation not only for the differential perception of the nature of power in bureaucracy and society.

The difference between the world of work and the world of social (symbolic) interaction is explained by Habermas as follows:

By "work" or *purposive-rational action* I understand either instrumental action or rational choice or their conjunction. Instrumental action is governed by *technical rules* based on empirical knowledge. In every case they imply conditional predictions about observable events, physical or social. These predictions can prove correct or incorrect. The conduct of rational choice is governed by *strategies* based on analytic knowledge. They imply deductions from preference rules (value systems) and decision procedures: these propositions are either correctly or incorrectly deduced. Purposive-rational action realizes defined goals under given conditions. But while instrumental action organizes means that are appropriate or inappropriate according to criteria of an effective control of reality, strategic action depends only on the correct evaluation of possible alternative choices, which results from calculation supplemented by values and maxims.[35]

In contrast, the world of society was characterized by communication among people about what they, as a society, wanted to accomplish and what means might properly be used. This kind of interaction Habermas calls "communicative action" or "symbolic interaction" because it is defined by shared symbols commonly arrived at in a social context. This view of society—as a world of communications set in a context of mutually perceived problems leading to a shared meaning of symbols—is entirely compatible with John Searle's concept of social language. It is, of course, totally incompatible with the machine language of modern bureaucracy and computers, which relates not to people's norms but to getting a piece of work done. (See Chapter 4.) Symbolic interaction, Habermas writes,

is governed by binding *consensual norms*, which define reciprocal expectations about behavior and which must be understood and recognized by at least two acting subjects. Social norms are enforced through sanctions. Their meaning is objectified in ordinary language communication.[36]

Society dies when science, technology, and bureaucracy demonstrate the superiority of technical work over social action in achieving the goal with which modern humans are preoccupied—the conquest of matter. But not only society dies; its ways of applying sanctions and its ways of power also die.

The rationality of language games, associated with communicative action, is confronted at the threshold of the modern period with the rationality of means-ends relations, associated with instrumental and strategic action. As soon as this confrontation can arise, the end of traditional society is in sight: the traditional form of legitimation breaks down.[37]

It is at this point that we experience the transmutation of traditional political power into technical power.

As long as people the world over are concerned with the quick and general delivery of the means for purely material survival that science, technology, and bureaucracy promise, we are tempted by the irresistible appeal of power based on control over material work and over people to do the work. This power, organized into vast institutions, is, because it controls both humans and matter as material tools, superior to political power related to organizing people through symbolic interaction toward cultural goals.

Here we find not only a description of the transmutation of power from political into technical and administrative, but an explanation for the death of public politics. When power can be properly exercised only by experts, because these demonstrate their ability to exert control over people and machines, then the claim of the old participants in politics, citizens and politicians, to have a part in controlling such power is rejected. In fact, both the citizen and the politician are disqualified from the new apolitics. They are replaced by functionaries, managers, and professionals. Habermas comments on this:

Old-style politics was forced, merely through its traditional form of legitimation, to define itself in relation to practical goals: the "good life" was interpreted in a context defined by interaction relations.[38]

The new substitute system is one of a "politics"* by experts and

---

* Put into quotation marks here for the same reason that "language" had to be put into quotations in Chapter 4: no one from the old system of politics would recognize technical and administrative decision-making today as politics in the old public sense.

administrators. These now make decisions not only for their proper sphere, technology and bureaucracy, but for all spheres of life.* Their ascendancy over politicians is assured as long as people bow to the superiority of expertise:

The solution of technical problems is not dependent on public discussion. Rather, public discussions could render problematic the framework within which the tasks of government action present themselves as technical ones.[39]

For this reason the new secret decision-making of bureaucratic politics is also forced to enter into an attempt to wipe out the realm of the old-style public politics. Following this bureaucratic takeover, it may be correct, as Habermas says, that "the new politics of state interventionism requires a depolitization of the mass of the population."[40] Further, to the extent that practical questions are eliminated, the public realm also loses its political function."[41] When politics becomes removed from designing means to reach ultimate social goals and instead concerns itself only with short-term maintenance of the internal standards of efficiency, reliability, and control that accompany the advent of bureaucratic decision-making, then it can no longer be called politics.

Thus Habermas presents, through an exposition of the changed meaning of power, an explanation for the replacement of polity by bureaucracy. Bureaucracy contains a different kind of power from that existing in society. This kind of power is incompatible with traditional politics as a way of reaching social goals but is, at least initially, superior to it in promising or reaching material goals. By the time that superiority could appear to lead to doubtful results, the personal investment of bureaucrats, and their inability to evade the psychological power grip exercised over them, makes a rethinking of the preference for bureaucratic over political systems impossible. Therefore bureaucratic power triumphs over political power. Bureaucracy replaces polity.

Martin Heidegger: The Politics of Possibility

Whereas Jürgen Habermas becomes concerned with repairing the breach in human trust that bad language practices cause,[42] the philosopher Martin Heidegger focuses on helping us recover ways of thinking about ourselves that are not shaped by the dominant institutions of modernity: science, technology, or modern organization.

Heidegger's argument is this: Modern man has lost the power to do political thinking. Instead he has developed a warehouse mentality. Successes with science lead us to believe that for every human problem there is a solution. Successes with technology lead us to believe that

---

* This expert control over decisions affecting the public is what Robert A. Isaak and I have previously labeled "apolitics."

eventually all solutions to human problems can be stored up in warehouses. Successes with modern organization lead us to believe that all that is stored in the warehouses of science and technology can be taken off the shelf when needed and can be distributed rationally to citizens acting as clients or consumers.* Tempted to act as a client or a consumer in order to get his share of what is on the shelf, the citizen himself is converted into a resource for the bureaucratic and technological warehouses. A simple example: "The current talk about human resources, about the supply of patients for a clinic, gives evidence of this."[43] Finally, as any manager knows: "Man becomes human material, which is disposed of with a view to proposed goals."[44] Man becomes a function of technology and bureaucracy.

This attitude reduces all problem-solving to decision-making over which solution "already on the shelf" is to be applied in a "given case." For example, in state-of-the-art industrial design today, designers assemble a new electrical motor on visual display terminals from a computerized list of available parts already in warehouses. Similarly, any new problem among bureaucratic clients is administered according to solutions already warehoused in old policies and programs authorized for a bureaucracy. Because of the intrusion of bureaucracy into politics, even new political solutions are designed according to standards already warehoused in the personnel, structures, and culture of the bureaucracy. Original political thinking is lost.

Original political thinking, like any original thinking, comes out of the pain of experience. "Experience, however, is according to its essence the pain in which the essential otherness of what is unveils itself in confrontation with that which we are used to."[45] People also suffer the pain of such experience when, for example, they are asked by technology to get used to the existence of electronic and mechanical devices that will almost infinitely prolong the biological life of a relative above and beyond what people essentially feel is a meaningful human life. The pain does not arise from the creations of technology; all such creations are designed to still any such outcries of pain. The pain arises when, confronted with what we have become used to—technology and rational administration— we suddenly flash back to a remembrance of humanity. All of modern civilization is designed to kill such pain.

Thinking—as the scientific accumulation in warehouses of solutions to all conceivable human problems—and as a process facilitating the withdrawal of such solutions from the warehouse when the time comes— reduces full thinking to the mere calculation of *probabilities*. This type of thinking denies us training in the thinking that opens up *possibilities*.

* Why we approach nature, including human nature, in this way has already been discussed in the section on Heidegger in Chapter 2.

Rational planning, trend projection, futurology—"the calculation of information about that which approaches Man as something that can be planned"[46]—replace politics as evocation: the calling up of that potential in the human being that enables us every day to leap ahead into a future no one can know.[47]

The great danger is binary thinking. This focuses our attention on what *is*—or is *not*. Binary thinking is in terms of either/or. Binary thinking is encapsulated in today's apotheosis of bureaucracy and technology, the computer. It limits our ability to see possibilities hidden even within the current tendency of modern civilization toward self-closure. As one commentator has said: "Binary logic is a defense against multiple realities."*

For example,[48] a Heideggerian analysis of the antagonism between bureaucracy and politics (American self-interested style) would try to overcome the binary juxtaposition "political/not-political" by raising a third possibility: "unpolitical." The unpolitical as third force is already contained in the civilization's current tension between politics (as self-interest) and the nonpolitics of bureaucracy (in which self-interested transactions are conducted under the cover of bureaucratic ideology such as standards of efficiency). Learning how to abandon binary thinking of "either/or" enables us to raise the possibility that an entirely new way of doing politics (neither self-interested nor bureaucratic) may be contained in our present bureaucracy/politics dilemma.

POST-BUREAUCRATIC POLITICS

Traditional American politics is a politics of self-interest. So the Founding Fathers conceived it and so it has stayed. The standards for self-interest politics are the personal passions and ends of individuals. In America, an individual can expect to ward off fear of untimely death at the hands of other individuals by acquiring property and hiring guards. Bureaucratized politics also is a fight for turf and survival. But now such fights have to be legitimated by bureaucrats' justifying their entry into politics in terms of the benefits that bureaucratic instrumental standards can provide the public: more bang for the buck (efficiency), formal equality (a fair chance at the goods for all), and so on. (See the section on Bureaucratic Culture in Chapter 2.)

A Third Political Arena

Now observe what happens when an individual well versed in the personal passions of interest politics and the impersonality and task-orientation of bureaucratized politics enters a situation in which neither

* Jay D. White, personal communication.

self-interest nor purely instrumental values are appropriate. A third political arena is formed. On occasion this happens on a large scale. When Congress, under the prodding of budget director David Stockman, largely set aside particular interests to pursue the public interest of budget reduction in 1981, the political process was temporarily transformed. In trying to discover the nature of a third type of politics emerging, we are here asking: What happens when a "facilitator" used to overcoming bureaucracy's structures (like division of labor and hierarchy) and used to overcoming petty personal politics enters a public political arena in which participants recognize the *public interest* as the appropriate goal? A "process politics" emerges.

Listen to Michael H. Halperin, an organizational consultant and trainer, speak of his experience as head of a local school board in Massachusetts:

I wasn't really interested in the finagling behind the scenes because it was a small committee; I didn't see the need for it. I would be more interested in setting up, say, goal-setting sessions and through developing a collaborative atmosphere get everybody to talk about what they thought the issues and priorities were.[49]

Here politics as the *shaping* of problems precedes, and perhaps even replaces, politics as the decision-making over which separate interests are satisfied. A leading consultant of our era, Donald Schön, reminds us that:

Underlying every public debate and every formal conflict over policy there is a barely visible process through which issues come to awareness and ideas about them become powerful. . . . These antecedent processes are as crucial to the formation of policy as the processes of discovery in science are crucial to the formation of plausible hypotheses. But our bias in favor of the rational, the "scientific," the well formed and the retrospective causes us to disregard the less visible process and to accept the ideas underlying public conflict over policy as mysteriously given.[50]

Halperin continues:

The commitment came not from individuals digging in their heels on positions they had staked out beforehand, but rather a willingness to engage in the process and to accept as a reasonable outcome whatever the group produced.

In short, the political facilitator says in effect to the members of the board: We may disagree on what the school system is about. But none of us disagrees that we have to have some goals. And none of you wants to be left out of the process of goal setting. Never mind the substantive issues that we all carried to the table, let's just all join in the process of determining what the goals might be. This gets participants into a problem-shaping mode and away from a mode assuming that choices are already brought ready-made to the table before discussion begins on what the problem is.

To the facilitator experienced in the politics of bureaucracy, "This is [as Halperin says] classic substance/process stuff." The political facilitator borrows from bureaucracy's experience that political fights over substances (different self-interest goals and human passions) can be sublimated under a process that commits participants to rational discussion of what a problem might be. Each participant contributes knowledge and perspective to the definition of the problem. However—and this is the crucial difference from bureaucratic politics—something new happens when the political facilitator carries such process facilitation over into a public interest situation. If everyone can be got to agree that what is at stake is not upholding instrumental values but the discovery of ends values in the public interest, a third political process is called for that is appropriate to the public-interest goal. The process politics of public interest situations avoids a bureaucratic trap of allowing rationality to become an end in itself. Everyone now accepts that rationality is simply one means by which to arrive at a public good: a good school system for children. Process politics also admits self-interest expression; but self-interest now is no longer legitimate as an end in itself, it must be legitimated as a means—a motivation—to serve and define the public interest.

Process Politics: Examples and Objections

The objection might be raised that such a facilitated politics would have a tendency to become bureaucratic if the only standards for success were themselves rationalistic standards. Halperin says, for example: "It was not that decisions were not made; it was just that they were *better framed.*" What is meant by "better"? The careless facilitator might be tempted, because of the rational bias of the process, to admit only standards that can stand rational calculation. On the other hand, it is entirely conceivable that the setting aside* of personal emotions and personal agendas might admit into the group observations and evaluations of knowledge that would not otherwise enter. Some such knowledge might derive from greater group willingness to speak of what constituents were actually saying, what had been expressed perhaps in similar process sessions with constituents. In such an environment, individuals might actually bring into the group knowledge that either a merely self-interested approach or a set of bureaucratic standards would prevent them from bringing in.

The temptation of bringing in bureaucratic values into problem-shaping according to "process methods" was certainly yielded to in Congress in 1985. Congress struggled with producing across-the-board cutbacks in the federal budget in the public interest of reducing the cost

---

* This does not mean suppressing such motives; it means admitting to them in order to overcome them.

of indebtedness on behalf of all citizens. In fact, through the Gramm-Rudman law, a bureaucratic process was invoked allowing cuts to be made according to bureaucratic values: for example, formal equality of suffering across agencies. However, in the 1981 budget-cutting effort, directed by budget director David Stockman, members of Congress had showed themselves capable of setting aside the pressures of constituency interests *and* the merely instrumental values of bureaucratic reasoning to produce a result in the public interest—once the general process of goal-setting in the public interest had been agreed to. That constituency interests could not be totally set aside should not obscure that a number of constituency-oriented budget amendments lost, leading Stockman to comment, "It was the kind of amendment that should have passed. The fact that it didn't tells me that the political logic has changed."[51] While interest politics has rebounded and while bureaucratic values are used to legitimate goals that cannot be justified in terms of constituency interests, the realization has dawned on many policy scientists that different policies are able to change the political process. These tend to be policies in which *everyone's* ox is in danger of being gored. They are policies in which reality—economic, social, or physical—can be shown to confront all Americans, not just those organized into interest groups. The postbureaucratic politics tends to deal with the growing recognition that interest politics and bureaucratized politics disable the polity from dealing with those issues that challenge its survival. It must be pointed out, however, that the postbureaucratic politics of survival is in its infancy, whether it takes place in the T-groups of modern organizations or in the polity itself. On one side lurk personal passions and interests and on the other the embedded faith that continued rationalization is the only alternative to the irrational basis of "dirty" politics. Against such probabilities for reversion and regression, the efforts of those advocating and processing a postbureaucratic politics are nothing less than heroic.

SUMMARY

Bureaucracy replaces politics. Bureaucracy does this in two ways. First, bureaucracy, trading on people's faith in its rationalistic values, moves into the public arena and competes successfully there with traditional political institutions. This is true both of corporate (private) and government (public) bureaucracy. Second, bureaucracy, by producing a knowledge gap between subordinates and managers, allows a truncated kind of interest politics to creep into bureaucracy itself. Within bureaucracy, this bureaucratized kind of politics, however, has lost *any* basis among *any* constituency: that is, its perpetrators are not forced as is any ordinary politician to touch base with a citizen constituency. Through division of labor, which reduces individuals' knowledge of the entire work process, and hierarchy, which allows bureaucratic politicians to exploit subordinates' dependency on superordinates for direction and coordination, bureaucracy generates a truncated internal politics that gives managers all the power they need without having to face up to any public responsibilities. There simply is no one in a position to judge whether a manager has exerted his or her powers legitimately in terms of the technical superiority of knowledge given him or her by hierarchy or whether he or she is pursuing personal passions or interests. Suffering of subordinates as such power increases is likely to increase also: they are forced to adhere to a rational culture of bureaucracy imposed on them while blindly tapping their way along dark corridors of power. Finally, a postbureaucratic politics may be emerging as a third-force or process politics in those cases in which organizations, public or private, are confronted with the fact that their own values and knowledge structure, separated from political guidance, are inadequate to even defining what are continuing problems of survival. Examples arise from markets that have not yet been completely rationalized and from citizens not yet completely pacified.[52] This third-force politics has begun to enter the political mainstream.

WHAT PEOPLE CAN DO

Surviving Political Attack
*Conrad P. Rutkowski**

How can you survive the politics of bureaucracy? There is one single lesson to be learned in the following cases of attack and defense; in Latin there is a handy phrase for it: *protege asinum*. Literally it means "Protect your donkey"; but the cases make the implied meaning clear. Here is how you might negotiate your way:

1. IN THE JOB INTERVIEW

MANAGER: "I see here you haven't held down many jobs for more than a year."
YOUR RESPONSE: "Well, how did you reach a conclusion like that?"

Express your puzzlement. Do not say, "But, but, I worked at So-and-So Company for three years." Say: "I don't understand. Are you sure you're talking about my résumé; do you have me confused with another applicant?" Put the interviewer on the defensive. Insist that he or she show where he or she got those conclusions from. Insist on an explanation. It is in the interest of employers to seek out, or create, weaknesses

---

* Dr. Rutkowski, a management and higher education consultant, has served as an executive assistant, aide, or administrator under two New York State Senate majority leaders, the governor of a state, and two university presidents.

in you that will put you in an inferior negotiating position. Professionals, especially, will tend to resent such slurs; and institutions that let their personnel managers or others get away with such tactics simply don't attract top professionals.

2. IN PAY NEGOTIATIONS

MANAGER, on Day One: How much money do you need? More than the fifteen thousand dollars you made in your last job, you say? Well, here we can go about eighteen or nineteen thousand.

MANAGER, on Day Two: Okay, here's our offer: $10,000.
Your intuitive response: You want to lunge across the desk at him. Don't do it.

YOUR RESPONSE: "Has someone told you to lower the offer from yesterday?" Do not blame the manager. Suggest that someone must have ordered him. He may then say, "Well, no, *I* did it." You then say, "Ohhhhh!"

Also, do not use the word "figure," use the word "offer."

The next step, after your "Ohhhh!" is to say: "Can you tell me why?" Keep on the offensive, but politely. Don't *let* the manager get you on the defensive, turn the question or the issue around. The best thing always is to answer a question with a question. Do not give an answer, because then the opponent keeps up with the questions. Force *him or her* into an answer.

3. IN A PROBATIONARY PERIOD

You are a professional. Every time you finish a piece of work, your manager either gives it back to you saying, "This is not what I want," or changes your product in some way. Confronted by you, your manager consistently refuses to give you any help: either by suggesting a pattern of mistakes you might be making or by suggesting a model for the kind of work she might want done. Her pattern is simply to criticize everything you do. At one point you say to her: "What are the standards that I must meet?" And she says, "Just follow your professional standards and you'll be okay by me."

That response is what is called a "cop-out" on her part. The more you follow your professional standards, the more this type will attempt to destroy you.

One type of response, which lets you reality-test whether there is actually anything wrong with your work, is to use the hairy-hand technique.* Give the manager two or three product options, all meeting

---

* So called after a legendary episode in the advertising business in which a client praises a painting of a thousand people smoking his cigarettes at a county fair but leaves the artist

the same order. Tell her which you think is the best, which is second-best, which is third. If the manager is using personal or political standards rather than task-oriented ones, she will consistently pick the product that you told her came in second or third in your evaluation; she'll never pick your number one choice.

At some point you must learn to suspect that both your integrity and judgment are being arbitrarily attacked. Keep in mind that people are very insecure and unsure, and they survive best by projecting. This is really not personal, in the sense that the manager's behavior is caused by anything you personally did. It originates in his or her own psychopathology. The trick is not to play into the hands of that pathology. A tip-off to such pathology should be obtained, if you suspect it at the interview stage, simply by finding out how many people have just left to create the need for replacements. If there is a relatively frequent turnover of staff, suspect pathology.

4. GETTING CREDIT FOR A PROJECT

Upon completion of a project your manager says to you: "Don't worry; I'll be sure to let the chief know how much you contributed to this project; there'll be no need for you to sign off on the report."

You, of course, know that your name will never appear on the report or in conversation.

One subordinate dealt with that by placing a piece of information in the report that he knew to be egregiously wrong but that he knew was outside the manager's field of competence. It has to be a piece of information that the manager's superordinate will catch.

The manager's only defense then is to point at you, and say: "But, I relied on Joe for that information." Rest assured, the manager's superordinate will at least suspect that the manager has tried to palm the report off on him as his own when it really wasn't. Make sure the piece of misinformation is both big enough to be noticed at the top and can be easily explained—but only by you.

Here we enter the difficult process of having to do one's political homework before acting in a given situation. Organizational structure may allow you occasionally to forward pieces of useful information voluntarily and directly to the top manager. A few weeks later that same piece can be slipped into a report you know your immediate supervisor will represent to the top manager as his or her own.

---

with the suggestion: "I'd like you to turn the faces of these people more to the side. This way we see them all from the back." The advertising director takes the distraught artist aside and says, "Next time use the hairy hand." "What's that?" the artist says. "Well," comes the answer, "paint in a guy with a lot of hair on back of his hand. The client will take one look and say, 'Get rid of that guy with the hairy hand!' That will satisfy his need to put his stamp on the final product."

Of course, if your supervisor and the top manager are close friends, the scheme will backfire. But, of course, you would not supply voluntary information to the top manager if you did not know something about his or her relations with your supervisor.

For extended games, you need to understand more than the structure. You also need to have inside dope. But above all, you need relationships—for example, with those whose needs you can serve regardless of the chain of command. If you have not been in your institution long enough to develop such relationships, indirect relationships may already be available: your secretary may be good friends with the top manager's secretary. Knowledge and relationships are the keys to political games.

5. At a Firing

At your firing, your manager says: "I'm sorry, it's nothing personal. You just didn't fit in with our needs. But here . . . [and at this point he grabs your elbow and propels you toward the door] . . . are some outplacement people waiting just next door for you. They'll find something suitable for you."

If you walk out that door, you will never get the chance again to have your manager debrief you. Such a debriefing is not only your right as a human being, it is a deeply seated need, and it is as important for the manager and the company as it is to you. Without such a debriefing the manager will never have to face up to his or her own role in the events leading up to your leaving the organization. And you will not have the benefit of coming to terms with those events. If you walk out that door, he (assuming it's a man) will never owe you anything again; he will never have to explain himself; he will never have to debrief you—or himself. "Nothing personal in this." Everything is personal because we take it personally.

There are several things you can do.

One: you can insist on a debriefing. Two: you have legal rights. Find out what they are. You have a right to be given a reason for dismissal. One experienced practitioner of office politics advises friends to suddenly fall on the floor and clutch their chest. Guilt. But not only that, the manager then has to worry about OSHA coming down, about precipitating a heart attack with what he has done. The manager is likely to want to call a doctor. "No . . . no . . . no . . ." the victim moans, "that's not necessary." The manager is left to swim in it. He is left with uncertainty. Turned against him is the one tool that managers normally use: because of their privileged position they do not have to tell anybody anything unless they want to. If he is not going to tell you what went on with your firing, you are now in a position not to tell him what is going on inside your body, for the health of which he is still legally and morally responsible. All the victim does is whisper: "My . . . my . . . my doctor told me to avoid stress . . ."

6. INTERIM EVALUATIONS AND PERFORMANCE APPRAISALS

Short of the mistakes we make on entry and on exit, there is the day-to-day experience of having to live with the organization, its structure, and its politics. Interim evaluations or performance appraisals can bring daily stress to a head.

Say your supervisor calls you in for such an evaluation and says, "You work well with me. Your coworkers say you work well with them. But you just haven't got what it takes for this kind of work. This kind of work is just not your kind of work." She (assuming it's a woman) is referring to the people you deal with who are your clients in casework or the things you physically work on, say you're making widgets. Your supervisor is really pointing to something very physical and concrete; she shows you where your work falls short of the section's goals. This is an ultimate indictment. And there may be some validity to it. You also are not sure, based on experience, that you are suited for case working or widget making.

Nevertheless, you have one need; that is to emerge from this situation with your integrity intact, so that you can still learn. Otherwise, if you let this destroy you and you leave the job—doubting that you are suited for this kind of work or perhaps for any kind of work—there is no future. What do you tell yourself? Never mind your supervisor. You are the one who now doubts whether you are suited for the work. You also are the only person who can tell whether you are suited for the work; the manager can only judge whether you fit in.

Do not do anything at the time. You simply indicate to your supervisor that this is a matter that you will have to give some thought to. You would be very grateful, you say, if she would address herself in a more detailed and specific way—even in writing (and of course she is going to resist this)—to the problems she perceives. For the moment, you simply say that this is the kind of assessment that requires a degree of time, consideration, and reflection, and that once you have these things lined up you would want to get back to her.

The temptation is to react instantaneously. But it is better to say, "I wasn't prepared for this. I wasn't really alerted to the contents of the agenda, or the meeting, or what was going to be talked about. So it's really not appropriate for me to respond at this time. This is obviously a serious matter, and I would want to take a degree of time. Then I will get back to you and then we can have a real discussion." This discombobulates her. What she wants to do is get you off guard, hit you with the bat, and then take off—and as far as she is concerned, it's a *fait accompli*.

First you want time. Two, you do not accept what she is saying. And what you are really saying is, "I am going to get back to you," which she really does not want to hear. The manager is likely to respond, "Well, there's no need to." You then say, "But I don't understand? That would really be unfair on your part, because you are really telling me this for the first time, and I would think that you would really want to be helpful in a situation like this. So I would assume that you really would want me to consider and reflect on what you have told me." Ask for particulars. Suggest that some of the supervisor's complaints "seem to border more on feelings on your part." Put her on the defensive. If she goes off the wall, as she is likely to, you keep your cool and simply add: "I am simply saying there would have to be more specifics, and what you have said would have to be concretized in terms of the work situation, in terms of specific tasks, specific responsibilities, specific assignments, and things of that nature."

In all these situations, there is only one thing we are talking about: *protege asinum!* There is an attack going on; a defense is required, but don't go on the defensive.

To understand this, you have to understand some of the fundamental workings of the human mind, at least in modern times. One profound truth in modern times is this: Behavior—that is, action—to a large degree tends to be unrelated to communication. With an employer or supervisor: keep in mind that it is not what they are saying that is important. That is camouflage. It is a mask. It is a psychological guise. It is what they are doing that is important. What they say is a pretext, not the text. Therefore what you can do is say, "Look, what you are saying is one thing, but what you are doing is something else." That will blow their minds. But you can do this only if the game is really all over and all you want is to go after them. It is not necessary to be nasty. You can say, "You are saying one thing, but you're doing something quite different." Then, if they say, "Well, I'm just trying to be decent and generous because . . . ," then you say, "What you're really saying is that I am terrible, and that is not so, and you and I *both* know that." The subordinate under attack needs to understand, for purposes of survival in or out of the organization, one thing: that his or her integrity is being questioned, if not attacked. No human being can tolerate such an assault without damage to himself or herself. We can learn from such attacks, and from our responses, and from the limits we see and feel in ourselves in being able to respond adequately. But the important thing is to respond.

It also helps to turn our attention onto managers and their motivations. What is it (we must ask ourselves) in managers—what is it in their circumstances, their blood, their genetics, their family?—that makes them want to attack subordinates so frequently and so consistently? Is it in their interest to do that? What do they gain from it? In short, we have to develop, to preserve our own sanity, some sort of theodicy, as Max Weber called it: a sense of God's way in the world—even if we don't believe in God—that helps us make sense out of the political experience in bureaucracy.

There is another way of putting this. I have found that most managers—including myself—are very good at dealing with things, paperwork, and so forth. The real test of managers comes in dealing with human beings. In any human situation, when people are faced with a crisis or with something they perceive as a crisis, they really have three options. Do nothing. Tackle it. Or, flee. The ethologists, those who study animal behavior, refer to the options as paralysis, fight, or flight. From the viewpoint of managers, as an example of people having to deal with people, this can be put into perspectives: To what extent, when they look out, do they see a threat, do things seem neutral, or do they see something that is pleasant? To the degree to which there is a threat, real or imagined, they then engage in one of those three behaviors. To the degree to which they are accountable to others—or to the degree they perceive themselves as being uncomfortable, an assault pattern will begin. In fact, the assault pattern is usually characteristic of bureaucrats, and the higher you go the more you can expect a fight. There is only one other viable alternative: silence, or doing nothing. But that really does not work. And then there is the option of getting someone else to do their dirty work.

There is a tendency on the part of bureaucrats and students of bureaucracy to try to make sense out of the assaultive behavior of superiors in terms of the actual superiority of knowledge they claim is derivative of their position, which they then misuse—perhaps even against the structures and the rationality of the culture that gave them the position. (See the section on "Bureaucratic Politics," above in this chapter.) But there is another dimension to this.

I once worked for two chief executive officers in a row in the same institution. The first took steps to develop an institutional structure around his office that provided for a staff that would keep him in touch with reality. You might say my job description required me to tell him the facts and when he might be heading in the wrong direction even, and especially, when it might be against my own narrow self-interest to do so. But there was another reason why I was able to walk into his office and tell him, "You're wrong on this one!" and why he would listen though he did not always follow my advice. There was a sufficient degree of self-assurance there, a sufficient degree of integrity, of self-worth, so that my CEO never felt assaulted, he never felt threatened. He felt he could afford to listen and still make his own judgments.

My next CEO comes on as a new leader and my boss without ever having run a major institution before. He immediately deinstitutionalized the office of the CEO. It was he and his secretary against the world.

In short, institutional structure can be helpful but only for people who have the strength and know-how—personal and moral—to use it. This is a matter of the mental makeup, the mental fatigue factor, and the mental ability of being able to deal with problems, structure, and staff. The really good decision-maker is the one who, as time goes on, has a greater degree of self-assurance, permits a greater degree of input, listens more, and becomes even more selective in terms of what he or she chooses to do. Out of this strength, he or she is able to learn without feeling threatened. This enhances one's ability to shape issues. Out of this strength, too, he or she is able to manage without threatening. No single factor ought to upset such a leader. The leading manager knows that there is no single factor at base or at fault in any event. It is a continuum that goes from the work to be done, through the people doing it, through the structures, to the manager, and back again. You have to treat reality as a continuum, and then you are on safe ground not only in terms of discussions with people, but you are on safe grounds in terms of self-analysis. The successful manager has to look at wholes as well as parts. At the managerial level (and above) everything comes together into wholes; below that it is divided into parts. Good managers move from situation to situation. They could follow the rules that govern wholes. But they know from experience that each situation is different because it is determined by the parts. This means that, as the manager moves from situation to situation, he or she has to make sure that the parts are the same, and if not must make adjustments. Especially during the learning phase of the job, the manager cannot afford to follow the rule of *protege asinum*; assault ultimately does not lead to safety. Learning does, and knowing when to lead.

NOTES

1. Max Weber, "Parliament and Government in a Reconstructed Germany," Appendix II to *Economy and Society* (New York: Bedminster Press, 1968), p. 1393.

2. John F. Kennedy quoted in Louis Harris, *The Anguish of Change* (New York: Norton, 1973), p. 15.

3. Marriner S. Eccles, *Beckoning Frontiers*, Sidney Hyman, ed. (New York: Knopf, 1951), p. 336; cited in Peter Woll, *American Bureaucracy*, 2nd ed. (New York: Norton, 1977), p. 207.

4. Loc. cit.

5. Woodrow Wilson, "The Study of Administration," *Political Science Quarterly*, 2 (June 1887), pp. 209–210; reprinted in Jay M. Shafritz and Albert C. Hyde, eds., *Classics of Public Administration* (Oak Park, Ill.: Moore Publishing Company, 1978), pp. 3–17; combined citation from p. 10.

6. B. Guy Peters, *The Politics of Bureaucracy: A Comparative Perspective* (New York: Longman, 1978), p. 32.

7. Woll, *American Bureaucracy*, p. 6.

8. James David Barber, *The Presidential Character: Predicting Performance in the White House* (Englewood Cliffs, N.J.: Prentice-Hall, 1972), p. 328.

9. Jimmy Carter, *Keeping the Faith—Memoirs of a President* (New York: Bantam, 1982), pp. 449–450.

10. Presidential scholar James David Barber has suggested that, given the recent merger of the technical values of campaign management with the older self-interested values of large corporations, Ronald Reagan was selected by his original millionaire supporters exactly for his actor's ability to follow a script provided by his "directors." Whether such directors are heads of corporations or heads of bureaucracies ultimately makes no difference; the management culture of today may simply select manageable politicians who fit the dominant pattern of values and practices.

11. Thomas P. O'Neill, Jr., "Congress: The First 200 Years," *National Forum*, vol. 54, no. 4 (Fall 1984), p. 19.

12. Quoted in Mark Green, with Michael Waldman, *Who Runs Congress?* 4th ed. (New York: Dell, 1984), p. 29.

13. Percentage change measured in constant dollars. Source for data: Gary C. Jacobson, "Money in the 1980 and 1982 Congressional Elections," in Michael J. Malbin, ed., *Money and Politics in the United States—Financing Elections in the 1980s* (Chatham, N.J.: Chatham House, 1984), pp. 38–69; citation from p. 40.

14. Quoted in Green, *Who Runs Congress*, p. 35.

15. Jeb Stuart Magruder in "Reflections on a Course in Ethics," conversation between Studs Terkel, Jeb Stuart Magruder, and William Sloan Coffin, Jr., *Harper's*, October 1973, p. 72.

16. Charles E. Lindblom, *Politics and Markets* (New York: Basic Books, 1977), p. 356.

17. Peter Woll, *American Bureaucracy*, 2nd ed. (New York: Norton, 1977), pp. 177–178.

18. This and the following quotation from a survey of opinion of high-level (GS 16–18) federal bureaucrats, in fact those who run the federal government, in Green, *Who Runs Congress?*, p. 185.

19. Michael Malbin, *Unelected Representatives: Congressional Staff and the Future of Representative Government* (New York: Basic Books, 1980), pp. 243–244.

20. Professor Raymond Cox III of Northern Arizona University, personal communication with the author, 1985. See also Raymond W. Cox III, "American Political Theory and the Bureaucracy," paper delivered at the annual meeting of the Midwest Political Science Association, Chicago, April 17-20, 1985.

21. U.S. Congress, Committee on Government Operations, Subcommittee on Intergovernmental Relations, *Confidence and Concern: Citizens View American Government* (Washington, D.C.: U.S. Government Printing Office, 1973), Part II, p. 115, and Part III, p. 61. The sample of elected officials was drawn from state and local incumbents in fifteen states.

22. Ibid, p. 60.

23. See Ralph P. Hummel and Robert A. Isaak, *The Real American Politics* (Englewood Cliffs, N.J.: Prentice-Hall, 1986), p. 83.

24. Harold D. Lasswell, *Politics: Who Gets What, When, How* (Cleveland: World Publishing, Meridian, 1958), p. 133.

25. Erik H. Erikson, *Young Man Luther: A Study in Psychoanalysis and History* (New York: Norton, 1958) and *Gandhi's Truth: On the Origins of Militant Nonviolence* (New York: Norton, 1969).

26. See Sanford J. Ungar, *FBI: An Uncensored Look Behind the Walls* (Boston: Little, Brown, 1976).

27. Howell Baum, "Psychodynamics of Powerlessness Among Planners," in R. P. Hummel, *The Bureaucratic Experience*, 2nd ed. (New York: St. Martin's Press, 1982), pp. 137–41; citation from p. 138.

28. Michael A. Diamond, "Psychological Dimensions of Personal Responsibility for Public Management: An Object Relations Approach," *Journal of Management Studies*, vol. 22, no. 6 (November 1985), pp. 649–67; chart from p. 654.

29. Ivar Berg, Marcia Freedman, and Michael Freedman, *Managers and Work Reform: A Limited Engagement* (New York: Free Press, 1978), p. 180.

30. Howell Baum, *Planners and Public Expectations* (Cambridge, Mass.: Schenkman Publishing, 1983) and Baum, "Sensitizing Planners to Organization," in Pierre Clavel, John Forester, and William W. Goldsmith, eds., *Urban and Regional Planning in an Age of Austerity* (New York: Pergamon Press, 1980), pp. 279–307, especially p. 302.

31. This may be the type of theoretical basis necessary for the interpretation of studies on affective responses to bureaucratic role structure as for example, Gerald Zeitz, "Bureaucratic Role Characteristics and Member Affective Responses in Organizations," *The Sociological Quarterly* vol. 25 (Summer 1984), pp. 301–18.

32. Jürgen Habermas, "Technology and Science as 'Ideology'," in Habermas, *Toward a Rational Society: Student Protest, Science and Politics* (Boston: Beacon Press, 1971), pp. 81–122. Citation from p. 92.

33. Ibid.

34. Ibid.

35. Ibid., pp. 91–92.

36. Ibid., p. 92.

37. Ibid., p. 96.

38. Ibid., p. 103. The argument that only citizens, because they are amateurs, are qualified to set societal goals and that experts and specialists are specifically disqualified from such activity is also made by Alfred Schutz in a classic article attempting to justify a return to the old-style politics: "The Well-Informed Citizen: An Essay on the Distribution of Knowledge," in Schutz, *Collected Papers* (The Hague: Martinus Nijhoff, 1964), pp. 120–134.

39. Ibid., p. 103.

40. Ibid., p. 103.

41. Ibid., p. 104.

42. See John Forester, "Critical Theory and Planning Practice," in Pierre Clavel, John Forester, and William W. Goldsmith, eds., *Urban and Regional Planning in an Age of Austerity* (New York: Pergamon Press, 1980), pp. 326–42.

43. Martin Heidegger, "The Question Concerning Technology," in Heidegger, *The Question Concerning Technology and Other Essays*, William Lovitt, tr. (New York: Harper & Row, Harper Torch, 1977), pp. 3–35; citation from p. 18.

44. Martin Heidegger, "What Are Poets For?" in *Poetry, Language, Thought*, Albert Hofstadter, tr. (New York: Harper & Row, Harper Colophon, 1975), pp. 89–142; citation from p. 111.

45. Martin Heidegger, "Zusatz" to *Parmenides*, vol. 45 of *Gesamtausgabe*, 2nd part, *Vorlesungen 1923–1944* (Frankfurt am Main: Vittorio Klostermann, 1982), pp. 246–50; my translation from p. 249. My thanks to Professor Fred Dallmayr of Notre Dame University for reading a trial paper on this definition of experience as laid down by Heidegger.

46. Martin Heidegger, "Die Herkunft der Kunst und die Bestimmung des Denkens," in *Denkerfahrungen* (Frankfurt am Main: Vittorio Klostermann, 1983), pp. 135–160; my translation from p. 143, the sentence in reference to contemporary science: "Sie verrechnet die Informationen über das, was als Planbares auf den Menschen zukommt."

47. On the nature of our existence as a "pro-ject," a hurling ourselves ahead of ourselves as in a leap in the dark, see Martin Heidegger, *Being and Time*, originally: *Sein und Zeit* (Tübingen: Max Niemeyer Verlag, 1976).

48. See Heidegger, "Die Herkunft der Kunst und die Bestimmung des Denkens," in *Denkerfahrungen*, cited above fn. 46, p. 158.

49. From a conversation with Michael H. Halperin, Feb. 19, 1986.

50. Donald Schön, *Beyond the Stable State* (New York: Norton, 1971), p. 123.

51. Quoted in William Greider, "The Education of David Stockman," *Atlantic Monthly* (December 1981), pp. 27–54.

52. I owe the concept of politics as the pacification of citizens to Theodore Lowi.

6

Bureaucracy Policy: Implementing the Critique of a Terminal World

Bureaucracy's partner, technology, has undergone deep study for the purpose of policy development and change. There is technology policy,[1] but there is no comparable bureaucracy policy. In public service and politics, the powerful and influential shun "mere" theory. Organization design and reform does not rest on theoretically founded analytic, scientific, and critical knowledge. Therefore, those who would bring about purely political solutions are not brought face to face with the logical consequences of their actions. Politics-based bureaucracy policy is not grounded in either the science of effective job relations, of work design, of the language and thought of work, the culture of work, or even the internal politics of work. Furthermore, theorists and analysts acquainted with such "technical" realities have failed to acquaint themselves with the "mere" practical realities of the conduct of politics and government and the design of administration in the United States. The great architectonic designs of the Brownlow, Hoover, and similar commissions that to this day constitute the structures of U.S. administration find no place in organization theory.[2] Little is known in academic circles about how managers actually think, which means little is known about what they do when they actually manage.[3] An entire generation of "young Turk" theorists and critics, while cutting across the practioner/theorist divide as consultants, has not developed the close political contacts and permanent working relationships of past influentials in the making of organizational and workforce policy. As a leader in the American Society for Public Administration has said bluntly of contemporary theorists:

They do not speak the language of policy and politics that is used by the people who make decisions about how the workforce will be managed.[4]

At the same time, the literature influential in the teaching of current and future public servants has been remarkably uncritical both scientifically and politically when it comes to understanding the inner imperatives of public bureaucracy and its social, personal, political, and civilizational implications. Critiques are rare.[5] When critiques are attempted, they tend not to be absorbed into the educational or political mainstream of the public service but to evoke defensive polemics[6] that are soon adopted as fact[7] and general defensive operations.[8]

The United States possesses no scientific institute of bureaucracy studies. Instead of a higher school to educate the corps of civil servants, it relies on hundreds of fragmented education programs distributed across colleges and universities. There, while dispute rages over whether public administration education is an art, a craft, or a science,[9] future managers are often forced into scholastic ways of thinking that have little relationship to the type of thinking they will have to do on the job. A general attempt is made, induced by the general culture of modernity with its bias toward rationalistic and scientific thinking and not by any policy decision, to place a helmet of rationalist/scientist thought on every managerial head. This runs against all evidence that many managerial problems do not present themselves in neat forms susceptible to rationalist or scientist solutions.[10] In the meanwhile, acute needs for practical knowledge are served by a separate world of training institutes and programs[11] as well as university public service programs[12] and academic and private consultancies.[13] While new ways of thinking, more appropriate to actual managerial experience, are able to flow into the public service through training programs and consultancies, the gap between managerial thinking and school thinking persists in those programs and consultancies that remain mainly under academic control.

In summary, the problem of public service education and training is this: Even where rationalist/scientist ways of thinking are taught, they are not rational[14] or scientific[15] enough to provide practitioners with adequate skills. At the same time, little is known in academe of the problems that managers actually face from within their own experience and of the actual thinking and managing operations they conduct; this has meant that very few actual managerial skills[16]—as distinct from specialist skills or general public administration socialization—are taught at all.

As in business administration,[17] reforms—but not a coherent policy of organizational design—are eventually carried into public management on the wings of force, leaving managers to deal with realities in the meanwhile without the support of an appropriate scholarly body of knowledge—analytical, scientific, theoretical, synthesizing—to fit their needs. Public managers take at best a neutral attitude toward scientific knowledge originating in academe, while expressing an appreciation for "practical" knowledge.[18]

The result is the division of the public service into two cultures: those who believe they know how things are supposed to work and are confident in being able to enact reality and those who know they know how things really work and are willing to adapt to reality.[19] Ironically, the first group tends to be composed increasingly of top administrators, especially political appointees, while the second group is increasingly composed of career hands-on managers and their subordinates.

The split in the two cultures has had tragic consequences in the 1980s when those with legitimate political intentions—validated in landslide electoral victories at the federal level[20] and preceded by a movement of spending limitations at the state level[21]—attempted to seize control of the bureaucracy with tools they did not fully understand.

BUREAUCRACY POLICY IN THE REAGAN ADMINISTRATIONS

The attempt of the Reagan administrations to reassert the predominance of politics over bureaucracy has offered the clearest example, in several decades, of the cost of trying bureaucratic reform with tools not understood. There can be no doubt that it was the intent of Reaganite bureaucracy policy to return to a prebureaucratic era in which society's ends values, as evoked and defined by a legitimately elected political regime, would once again be put in charge over the instrumental values and practices of bureaucracy that had become a system of nonlegitimate domination.[22] Some methods of regaining political control were, in fact, traditional: for example, the substitution of partisan and personally loyal top administrators for administrators drawn from the career staff. However, many of the methods themselves actually drew on bureaucratic standards and practices. The politicians were seduced by bureaucratic thinking of the type that says: When strict top-down control is exercised over policy and when discretion in implementation is strictly limited and supervised, then products and services compatible with the values of the political masters will result. This is true only under conditions of cultural consensus in which formal social and political channels can be relied on to produce policies in touch with reality. We can expect that in a time of cultural dissensus in which political channels include pressures emanating from bureaucracy itself, which has become its own social and cultural force, the solution to political mastery over bureaucracy is not that simple. Those in the Reagan presidency may have sensed this, as evidenced by their heavy emphasis on trying to do away with bureaucratic institutions apart from making efforts to control them.

Even a beginning analysis of the Reagan effort reveals its inner contradictions. Bureaucracy requires inequality of knowledge socially, emphasis on instrumental values culturally, organizational identity psychologically, quantitative thinking and top-down information cognitively and linguistically, and the preeminence of administration over politics. Politics requires the assumption of a basic knowledge equality among independent citizens who shape the political definition of their problems through free communication by reference to the ultimate ends values of their culture. At least the Reagan rhetoric sought to reestablish such a politics as master over administration as tool. What actually was done, however?

Social Structure: Hierarchy versus Knowledge Equality

The basic power of bureaucratic control arises when knowledge of work among workers is divided so that each worker must look upward to a manager for guidance. In order to win control over the bureaucracy, the Reagan administration was, from the beginning, advised to divide knowledge.

In the words of one conservative ideologist:[23]

Control over the process [of implementing a planned agenda and formulating a new one] must be retained by the political executive and his immediate political staff. Very little information will be put in writing. Career staff will supply information, but they should never become involved in the formation of agenda-related policy objectives. Similarly, once controversial[24] policy goals are formulated, they should not be released in total to the career staff. Thus, the political executive and his political staff become "jigsaw puzzle" managers. Other staff see and work on the individual pieces but never have enough of the pieces to be able to learn the entire picture.

By operating in this fashion, the political executive maintains control over his political agenda and his political opponents can only guess what the political executive is after.

To the extent that such thinking pervaded the Reagan administration, the politicians adopted the methods of the enemy—bureaucracy—to control bureaucracy. *Knowledge* was to be divided *among* subordinates (division of labor) and clear *levels* of knowledge (hierarchy) were to be established (see Chapters 1, 2, and 5). In addition, there would be reliance on top-down *information*, not on reciprocal *communication* between career staff and political appointees (see Chapter 4). Only one antibureaucratic method is in evidence: keeping information from being put in writing.

From our analysis of how bureaucracy functions, however, we know this:

1. When career staff is not involved in policy formulation, policymakers deny themselves knowledge of *how* and *whether* what they want done can be done: they are out of contact with the reality of implementation: tools, people, practices, impacts, outcomes (see Chapter 2).
2. When any bureaucrat—but especially top career staff—is denied "the entire picture," the bureaucrat is unable to make any kind of judgment—political or administrative—as to what needs to be done in programs and subprograms below in order to make sure that all the pieces eventually will fit together into the product sought by the masters.
3. Ultimately, when any bureaucrat is kept guessing, the tendency is to take less and less risk by working and to spend more and more time guessing. Work tends to cease (see Chapter 4).

The first Reagan director of the Office of Personnel Management admitted that "even in terms of what it thinks it wants to do, [the Reagan administration] needs very much the advice of the career civil servant who knows how the system really works."[25] Nevertheless, by 1984, 40 percent of Senior Executive Service managers who entered SES in 1979 had left the government, 22 percent of career executives said they were planning to leave, and 72 percent of career executives said they would not recommend a career in the federal government to their children.[26]

Culture: Ends Values versus Instrumental Values

Culturally, the basic values of bureaucracy tend to be those that can be reduced to numbers; quantity not quality rules (see Chapter 2).

In one of the most powerful attacks on bureaucracy, the Reagan administration mobilized traditionalist members of the business community into what became known as the Grace Commission. The mandate of the commission was to increase *efficiency* and reduce *costs*. A total of $424.5 billion in possible savings was projected.[27]

While the concern with reducing public investment in government could be said to represent a general social value—beginning with state spending limits and culminating in the Republican campaign of 1980 in which a balanced budget was promised (but not delivered) and subsequent budget-balancing efforts by both parties—the method chosen by the Grace Commission was a classic bureaucratic one. In the words of Eugene B. McGregor, Jr., this method focused on "a standard fare of 'volume up, costs down' recommendations that public managers have come to expect from the business community."[28]

The question was: *Which* business community? While large segments of the business community continued to pursue organizational and management methods oriented toward traditional corporate-bureaucratic values such as

$$\frac{\text{high volume}}{\text{low costs}} = \text{efficiency,}$$

as many as 41 percent of those companies with more than five hundred employees had installed worker/management participation programs by 1982.[29] Especially, the auto industry, challenged by the quality of Japanese products, turned toward an emphasis on work *effectiveness*, rather than a single-minded focus on *efficiency*, with one major manufacturer installing quality of working life programs in ninety of its plants by 1981.[30] This was not the business community that the Grace Commission represented.

Despite the cultural upheaval in the values of the business community itself and a decade-long record of effectiveness-oriented practice[31] and analysis[32] and theory[33] in public administration, the Grace Commission chose not to let a thousand flowers bloom but resorted to traditional top-down budgeting, accounting, and personnel practices to attempt to obtain control over the ranks. Against the understanding that this tempts line managers to hide actual practices behind paper reports, a fact obscured by a heavy hand at the budget-cutting axe, we know from our study of social relations on the job (Chapter 1) and internal politics (Chapter 5) that true control requires cooperation from the ranks. In the words uttered as far back as 1973 by two leading policy analysts, ". . .we do think it makes more sense to conceive of 'organization' in an extended sense so that it encompasses those whose cooperation is necessary for a program to be carried out."[34]

The Grace Commission purposefully seemed to ignore growing business experience, policy practice, and critical organization theory that culminated—in the business sector—in the summary of a new organizational culture presented by Peters and Waterman in *In Pursuit of Excellence*.[35] (See the discussion of Peters and Waterman in Chapter 2 of this book.) By using traditional values of business bureaucracy to control public bureaucracy, the commission produced, in the public sector, a situation in which procedure threatened to overwhelm substance.[36] Where the new culture recognized that "most members of the organization should be innovators," the Reagan administration had a great deal to fear from such innovation: not the least of which was the possibility that its conservative political agenda would be undermined unless bureaucrats were controlled. Control as the solution, however, ignores the fact that hierarchy as a reliable chain of command works only when a culture already exists that can accept hierarchy. Most bureaucrats in the federal Civil Service could be expected for reasons of bureaucratic psychology and citizenship to obey the chain of command. But failure to engage their active and innovative collaboration in the implementation of new programs would inevitably have to be considered a challenge to their professional competency and bureaucratic status, evoking not only fear for their jobs but anxiety as to who they were and what all their laboring amounted to. The morale crisis in the Senior Executive Service can be read as reflecting this anxiety.

Psychology: Personality versus Identity

Psychologically, the Reagan administration acted correctly according to theoretical standards in confronting personnel of institutional identity with politically committed personalities. Personality characterizes the psychology of free citizens with their own power base, while identity characterizes the institutionalized, whether manager or functionary (see Chapter 3).

Psychological organization theory would predict that political leadership in top posts can be accepted by those below because they have been socialized into a _psychology of dependence_ suitable to hierarchical structure. The political masters used the bureaucratic psychology against itself.

Only when the existence of a position, work group, section, bureau, or agency itself is put in question, would legitimate political leadership give rise to _anxiety levels_ counterproductive to getting work done.

If the use of political appointees is to be questioned,[37] it must first be put into the context within which the Reagan policy makers believed they found themselves. If, as one analyst concluded, they found themselves in the context of "a highly ideological president, a clear agenda, a permanent government openly hostile to the president's program," then the legitimate political remedy and one acceptable at the highest bureaucratic levels would logically be the deployment of political partisans. This, in fact, was done; Table 6.1 illustrates the particular impact the policy had on agencies targeted for major shifts in program priorities.

To the extent, however, that belief in fiscal conservatism, widely distributed throughout the general population, also cut through those citizens who happened to function as bureaucrats, the Reaganites' expectations of hostility may well have been exaggerated. In fact, one pair of interviewers arrived at this summary of their experience with career managers:

With rare exceptions, we did not find career managers who were "openly hostile" or even strongly opposed to the Reagan policy initiatives. We were told in every

Table 6.1
GROWTH OF POLITICAL APPOINTEES* IN SELECTED AGENCIES—
SEPTEMBER 1980 TO SEPTEMBER 1982

| | Percentage of Executives | |
Agency	1980	1982
Consumer Product Safety Commission	7	18
Department of Education	35	40
Federal Home Loan Bank Board	33	50
Federal Trade Commission	5	23
General Services Administration	5	19
National Aeronautics and Space Administration	0	8

* Noncareer or limited appointees.
Source: Edie N. Goldenberg, "The Permanent Government in an Era of Retrenchment and Redirection," in Lester M. Salomon and Michael S. Lund, eds., *The Reagan Presidency and The Governing of America* (Washington, D.C.: Urban Institute, 1984), p. 369.

agency in which we interviewed that some cutbacks made sense, that fiscal conservatism was important, and that Washington does, indeed, suffer from bureaucratic bloat. We were also told, however, that for "responsive competence" to be real and not merely myth, the realities of career expertise and the need for career management responsibility must be recognized and accepted.[38]

In a later study, the same analysts concluded that political appointees had come to hold the competences of specific career officials immediately below them in high esteem—but had not changed the opinion about career officials in general that they held upon entry into their positions.[39]

Thus, while it may be that "loyal and competent supporters in key executive positions can be a potent tool of administrative leadership,"[40] excessive use of the anxiety dynamics built into bureaucracy (see Chapters 3 and 4) may well have contributed unnecessary costs to the personnel policy. Among such costs will be the inability of bureaucrats to fit themselves into their proper subordinacy position vis-à-vis political managers when the existence of themselves or their enveloping and identity-giving institutions is threatened.[41] While exit increased and decline in morale was reported,[42] it is likely that the increase in defensive self-system operations[43] will be openly displayed only on rare occasions[44]—while the bottom-line costs will be obscured by budgeting and reporting systems that measure nominal actuality, not possibility.[45]

Language and Thought: Control versus Flexibility

Those who want to control bureaucracy must be able to dictate the words and grammar used for human communication. Bureaucratic communication determines terms from the top down instead of through reciprocality and is monologic rather than dialogic; it is information (see Chapter 4). Similarly, bureaucratic thinking rests on the assumption that all behaviors and cases can ultimately be brought under the explanation and control of a few fundamental rules external to and above specific instances; operative thinking by analogy is the result, testing reality for adherence to rules (see Chapter 4). Control exists where the masters of bureaucracy can dictate the terms of discourse and the categories of thought.

The Reagan administration's turn to top-down budgeting as a replacement of what a leading budget analyst called an insular, bottom-up process[46] forced all bureaucrats with budgetary interests toward greater emphasis on thinking in quantitative terms in general and to communicate in the categories and terms defined by the Office of Management and Budget. If these categories and terms were no longer "objective"—meaning in tune with bureaucratic values—but politically loaded, adherence to a centralized budgetary language could nevertheless be forced on threat of being left out of the funding process altogether. Even Congress fell under the magical sway of those who defined the budgetary language, with success in 1981 assured by congressional acceptance of a Reaganite redefinition of the budget reconciliation process.

By its own terms, the first Reagan budget may be called successful; while it did not get rid of the mounting deficit, it achieved more than any previous attempts to cut budgets, "saving" $44 billion. However, when quantitative savings of the top-down budgeting process are related to likely compensatory activity in the agencies, some costs begin to emerge.

Above all, we would not expect any budgeting system that relies totally on top-down definition of reality purely in terms of *quantitative* and *procedural* categories to ever be able to encompass the *qualitative* and *substantive* experience of management at the programmatic level (see Chapter 4). The necessity to deal with heavy-handed procedural systems forces managers to "rely upon traditional, computational decision strategies even when it is apparent that those will not solve the problem, and may even worsen it."[47] A dual reality results: one an enacted reality, the other a practiced reality. The reason central budgeting systems have historically been confronted by multiple agency budgeting systems is the same as the reason for the incompatibility of management information systems at the center and the periphery: "the clash between managerial and analytical perspectives, with the core categories appropriate for one purpose quite different from those helpful for the other."[48] Given present reporting systems—which institute an enacted picture of reality and permit no exploration of missed opportunities—we will never know what the ratio of costs and benefits of the use of budgetary threat is in actually forcing compliance from managers in seeing to it that work is done.

Politics: Administrative Technique versus Political Evocation

We live in an age in which administration increasingly supersedes politics (see Chapter 5). This means not only that we more and more rely on management and managers to run our lives, but that we are tempted to use management analytic techniques to define what our lives and our problems are all about. This latter tendency has been criticized by both the political left[49] and the political right.[50]

The Reagan administration clearly perceived the conflict between politics and management—but it did so in traditional society versus bureaucracy terms, strangely blind to three problems that had arisen since the preeminence of politics was asserted two hundred years earlier. The Reagan administration ignored:

1. The rise of the corporate bureaucracy.
2. The transformation of society as the result of the rise of public bureaucracy as part of not only the permanent government but as the dominant force in society itself.
3. The creeping use of bureaucratic—managerial and technical—terms to define reality *even* on the part of politicians, including members of the Reagan administration.

The use of the Grace Commission, dominated by traditionalist members of private enterprise, to attempt to seize hold of the public bureaucracy could only mean using corporate bureaucratic tools to try to control public bureaucracy. A smaller public bureaucracy might result. But it would be shot through with obsolescent quantitative and procedural techniques tailored, at best, to traditional private enterprise but not the public sector.

The administration treated bureaucracy as a cancer that could be surgically removed from the body politic, or at least forced into remission. In doing so, it ignored the fact that bureaucracy had transformed the body politic, so that politics is now more part of the bureaucratic society and bureaucracy less part of the political society.

Finally, in its quest for control, the administration used any tool at all that came to hand as long as it promised short-term change. As a result, as we could have predicted and do predict, the long-term effect of Reaganization is a strengthening of the bureaucratic mentality not only among bureaucrats but among politicians and citizens, who now expect terms like control, efficiency, and productivity to apply even to political operations.

The major success of the Reagan administration, given these constraints, was to reassert the preeminence of "politics" in the evocation of issues and in the convocation of the national political community (see

Chapter 5). But whether such a call for a return to an evocative politics could succeed when those who were to hear it would interpret it in bureaucratic terms was in serious doubt.

THE NEED FOR BUREAUCRACY POLICY

What is bureaucracy policy? If we had one, what would it look like? Who would have an interest in bureaucracy policy? What present conditions would be changed by it?

Before 1970 it would have been unusual to speak of technology policy.[51] Technology policy arose out of decreased national support for science, increased fear of technology, and residual hopes that technology could provide the quick fix to the problems it created.[52] Technology policy is the political expression of a national concern over the pathways that are opened up and foreclosed by applying hard-science solutions to human problems. A growing concern for bureaucracy policy reflects a similar need for publicly examining, formulating, debating, and deciding political preferences regarding the pathways we take and are forced into when we are at work—whether in the public or in the private sector. It reflects the growing recognition not only that work shapes our lives but that many of the structures of work today shape our lives negatively, both quantitatively and qualitatively. The recognition by the American auto industry that hierarchical structures had bottom-line costs so severe that they threatened the continued existence of the industry is the beginning of recognizing the need for conscious choice between fundamental assumptions about structuring work. The Reagan administrations' attack on the public bureaucracy opened up the question of what kind of structures of public service work are good for the country as well as for those who are public servants.

If technology policy is the public design of structures of natural science applications to society, then bureaucracy policy is the public design of human science applications—human science understood broadly—to problems of work. To a large extent, the impetus for a separate bureaucracy policy comes from the recognition that previous reliance on natural-scientific design of work must be (and is increasingly being) balanced by new insights derived from the social sciences, about what actually gets people to work and do good work. These insights come from postmodern interdisciplinary recombinations of the traditional social sciences, from widespread work practices and consulting practices, and from a culture change in which people increasingly take a postmodern stance toward life.

At root of the need for bureaucracy policy is a questioning of the good that society hopes to obtain from bureaucracy itself. For, while bureaucratic structuring of work has produced the benefits of mass production and mass governance, the society has, over the last twenty years, developed an inventory of costs for this form of organization. Bureaucracy policy, ironically, is the result of progressive public disillusionment with bureaucracy. "Among the ironies of our day," comments the dean of mainstream public administration, "is the fact that New Left often joins Old Right in opposition to the solution of problems through governmental means, in praise of local solutions through personal action.[53] Ideologically, this longing to return to a simple, prebureaucratic day played itself out in the antibureaucratism of the Reagan administration; it is, however, unlikely that such a solution will be permanent just when economy, government, and culture are moving ahead into a postbureaucratic era. There is a need to move back to the examination of the fundamental assumptions that made bureaucracy tick; but from there the country will move ahead to discovering why it won't tick anymore, what the costs would be of artificially restoring the dominance of pure bureaucracy, and what the policy alternatives to bureaucracy are. We can briefly summarize what we have said throughout about the costs of bureaucracy.

The structuring of work through bureaucracy is responsible for costs for human relations in society. These include the shaping of solutions to human problems according to instrumental rather than end values; the psychology of bureaucrats and clients; deadend thinking mandated by bureaucratic language and thought; and the diversion of the innovative and evocative flow of politics into closed-systems (administration) of who gets public goods, when, how. In summary, the human costs of bureaucracy are these:

Socially: Bureaucracy works precisely because it breaks down reciprocal human relations natural to society and restructures them into artificial relations of top-down control. The operative hypothesis is: The more work (knowledge of work) can be divided, the more there is a need for hierarchy. Top-down control is assured through the division of labor. We can express the transformation from society to bureaucracy in terms of widely prevalent icons. Social relations are normally depicted as a flow between discrete individuals, while organizational relations are depicted as structured channels set up not between people but between offices or roles (see Figure 6.1). The cost of this transformation is the ripping apart of society's fabric and its reconstitution as organization. For a democratic society, the loss of reciprocity in society construction means the loss of democracy. Since the values of the new organization are not compatible with social values—they are instrumental and not ends values—the result is nonlegitimate domination. In nonlegitimate domination, a society turns to rulers to solve its problems without first examining whether the tools used by the rulers are compatible with the basic values of the society.

Culturally: The internal values of that form of organization we call

Figure 6.1
Social Relations in Society and Bureaucracy

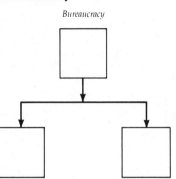

bureaucracy not only may contradict but may show a lack of concern and care for the foundation values of the culture at large. Society knows what it is all about by direct participation of people in the construction of core values. These are then directly accessible to each individual for making sense out of and guiding life. In contrast, the ultimate goals of the bureaucratic organization are held closely at the top and knowledge about them is distributed only partly through the division of labor and levels of hierarchy. Foundation values are permanently embedded in job and work structures that brook no participation, redefinition, discussion, or even awareness from those occupying work roles (see Figure 6.2).

The immediate danger is a growing gap between what the organization means to those who think they are in control of it and those who do the work.

Psychologically: Society relies on citizens who are individuals of psychological integrity. This integrity is broken apart by the demand of

Figure 6.2
Core Values in Society and Bureaucracy

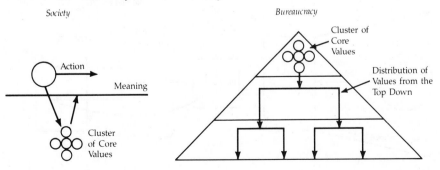

Figure 6.3
Psychological Structure in Society and Bureaucracy

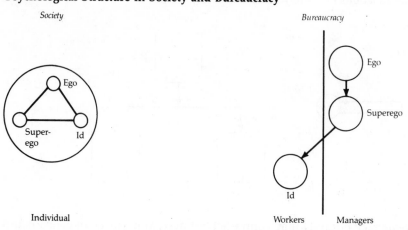

bureaucratic organizations that functionaries surrender to management their judgment over whether they *should* do something or not (conscience) and over whether it is done well when they do it (mastery) (see Figure 6.3).The cost of fragmenting the psyche is evident in behavior in every position of the workplace: creative and innovative work responsibly carried out cannot be expected to arise from *within* bureaucratic inmates, it must be controlled from *without*. But this means management. While management from the top-down produces benefits—such as control and efficiency—the more management there has to be from the top the less an organization can expect bottom-up knowledge of work and work problems to be originated and applied judiciously from below. The quality of goods and services, dependent as it is on sound judgment and mastery at the point of production or delivery, after an optimal point declines in

Figure 6.4

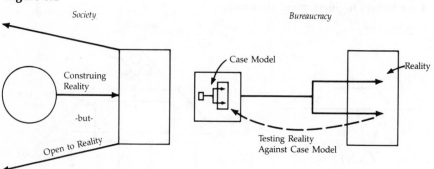

Figure 6.5

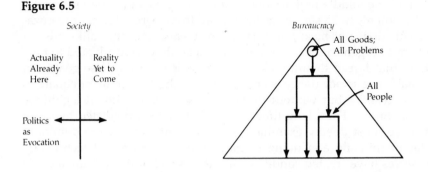

inverse proportion to the increase of top-down management activities. In deliberations on bureaucracy policy, the society will get a chance to decide whether sacrificing the existence of its fundamental constitutive units—individuals of psychological integrity—is worth the mass production and mass control benefits of bureaucracy.

Linguistically and thoughtfully: The language and thought of bureaucracy lend themselves more to a world in which it can be assumed that all human problems have already been solved. If so, this would require merely the kind of language and reasoning that enables bureaucrats to decide who fits into which case of already available and warehoused solutions (see Figure 6.4). A bureaucracy policy would examine especially whether bureaucratic language and scientific/technological thought are adequate to deal with the very problems for human life—endangering, threatening, or seducing it—that science and technology themselves have produced.

Politically: The society has to discuss and decide whether it will be satisfied with politics as mere decision-making over who gets the goods when and how. For this role, administration is much better equipped. The other choice is to see whether politics can be resurrected as the process convoking the national community for the purpose of evoking new ways of dealing with problems unheard of before. If politics is really administration, then society may want to continue the surrender of politics and the polity to those who are trained to administer (see Figure 6.5).

POST-BUREAUCRATISM AND BUREAUCRACY POLICY

For decades, theorists have developed models of organization to serve as alternatives to bureaucracy: a post-bureaucratism for bureaucracy policy. Reality may have caught up with the models. As yet, the masters of hierarchical organizations believe themselves in charge. But actual practices, and the middle-rank to lower-rank managers and supervisors who installed them, have simply walked away from purely formal organization. This does not mean, and has never meant, that the ranks are not obedient to organizational goals; it does mean they have adapted to new realities that forced them to take up new tools to reach those goals. An informal bureaucracy policy is emerging from the bottom up adequate to the new realities but without public discussion and without legitimate political control. For a long time, a change has been predicted by those who have most deeply examined the forces inherent in the dominant modes of thinking and doing of modernity.[54] Science and technology themselves have created conditions under which traditional bureaucratic forms of organizing are no longer necessary or functional. "Some of the sources of the counterrevolution," writes Dwight Waldo, "are in a general sense, the same as those of the organizational revolution: science and technology. But the sciences and technologies involved are increasingly advanced; and their use in production demands, or at least makes possible, *new* forms of human interaction: forms that are unbureaucratic."[55] Other sources of the new organizational revolution, however, are cultural and civilizational rather than scientific and technical.

There seems to be general recognition on the part of a large and increasingly dominant segment of students and practitioners of postbureaucratic organization policy that the following realities are taking over:

Organizational Social Structure: There is a surprising scarcity of research on the actual activities and thinking of public managers.[56] Yet, those in close touch with federal managers—GS 13 to GS 15, for example—conclude that program management is the state of the art model toward which many of those who run the nation's business from day to day strive.[57] This sense of actual practices has percolated upward to the very top of administrative theorists, whose leading representative has commented, "In general, the more knowledge that is necessary to run a contemporary society, and the more specialization that is a consequence, then the more the need of and potential for *horizontal* rather than vertical cooperative arrangements."[58] In actual consulting and training, this leveling of managers and subordinates has been the standard practice for as long as forty years,[59] impacting more on the program level while leaving the skeleton of the overall larger administrative structure intact (see Figure 6.6). While the icon of hierarchy still holds *external* to programs, within programs a new icon emerges of managers and functionaries working together in functional equality orienting themselves to and reflexively enacting the field of their situation (see Figure 6.7).

Within the operational field, the unit of analysis is *analytically* the dyad formed by manager and functionary (subordinate, specialist, or professional); *practically* it is the cluster of dyads that constitutes the team.

Figure 6.6

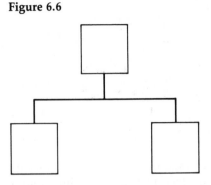

Each member of the dyad orients himself or herself to the other by reference to the individual's knowledge of the situation. They construe the meaning of their interaction by reference to that field of the situation and construct their interactions accordingly.

Dyads in program settings may be nonlegitimate in that they cannot draw on such official reward systems as that of the Civil Service, which still metes out rewards top-down to individuals rather than to teams. However, dyads may be put in place contractually through labor agreements, as has happened in the U.S. Department of Labor where "employees have the right to propose new and innovative ways to carry out the mission or function of the department . . . [and] when feasible the Department will implement the plan." If the employee's plan is rejected, the department has to explain, in writing, why.[60] Similar moves are reflected in Management by Objectives (MBO), which forces managers to reveal to subordinates some sense of the goals that managers themselves must meet in order for employees to be able to innovate suitable operations.[61]

Organizational Culture: The shift from vertical social relations toward horizontal ones, so work can be done, is matched by new values more

Figure 6.7

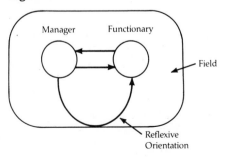

Figure 6.8

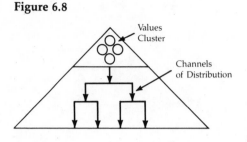

suited for work than for control. The change in icon is from hierarchy, where goal values are located at the top (see Figure 6.8), while instrumental values are embedded in organizational structure, to an icon depicting the individual (dyad or team) as open to and immersed in the values dictated by the work itself (see Figure 6.9). In American industry, this shift was made necessary by loss of market share when top-down quantitative design of work processes moved production lines so fast as to deprive workers of the time and space to develop sensitivity to values of work emanating from the work itself.[62] However, bureaucracy's public has been making similar demands for quality of public product and service delivery at least since the 1960s, with corresponding changes in public participation and policy analysis and evaluation toward such qualitative concerns as impact and outcomes.[63] Worker orientation toward the values of working demanded by the objects of work themselves is on the increase. Work values are emerging from an era of enforced silence that has lasted throughout modernity.[64] This emergence brings with it entirely new ways of thinking and speaking.[65] These must now be officially formulated and recognized. We face a cultural crisis without compare for our time: work values and control values may not be compatible and a balance between them will have to be worked out. A second issue for the public to decide will be to what extent to sacrifice the benefits of rational/scientific instrumental values. Some of these must be

Figure 6.9

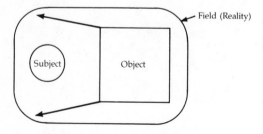

Figure 6.10

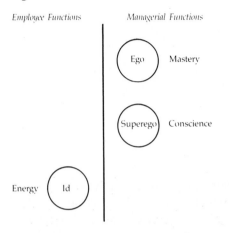

Employee Functions   *Managerial Functions*

Ego   Mastery

Superego   Conscience

Energy   Id

given up. Only then will public servants be able to pursue work in its own terms and in terms of its benefit to the community.

Organizational Psychology: Knowledge of work values and knowledge of social purposes are not possible for people whose cognitive and emotional abilities are truncated by management taking over their functions of mastery and conscience through hierarchy and the division of labor. The splitting of the psyche between management and labor (see Figure 6.10) can be and is being remedied by mutual support agreements between managers and subordinates. Especially in team situations and in functional collaborations between managers and professionals, each side retains functions of mastery and conscience appropriate to it. Increasingly we are becoming aware of the absurdity of expecting workers to show self-integrity, innovation, judgment, and responsibility in bureaucratic systems designed to trade such characteristics for top-down control, compliance with routines, obedience, and surrender of personal responsibility to the organization. Public deliberation of bureaucracy policy will weigh the costs and benefits of such trade-offs.

Where new psychological forms have emerged and are emerging, the new icon is one of managerial nurturing of coworkers' abilities to do good work and to judge whether it is for the benefit of society. The social icon of the dyad as prime unit of analysis suggests overlapping and complementary functions carried out by manager and subordinate in a mutually supportive fashion (see Figure 6.11). In a true dyad one type of ego functions may be carried out by a professional subordinate—for example mastery functions directly related to a specific piece of work—while other ego functions—for example, mastery functions related to working out relations with a bureau's environment—may be carried out by the

Figure 6.11

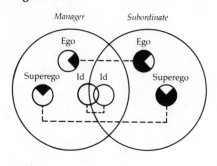

manager.[66] Without public examination and deliberation, however, it will be impossible to formulate ways in which dyads and teams can develop an appropriate form of community-directed conscience; such deliberations will cover general public expectations about the purpose and form of the private economy and public bureaucratic institutions, and citizenship education for both.[67]

Organizational language and thought: Control-oriented citizens, politicians, and administrators have observed with loathing and horror the development of a popular language open more to discovery than to control. The modern icon (see Figure 6.12), that ideas and language are valid to the extent that they find their analogy in a physical operation,* is replaced by an icon of openness to reality (see Figure 6.13), in which language does not encompass and control reality but is, on the contrary, encompassed and controlled *by* reality. The new language of attunement

Figure 6.12

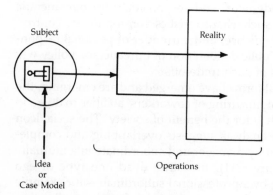

* In bureaucracy, reality has existence if it conforms to a reality model contained in a case description.

Figure 6.13

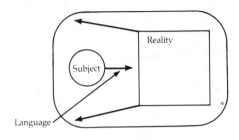

does not designate reality, it refers to it; in particular uncertain conditions of ongoing discovery, language uncertainty merely points to it. Condemned in their most widespread form as pop language or psychobabble, the emerging dialects of the language of attunement nevertheless serve to communicate. Professionals deeply involved in organizational consulting speak such dialects to open up communications. These serve to free organization members from the dictatorship of top-down definition of language and analogous reasoning.[68] Where a new language is in the making, a culture is in transformation. Two characteristics—ambiguity and openness to reciprocal construction of meaning by participants—reflect the function of the new language: to bridge old and new meanings and to reflect the growing power of reciprocal and horizontal relationships against one-way, top-down relationships.

The growth of new realities and new language is accompanied by a decline of faith among the intellectual elite both in such traditional modern values as progress and in the usefulness of the dominant carrier of modern knowledge: technical information.[69]

Organizations and Politics: Modern organizations obtain their power from a breach of trust in social relations, from a breach of faith in human values, from a breach of the human psyche, from a breach of thought that separates the thinker from reality and the speaker from language, and, finally, from a breach in the political system. The political breach not only separates tools from the master but puts tools ahead of the master. Bureaucracy succeeds as a surrogate political system only by substituting redefined bureaucratic goals for true political goals: for example, permanent prehostility for peace.[70]

Given the numbers of people employed in structures that make such breaches a permanent part of our reality, it is the task of politics today to bridge them. A complex picture emerges in which the public is asked to bridge not only the gap between divided labor or the gap between labor and hierarchy, but the gap between bureaucracies and politics (see Figure 6.14). This is a mechanical picture of the size of the problem that

Figure 6.14

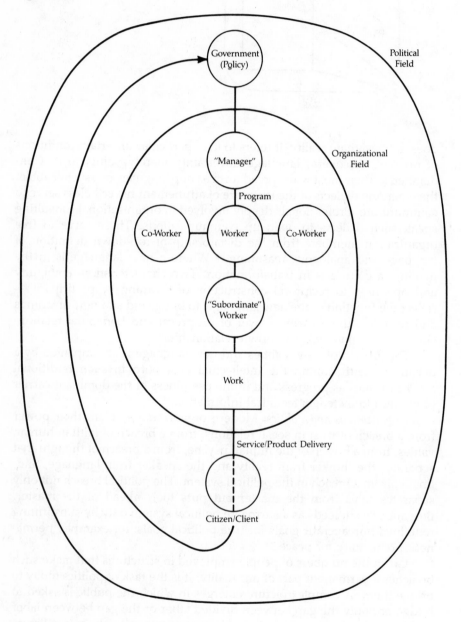

bureaucracy policy faces today. It is, however, only a mechanical answer to a problem that has, to begin with, been reduced to mechanical terms. Clearly a solution does not depend on more mechanics, though the mechanisms that exist cannot be ignored or abandoned. There is no way back to a premodern picture of the universe—either of human life in general or of organized life.

The citizens and politicians who help design a postmodern bureaucracy policy, by recognizing changes already in progress and giving them legitimacy, start doing so by viewing the world in terms entirely different from those of traditional science. They also set aside compensating approaches that merely seek to repair what science has ripped asunder. Among the new assumptions about the nature of the world, these are already clear:

1. *Socially*. The unit of analysis is not the lone individual, but the dyad and combinations of dyads: teams in fields.
2. *Culturally*. Values are derived from *what* a thing is (quality), not from *how much* there is of a thing (quantity).
3. *Psychologically*. Our emotional being is shaped by the fact that we are born into the world already in the company of others and that our first experiences are those of the mother/child unity, not of separateness.
4. *Linguistically/thoughtfully*. We come to knowledge in unity with reality, including the work we encounter and those we work with; we communicate, as against inform, when we construct language in the company of others.
5. *Politically*. We are at our political best not when we struggle for power over deciding who gets what, when, how of those goods and services that have already been valued and created, but when we convoke the political community to formulate values that do not yet exist.

For this postbureaucratic political experience there is as yet no icon, we can only point in the direction from which it might come.

None of us can yet know how well we will succeed in bringing about a political solution to the gap between the enacted actuality of modern organization and the emerging reality of postmodern work. We can only try. We do know what is at stake: nothing less than the re-creation of human values that has been the concern of human beings from the beginning of time. For the receding tide of modernity, Max Weber's ominous words still stand: Fate, in modern times, is the consequence of man's action contrary to his intentions. But for realists by profession and optimists by obligation, there is also the growing realization of postmodernity: that neither the divinity of gods nor the power of men alone speaks our true fate, but rather that we utter our fate when we accept the human condition.

NOTES

1. On the history of technology policy, see W. Henry Lambright, *Governing Science and Technology* (New York: Oxford University Press, 1976).

2. Personal communication from Charles Levine, March 26, 1986.

3. See the papers of the panel "Is There a Need for Theory or Theorists in ASPA or the Profession?", annual Convention of the American Society for Public Administration, Anaheim, Calif., April 13–16, 1986.

4. Private communication, author anonymous, dated July 10, 1985.

5. The critical work on bureaucracy by Max Weber is in the main ignored in public administration. Recent critical works include Robert B. Denhardt, *In the Shadow of Organizations* (Lawrence, Kans.: Regents Press of Kansas, 1981); Howell Baum, *Planners and Public Expectations* (Cambridge, Mass.: Schenkman Publishing, 1983); Pierre Clavel, John Forester, and William W. Goldsmith, eds., *Urban and Regional Planning in an Age of Austerity* (New York: Pergamon Press, 1980); Michael M. Harmon, *Action Theory for Public Administration* (New York: Longman, 1981); Michael M. Harmon and Richard T. Mayer, *Organization Theory for Public Adminstration* (Boston: Little, Brown, 1986); and Frederick C. Thayer, *An End to Hierarchy and Competition: Administration in the Post-Affluent World*, 2nd ed. of *An End to Hierarchy! An End to Competition!—Organizing the Politics and Economics of Survival* (1973), (New York: Franklin Watts, 1981).

In the mid 1970s, one study using small samples found academicians to be in general uncritical of public bureaucracy while citizens were critical. The authors concluded, "This raises the question, if there are dissatisfactions with the current relationships between bureaucratic and political structures, who is to detect and publicize them? Avowedly we can but speculate, yet on the basis of these findings we suspect such advocacy is not likely from the academic students of public administration. Our study suggests they are more adept at fulfilling the maintenance function rather than the change function of education." Dean L. Yarwood and Dan D. Nimmo, "Perspectives for Teaching Public Administration," *Midwest Review of Public Administration*, vol. 9, no. 10 (January 1975), pp. 28–42; citation from p. 42.

6. The classic in this genre: Charles T. Goodsell, *The Case for Bureaucracy—A Public Administration Polemic*, 2nd ed. (Chatham, N.J.: Chatham House, 1983); see also Goodsell's bibliography for other defensive works.

7. For example, in Perry Moore, *Public Personnel Management—A Contingency Approach* (Lexington, Mass.: Heath, Lexington Books, 1985), p. 11 and the reference to Goodsell's book p. 22, Footnote 11, which fails to mention the original subtitle, "A Public Administration Polemic."

8. See The Blacksburg Manifesto.

9. See, for example, R. G. Collingwood, *An Autobiography* (Oxford, England: Clarendon Press, 1939, repr. 1967), p. 104: "If you act according to rules, you are not dealing with the situation in which you stand, you are only dealing with a certain type of situation under which you class it. The type is, admittedly, a useful handle with which to grasp the situation; but all the same, it comes between you and the situation it enables you to grasp."

10. For a recent restatement of the argument that public adminstration knowledge to be useful must meet the standards of positive science, see Howard E. McCurdy and Robert E. Cleary, "Why Can't We Resolve the Research Issue in Public Administration?", *Public Administration Review*, vol. 44 (January/February 1984), pp. 49–55; and "A Call for Appropriate Methods," *Public Administration Review*, vol. 44 (November/December 1984), pp. 553–54.

11. In the federal Civil Service, the relevant institutes are the three federal executive seminar centers at Kings Point, New York; Denver, Colorado, and Oak Ridge, Tennessee. At the level of supervisory training, agencies design their own training needs, with little control from the Office of Personnel Management.

12. Recent studies of university public service assistance to state government officials and local government managers found gaps not only between the research priorities of the academicians and the practitioners but in the skills practitioners expect from academicians. Joseph W. Whorton, Jr., Frank K. Gibson, and Delmer D. Dunn, "The Culture of University

Public Service: A National Survey of Perspectives of Users and Providers," *Public Administration Review*, vol. 46, no. 1 (January/February 1986), pp. 38–47.

13. The split between the kind of knowledge preferred by academicians and desired by practitioners continues in consulting. While practitioners express confidence in university-sponsored training programs, academicians' confidence in such programs is lower. Similarly on the problem of translating theory into practice, practitioners prefer university-sponsored training programs to university-based consultants. James S. Bowman, "Managerial Theory and Practice: The Transfer of Knowledge in Public Administration," *Public Administration Review*, vol. 38 (November/December 1978), pp. 563–69. See also Thomas Vocino, Samuel J. Pernacciaro, and Paul D. Blanchard, "An Evaluation of Private and University Consultants by State and Local Officials," *Public Administration Review*, vol. 39 (May/June 1979), pp. 205–10.

14. The preeminent form of rational skills is quantitative skills. But when a public administration educator is asked, "Where does public service get its accountants from?" the educator must answer: "From the private sector, or through hands-on training on the job." Most master of public administration programs require students to complete a single course in budgeting or financial management. When researchers asked the question, "Can the curriculum satisfy practitioner needs?," their answer has had to be: "Programs as a whole do seem to be out of step with practitioner preferences. . . ." Gloria A. Grizzle, "Essential Skills for Financial Management: Are MPA Students Acquiring the Necessary Competencies?", *Public Administration Review*, vol. 45, No. 6 (November/December 1985), pp. 840–44; citation from p. 843.

15. Oral communication about a survey of Ph.D. and D.P.A. dissertations conducted by Jay D. White for presentation to the Task Force on Research in Public Administration, National Association of Schools of Public Affairs and Administration. On interpersonal and intrapersonal skills, see Robert B. Denhardt, "Action Skills in Public Organizations," in Denhardt and Edward T. Jennings, Jr., eds., *Toward a New Public Service*, forthcoming.

16. The distinction is one between skills involving judgment and skills involving knowledge based on science and pure reason (mathematics).

17. The classical recent case in business administration is that of the growth of worker/management consultation practices, which has been brought about because of the impact of high-quality industrial products of the Japanese competing successfully with American products.

18. See Elmer D. Dunn, Frank K. Gibson, and Joseph W. Whorton, "The Problem-solving Relevance of Political Science: An Exploration of the Attitudes of State and Local Policymakers," paper presented at the 1985 annual meeting of the American Political Science Association, New Orleans, Aug. 29–Sept. 1, 1985.

19. See, for example, Donald A. Schön, *The Reflective Practitioner: How Professionals Think in Action* (New York: Basic Books, Colophon, 1983), and R. P. Hummel, "Good Work/Bad Work: The Silent Psychology of Belaboring the Object—Introduction to Technological Development," paper presented at the First Cornell Symposium on the Psycho-Dynamics of Organizational Behavior and Experience, New York City Center of the New York State School of Industrial and Labor Relations, Oct. 1–2, 1983.

20. See Gerald Pomper et al., *The Election of 1984—Reports and Interpretations* (Chatham, N.J.: Chatham House, Inc., 1985), pp. 67–68.

21. See, for example, Warren E. Miller, "Crisis of Confidence: Misreading the Public Pulse," *Public Opinion*, vol. 1 (October-November 1979), pp. 9–15 and 60.

22. "Nonlegitimate domination" is Max Weber's term for regimes that do what people want them to do without prior legitimation of the values that such regimes bring with them. See Max Weber, *Economy and Society* (New York: Bedminster Press, 1968), e.g., pp. 1274–76.

23. Michael Sanera, "Implementing the Mandate," in Stuart M. Butler, Michael Sanera, and W. Bruce Weinrod, eds., *Mandate for Leadership II: Continuing the Conservative Revolution* (Washington, D.C.: Heritage Foundation, 1984), pp. 514–15.

24. Emphasis added; Sanera proposes an even more restricted distribution of knowledge about controversial objectives to career personnel than about noncontroversial objectives.

25. Donald J. Devine, "Career-Political Interface," *The Bureaucrat*, vol. 11, no. 3 (Fall 1982), p. 40.

26. Testimony before House Civil Service Subcommittee reported by Hugh Heclo, "A Government of Enemies?" *The Bureaucrat* (Fall 1984), pp. 12–14; data from p. 12.

27. President's Private Sector Survey on Cost Control, J. Peter Grace, chairman, *War on Waste* (New York: Macmillan, 1984).

28. Cited in Charles H. Levine, ed., *The Unfinished Agenda for Civil Service Reform—Implications of the Grace Commission Report* (Washington, D.C.: Brookings Institution, 1985), p. 6.

29. New York Stock Exchange [report on work-related employee programs], reported in William Serrin, "Giving Workers A Voice of Their Own," *New York Times Magazine*, Dec. 2, 1984, pp. 125–37.

30. General Motors.

31. The public service had, since the social upheavals of the late 1960s and partly as a response to public concern with the substance of program output, shifted its policy analysis and program evaluation tools from an emphasis on mere efficiency and output to the study of impacts and perceived outcomes.

32. For the development of an effectiveness-oriented policy analysis and program evaluation, see, among others, Ralph P. Hummel and Robert Allen Isaak, *The Real American Politics* (Englewood Cliffs, N.J.: Prentice-Hall, 1986), pp. 234–39.

33. A handy starting point for effectiveness-oriented theory, though it excludes important earlier individual contributions, is Frank Marini, ed., *Toward a New Public Administration—The Minnowbrook Perspective* (Scranton, Pa.: Chandler Publishing, 1971).

34. Jeffrey L. Pressman and Aaron Wildavsky, "Preface to First Edition [1973]," *Implementation*, 2nd ed. (Berkeley: University of California Press, 1979), p. xxii, Footnote 4.

35. Thomas J. Peters and Robert H. Waterman, Jr., *In Search of Excellence—Lessons from America's Best-Run Companies* (New York: Warner Books, 1984), p. 285.

36. Finding of National Academy of Public Administration, *Revitalizing Federal Management: Managers and Their Overburdened Systems* (Washington, D.C.: National Academy of Public Administration, 1983). For the traditionalist bias of the Grace Commission see George W. Downs and Patrick D. Larkey, *The Search for Government Efficiency—From Hubris to Helplessness* (New York: Random House, 1986), p. 262.

37. For a critical series of biographies of top Reagan administration appointees, see Ronald Brownstein and Nina Easton, *Reagan's Ruling Class—Portraits of the President's Top One Hundred Officials* (New York: Pantheon, 1983).

38. Patricia W. Ingraham and Carolyn Ban, "Is Neutral Competence a Myth?—The Policy Environment of the Career Executive in the Reagan Administration," draft paper prepared for delivery at the 1985 annual meeting of the American Political Science Association, New Orleans; quoted by permission of the authors.

39. Personal communication from Patricia W. Ingraham regarding paper prepared for the 1986 annual convention of the American Society for Public Administration, Anaheim, Calif.

40. Lawrence E. Lynn, Jr., "Managers' Role in Public Management," *The Bureaucrat*, vol. 13, no. 4 (Winter 1984-1985), p. 20.

41. Among such costs are increasing energy devoted to such defensive operations as the creation of professional associations, increased reliance on unionization, appeals to the Merit System Protection Board, lawsuits, and lobbying in Congress—to say nothing of passive noncollaboration: not bringing to bear knowledge and insights that are only to be had by those who have their hands on the bureaucratic tools at any level.

42. Data and testimony presented to the House Post Office and Civil Service Committee hearings on the Senior Executive Service in 1984, as reported by Heclo, op. cit., cited above footnote 26.

43. See article by Michael A. Diamond in Chapter 3.

44. Such as for example Michael Maccoby's current study of the U.S. Department of State or his previous study of the U.S. Department of Commerce. On the latter: Michael Maccoby et al., "Bringing Out the Best: Final Report of the Project to Improve Work and Management in the Department of Commerce, 1977–1979," Project on Technology, Work, and Character, Harvard University, Discussion Paper No. 91D, John F. Kennedy School of Government, June 1980.

45. Analysts will decide for themselves how useful, in the exploration of uncharted possibilities, are such policy simulations as those undertaken in John L. Palmer and Isabel

V. Sawhill, eds. *The Reagan Record* (Cambridge, Mass.: Ballinger Publishing, 1984), Appendix B, pp. 355–62. Some lessons, however, might be drawn from the growing practice of Human Resource Accounting in the private sector.

46. Allen Schick. See also Virginia A. McMurtry, "OMB and Financial Management," in Congressional Research Service, Library of Congress, *Office of Management and Budget: Evolving Roles and Future Issues* (Washington, D.C.: U.S. Senate Committee on Governmental Affairs, Feb. 1986), pp. 269–303.

47. Donald E. Klingner and John Nalbandian, "Judicial Influence on Public Agencies: Negative Impact on Organizational Design and Effectiveness," unpublished paper, July 16, 1981, p. 14; available from the authors at Florida International University and the University of Kansas, respectively.

48. Schick, op. cit., pp. 423–24 in Joseph A. Uveges, Jr., ed., *The Dimensions of Public Administration* 2nd ed. (Boston: Holbrook Press, 1975).

49. See Chapter 5, section on Jürgen Habermas.

50. See Hummel and Isaak, *The Real American Politics*, Chapter 7, section on "The End of Deliberation."

51. W. Henry Lambright, *Governing Science and Technology* (New York: Oxford University Press, 1976), p. 186.

52. Loc. cit.

53. Dwight Waldo, quoted in James M. Elden, "Radical Politics and the Future of Public Administration in the Postindustrial Era," in Dwight Waldo, ed., *Public Administration in a Time of Turbulence* (New York: Chandler Publishing, 1971), p. 21.

54. We may think here of philosophers such as Martin Heidegger, who predicted that technology would reveal from out of its own character ways of dealing with the world that are no longer technological; but it would be more directly appropriate to look to such innovators in organization research and theory as Joan Woodward, who recognized as far back as the late 1950s that growing differentiation in types of organizations required growth in the variety of organizational designs. Joan Woodward, *Management and Technology* (London: Her Majesty's Stationery Office, 1958). Woodward's thinking is reflected in contingency theory today.

55. Dwight Waldo, "Public Administration Toward Year 2000: The Framing Phenomena," in Frederick S. Lane, ed., *Current Issues in Public Administration* (New York: St. Martin's Press, 1982), pp. 499–512; citation from p. 509.

56. Hal G. Rainey, "Public Organization Theory: Current Contributions and Research Directions," paper prepared for presentation at the 1984 annual meeting of the American Political Science Association, Washington, D.C., Aug. 30–Sept. 2, 1984, p. 19.

57. For example, Dail Neugarten, basing her observations on her experience as trainer for the Western Executive Seminar Center of the U.S. Government, in Denver, Colorado.

58. Waldo, "Public Administration Toward Year 2000: The Framing Phenomena," citation from p. 509.

59. Organization Development dates back, according to a founder, Carl Rogers, to 1947.

60. Reported in Barbara Palmer, "The 10-to-3 Ethic," Charles Peters and Jonathan Alter, eds., *Inside the System—Readings from the Washington Monthly* (Englewood Cliffs, N.J.: Prentice-Hall, 1985), pp. 235–42; citation from p. 239.

61. Author's own experience with orienting battalion chiefs toward MBO in the Fire Department of the City of New York.

62. See R. P. Hummel, "The Two Traditions of Knowledge: Quality Management and the Crisis of Quantity," in Donald J. Calista, ed., *Bureaucratic and Governmental Reform*, vol. 9, *Public Policy Studies Series: A Multivolume Treatise* (New York: JAI Press, 1986); Hummel, "Work," paper presented to the annual meeting of the American Society for Public Administration, April 16–20, 1983, New York City; and Hummel, "Quality Management of Work," paper presented at the Roundtable on Quality Management, annual meeting of the American Political Science Association, Aug. 29–Sept. 3, 1985, New Orleans.

63. See Pressman and Wildavsky, *Implementation*, cited above, fn. 34.

64. R. P. Hummel, "Good Work/Bad Work," cited above, fn. 19.

65. See Chapters 2 and 4; see also Donald A. Schön, *The Reflective Practitioner: How Professionals Think in Action* (New York: Basic Books, 1983).

66. Attempts to reconcile psychological differences between managers and functionaries

The Bureaucratic Experience

have been and are being carried out by psychoanalytic consultants to both private and public bureaucracy: for example, by Michael Maccoby in twelve major corporations and in the U.S. Commerce and State departments.

67. The extent to which a rescue of personality from mere institutional identity is possible without far-ranging reformulation of the cost-benefit-oriented market system itself would be questioned by economics-based organization theorists like Alberto Guerreiro Ramos; see his *The New Science of Organizations: A Reconceptualization of the Wealth of Nations* (Toronto: University of Toronto Press, 1981). The present work, however, argues that modern economics, as well as science and technology, have reached their own limits—and that transformations in economic, scientific, technological, and organizational values and practices are already being undertaken.

68. The language of attunement shows a surprisingly wide distribution, ranging from its use by philosophers (for example, Martin Heidegger) to psychologists (Carl Rogers, Eugene Gendlin) to professional consultants (for example, Organization Development) to popular use (for example, in such expressions as "What I hear you saying is . . ." and "You have to tune in to things.").

69. For example, one recent study of a case of attempted innovation concludes with two statements inconceivable in a serious policy study of even a few years ago: First, that "There is little or no intrinsic value to innovation," and, second, that "technical information can do little to rationalize decisions . . . where there are a large number of official and unofficial actors with highly divergent interests and values. . . ." Barry Bozeman and J. Lisle Bozeman, "Technical Information and Policy Choice: The Case of the Resource Recovery Nondecision," In Barry Bozeman and Jeffrey Straussman, *New Directions in Public Administration* (Monterey, Calif.: Brooks/Cole, 1984), pp. 184–94; citations from pp. 193 and 194, respectively.

70. The U.S. Department of Defense redefinition of peace was reported Nov. 28, 1984, on ABC Television News. "Permanent prehostility," however, is not a late modernism; it accords with the definition of peace as the readiness for war logically deduced at the beginning of modern times (1651) in Thomas Hobbes, *Leviathan*, Michael Oakeshott, ed. (Oxford: Basil Blackwell, undated), p. 82: "The nature of war, consisteth not in actual fighting; but in the known disposition thereto, during all the time there is no assurance to the contrary. All other time is PEACE." It follows that no modern-thinking government can guarantee peace, only readiness for war.

Index